International Protection of Performers' Rights

International Protection of Performers' Rights

OWEN MORGAN

HART PUBLISHING
OXFORD AND PORTLAND, OREGON
2002

Published in North America (US and Canada) by
Hart Publishing
c/o International Specialized Book Services
5804 NE Hassalo Street
Portland, Oregon
97213-3644
USA

Distributed in Netherlands, Belgium and Luxembourg by
Intersentia, Churchillaan 108
B2900 Schoten
Antwerpen
Belgium

Hart Publishing is a specialist legal publisher based in Oxford, England.
To order further copies of this book or to request a list of other publications please write to:

Hart Publishing, Salters Boatyard, Folly Bridge,
Abingdon Rd, Oxford, OX1 4LB
Telephone: +44(0)1865 245533 Fax: +44(0)1865 794882
email: mail@hartpub.co.uk
WEBSITE: http//:www.hartpub.co.uk

British Library Cataloguing in Publication Data
Data Available

ISBN 1–84113–285–3 (hardback)

Typeset by J&L Composition, Filey, North Yorkshire
Printed and bound in Great Britain by
T J International, Padstow, Cornwall.

Acknowledgements

I would like to thank Margaret and Mark for their patient forbearance and their unfailing support throughout my work on this project. I would also like to thank Dr Andrew Christie for his encouragement and wise guidance. Finally, I would like to acknowledge my father.

Contents

Table of Cases ix
Table of Legislation xii

PART I INTRODUCTION

1 Introduction 3

PART II DEVELOPING THE ANSWERS

2 Defining a Performance 13
3 The Arguments for Performers' Rights 31
4 Technology and the Development of Performers' Rights 53
5 Other Protection for Performers 75
6 Performers and the Structure of Ownership 97

PART III THE STRUCTURE OF PROTECTION

Historical Interlude 119
7 National Treatment and the Protection of Foreign Performers 125
8 The Right Holder and the Subject Matter of Protection 137
9 The Primary Economic Rights 153
10 The Extended Rights 181
11 Limitations and Exceptions and Reservations to the Guaranteed Rights 203
12 Duration of the Rights 217
13 An Audiovisual Performances Treaty? 227

PART IV CONCLUSIONS

14 Conclusions 241

Bibliography 253
Index 265

Table of Cases

AUSTRALIA

Conagra Inc v McCain Foods (Aust) Pty Ltd 23 IPR 193 91
Elders IXL Ltd v Australian Estates Pty Ltd (1987) ATPR ¶40–832................91
Henderson v Radio Corp Pty Ltd [1960] SR (NSW) 576 88
Hogan v Koala Dundee Pty Ltd (1988) ATPR 40–902....................................91
Hogan v Pacific Dunlop Ltd (1988) ATPR ¶40–914..................................89, 91
JC Williamson Ltd v Metro-Goldwyn-Mayer Theatres Ltd (1936) 56 CLR 567..82
Milpurrurru v Indofurn Pty Ltd (1995) 30 IPR 210 41
Moorgate Tobacco Co Ltd v Philip Morris Ltd (No 2) (1985) 59 ALJR 77 47
Sony Music Australia Ltd and Michael Jackson v Tansing (t/a as Apple House) (1993) 27 IPR 649...48, 101

HONG KONG

Shaw Bros (Hong Kong) Ltd v Golden Harvest (HK) Ltd [1972] RPC 559 92

SINGAPORE

Star Industrial Co Ltd v Yap Kwee Kor [1976] FSR 256 91

UNITED KINGDOM

A Schroeder Music Publishing Co Ltd v Macaulay [1974] 3 All ER 616 78
Abernethy v Hutchinson (1825) 47 ER 1313..79, 81
Ad-Lib Club Ltd v Granville (1972) RPC 673 91
Barnes v Jarvis [1953] 1 All ER 1061 20
Bassey v Icon Entertainment plc [1995] EMLR 596 81
Board of Governors of the Hospital for Sick Children v Walt Disney Productions Inc [1967] 1 All ER 1005...82
Clayton-Greene v De Courville (1920) 36 TLR 790 88

De Mattos v Gibson (1859) 45 ER 108 80
Ekland v Scripglow Ltd [1982] FSR 431 ....62, 81, 165
Erven Warnink BV v J Townend and Sons (Hull) Ltd [1979] 2 All ER 927 90
Godfrey v Demon Internet Ltd [2001] QB 201 194
Godfrey v Lees [1995] EMLR 307 84
Harrison and Starkey v Polydor Ltd [1977] FSR 1 92
Helliwell v Piggott-Sims [1980] FSR 582 61
Law Debenture Trust Corporation v Ural Caspian Oil Corporation Ltd [1993] 1 WLR 138 80
Lord Strathcona SS Co Ltd v Dominion Coal Co [1926] AC 108 80
Marbe v George Edwardes (Daly's Theatre) Ltd [1928] 1 KB 269 45
Morrison Leahy Music Ltd v Lightbond Ltd [1993] EMLR 144 199
O'Sullivan v Management Agency and Music Ltd [1985] 3 All ER 351 78
Reformation Publishing Co Ltd v Chrysalis Records Ltd, unreported Court of Appeal Oliver and Nourse LJJ 15 November 1985 62
Rickless v United Artists Corp [1988] QB 40 ....81, 115
Serville v Constance [1954] 1 All ER 662 93
Shelley v Cunane [1983] FSR 390 90
Silly Wizard Ltd v Shaughnessy [1984] FSR 163 85
Silvertone Records Ltd v Mountfield [1993] EMLR 152 78
Sim v HJ Heinz Co Ltd [1959] 1 All ER 547 89
Sports and General Press Agency Ltd v 'Our Dogs' Publishing Company Ltd [1917] 2 KB 125 80
Swiss Bank Corpn v Lloyds Bank Ltd [1979] 2 All ER 853 80
Thornton v Shoe Lane Parking Ltd [1971] 2 QB 163 80
Tolnay v Criterion Film Productions Ltd [1936] 2 All ER 1625 45
Warner Bros Pictures Inc v Nelson [1936] 3 KB 160 78
Zang Tumb Tuum Records Ltd v Johnson [1993] EMLR 61 78
ZYX Music GMbH v King [1995] EMLR 281 84

UNITED STATES OF AMERICA

A & M Records Inc v Napster Inc 114 F Supp 2d 896; 239 F 3d 1004 55
Allen v National Video Inc 610 F Supp 612 89
Benson v Paul Winley Record Sales Corp 452 F Supp 516 88
Bleistein v Donaldson Lithographing Company 47 L Ed 460 42
Ettore v Philco Television Broadcasting Corporation 229 F 2d 481 ....62, 82
Gilliam v American Broadcasting Corporation 538 F2d 14 ....57, 87–8
Jarvis v A & M Records 827 F Supp 282 56
King v Mister Maestro Inc 224 F Supp 101 47
Midler v Ford Motor Co 849 F 2d 460 89
RCA Mfg Co Inc v Whiteman 114 F2d 86 80

Shostakovich v Twentieth Century Fox Film Corp 80 NYS 2d 575 (1948) 45, 88
Ventura v Titan Sports Inc 65 F3d 725.....82
Waits v Frito-Lay Inc 978 F 2d 1093.....89
Waring v Dunlea 26 F Supp 338 80
Waring v WDAS Broadcasting Station Inc 327 Pa 433.....65, 102
Zacchini v Scripps-Howard Broadcasting Company 53 L Ed 2d 965 63

Table of Legislation

AUSTRALIA

Copyright Act 1968
s 10 17
s 28(1) 18
s 35 105
s 89 83
s 93–5 85
s 97–9 85
s 119 115
s 248A 16
s 248A(1) 16, 21, 22, 71, 99, 141, 142
s 248A(1)(a–e) 17
s 248A(2) 18, 251
s 248A(2)(a) 18
s 248G 94
s 248J 94
s 248N 111, 218
Part XIA 16, 17, 72
Copyright (International Protection) Regulations 1969
Reg 4A(2–3) 99
Reg 4B(2) 72
Reg 4B(2)(d) 99
Trade Practices Act 1974
s 52 48
s 52(1) 48
s 82(2) 91
Copyright Amendment (Digital Agenda) Act 2000 201
s 26 194
s 39 194
s 42 194
s 87 194
s 95 194

CANADA

Copyright Act 1985
s 2 16

EUROPEAN COMMUNITY

Directives

Council Directive 92/100/EC of November 19, 1992 on rental right and lending right and certain rights related to copyright in the field of intellectual property 73, 201
Art 2(5) 72, 114
Art 2(7) 72
Art 4(1–2) 114

INTERNATIONAL

Agreement Establishing The World Trade Organisation Done At Marrakesh, 1994
Art ii(2) 121
Agreement On Trade-Related Aspects Of Intellectual Property Rights, Annex 1C to The Agreement Establishing The World Trade Organisation Done At Marrakesh 1994 (TRIPS) 6, 31, 98, 119, 122, 125
Art 1 130
Art 1(1) 121
Art 1(3) 130–2, 143
Art 2(1) 89
Art 2(2) 123
Art 3 ....130, 183
Art 3(1) 130–3
Art 4 ....130, 183
Art 6 183
Art 9(1) 196
Art 11 ....184, 186–7, 211
Art 13 210–11
Art 14 ....65, 158–9, 163, 186, 244
Art 14(1) 94, 138, 143, 150, 158–9, 162–3, 167, 187, 189, 210–11, 248
Art 14(2) 163
Art 14(3) 163
Art 14(4) 186–8, 190

Art 14(5) 222
Art 14(6) 143, 163, 210–11, 222
Art 28 183
Art 70(1) 222, 224
Art 70(2–4) 222
Art 72 211
Part II 65
Berne Convention For The Protection Of Literary And Artistic Works, Brussels Act 1948
Art 7(1) 220
Berne Convention For The Protection Of Literary And Artistic Works, Paris Act 1948....41, 83, 119, 120, 122
Arts 1–2....170, 196
Art 2(1) 18, 140
Arts 3–5....170, 196
Art 5(1)....85
Art 6 ....170, 196
Art 6*bis* 86, 196
Art 6*bis*(1) 148, 197
Art 6*bis*(2) 224
Art 7 ....170, 196
Arts 7(1–2) 85
Art 8 ....170, 196
Art 9 ....86, 170, 196
Art 9(1) 161, 168, 170
Art 9(2) 205–10
Art 9(3)....161
Art 10 ....170, 196
Art 10(2) 208, 213
Art 10(3) 196
Art 10*bis*(2)....208
Art 11 ....86, 170, 196
Art 11*bis*(2) 194, 196
Art 11*bis*(3)....208
Arts 12–14 ....170, 196
Art 14*bis*(2–3) 233
Art 15 ....170, 196
Art 15(4) 41
Arts 16–17 ....170, 196
Art 18....170, 196, 222–3
Art 18(1–4) 222
Arts 19–21 ....170, 196

Convention Establishing The World Intellectual Property Organisation Signed At Stockholm 1967
Art 2(viii) 65
Convention For The Protection Of Producers Of Phonograms Against Unauthorized Duplication Of Their Phonograms 1971
Art 7(1) 6
Convention Relating To The Distribution Of Programme-Carrying Signals Transmitted By Satellite 1974
Art 6 6
International Convention For The Protection Of Performers, Producers Of Phonograms And Broadcasting Organisations 1961 (Rome Convention)....................6, 98, 119–25
Art 1 ....123, 220
Art 2(1)....................128
Art 2(1)(a)....................128
Art 2(2) 128–9, 133
Art 3(a)....................15, 19, 26, 94, 99, 129, 137–50
Art 3(b) 3, 163, 173
Art 3(d)....................173
Art 3(e) 55, 161, 164
Art 3(f) 155
Art 4 127–31
Art 5....................127–9, 175, 210
Art 5(3)....................210
Art 6 ....127–9, 210
Art 6(2)....................210
Art 7 ....76, 128, 147, 149, 154, 159, 166, 207, 221, 249
Art 7(1) 209–10, 246
Art 7(1)(a) 149, 155–6, 159, 248
Art 7(1)(b)....................156, 161–2, 166, 248
Art 7(1)(c) 164–8, 249
Art 7(1)(c)(i) 165
Art 7(1)(c)(ii) 165, 167
Art 7(1)(c)(iii) 165
Art 7(2) 169, 209
Art 7(2)(1) 156–7, 169
Art 7(2)(2–3)....................157
Art 9 ....26, 140–5, 151, 161, 251
Art 10....................168
Art 11....................129, 147, 195
Art 12....................129, 172–6, 221
Art 14 ....129, 220
Art 15....................129, 165, 207–10

Art 15(1), 207–8
Art 15(1)(c) 16–5, 169
Art 15(1)(d)....................208
Art 15(2) 165, 208–11
Art 16....................129, 177, 210
Art 16(1) 174, 210
Art 16(1)(a) 173–5, 210
Art 16(1)(a)(i) 174
Art 16(1)(a)(ii) 174
Art 16(1)(a)(iii) 174, 175
Art 16(1)(a)(iv) 174, 175, 221
Art 17 210
Art 19 ....166–8, 220–1, 249
Art 20(2) 221
Art 21 153
Arts 23–4 140
Art 31 210

Paris Convention For The Protection Of Industrial Property, Stockholm Act 1967
Arts 1–2 89
Art 2(1)....................91
Arts 3–10 89
Art 10*bis*(1) 89, 90
Art 10*bis*(2) 89
Arts 11–12 89
Art 19....................89

Vienna Convention On The Law Of Treaties 1969
Art 2(1)(d) 173, 206
Art 31 ....185, 190
Art 31(1) 170
Art 31(2)(a)....................170
Art 32 ....142, 190

WIPO Copyright Treaty 1996
Art 1(1)....................189
Art 1(4)....................170
Art 6(1)....................184
Art 7....................189
Art 7(1)....................189
Art 8 ....191, 194
Art 8(2)....................185

WIPO Performances And Phonograms Treaty 1996
Art 1(1–2) 123
Art 1(3) 123, 189
Art 2 ....132, 159
Art 2(a) 15, 26, 94, 132, 137–8, 143–5, 149, 151
Art 2(b) 3, 164, 185, 249
Art 2(c) 163, 185, 229
Art 2(e) 177, 184
Art 2(f) 56, 159
Art 2(g) 56, 155, 160, 177
Art 3 132
Art 3(2) 98, 132, 138
Art 3(3) 132
Art 4 132
Art 4(1–2) 133
Art 5 148
Art 5(1) 148, 197–8, 224
Art 5(2) 111, 115, 158, 224
Art 6 159
Art 6(i) 159–61, 248
Art 6(ii) 163
Art 7 168–71
Art 8 ....183–4, 188–9
Art 8(1) 183–5
Art 8(2) 185
Art 9 184–9
Art 9(1) 188
Art 9(2) 190
Art 10 ....178, 18–4, 193–4, 212
Art 11 ....168, 171
Art 12 184
Art 13 ....184, 189
Art 14 ....178, 194
Art 15 ....132–4, 176–8, 183
Art 15(1) 176, 178, 230
Art 15(2) 177
Art 15(3) 133, 177, 214
Art 15(4) 178
Art 16 ....171, 185–6, 212–13
Art 16(1) 211–14
Art 16(2) 171, 212–14
Art 17(1) 222
Art 20 104

Art 21 ....177, 214
Art 22 222
Art 22(1) 222, 224
Art 22(2) 224

NEW ZEALAND

Fair Trading Act 1986
s 9....90
s 43(5)....91
Copyright Act 1994
s 169 ....16, 107
s 196(2) 108
s 197(1)(b)....108

UNITED KINGDOM

Public Health Amendment Act 1890
s 5....20
Copyright, Designs and Patents Act 1988
s 1....83
s 3....17
s 9....85
s 11 ....85, 105
s 13–14 85
s 101 115
s 180(2) 16, 21, 71, 107, 141–2, 251
s 182....94
s 182C....201
s 183–4 94
s 185 107
s 185(1) 107
s 186–8 107
s 191B....72, 111, 115, 218
s 191L....115
s 192A....115
Part II 81

UNITED STATES OF AMERICA

Copyright Act 1976
§ 201(b) 87, 105, 232
Digital Millenium Copyright Act 1998 201
Title II 194

Part I

Introduction

1

Introduction

I THE NATURE OF THE PROBLEM

IN A WORLD that increasingly uses digital technology, it is worth remembering that for thousands of years performances were made without the aid of any technology at all.[1] Those performances were all marked by two factors that hold good today. In the absence of technology: (i) a performance exists past the time of its presentation only in the memory of a spectator physically present when the performance was given; and (ii) the communication of a performance is limited to spectators physically present in the immediate vicinity of the performance at the time it is presented. It is only in the last 130 years, since the development of the phonogram, that technology has been developed that has allowed performances to be exploited; previously, they had been transitory.[2] Sophisticated means of fixing performances and of broadcasting or communicating them to the public have forever changed the relationships between performers, performances and audiences. In doing this, technology has forced the law to confront the problem of protecting performers against the unauthorised exploitation of their performances.

'Exploitation' is a term that is used frequently in the following chapters. It is an important term that covers all those activities that enable a performance to be made available to the public, that give the public access to the performance. These are the activities by which a performance is fixed, broadcast and communicated to the public.[3] Exploitation also includes the various ways in which a performance can be reproduced once it has been initially fixed. Reference will sometimes be made to the technology of exploitation. By contrast, 'production'

[1] Schechner suggests that performances date from Paleolithic times. R Schechner, *Performance Theory* (Routledge, New York, 1988) xiii.

[2] In the law of performers' rights, the most recent definition of a phonogram is provided in Art 2(b) of the WPPT: '"phonogram" means the fixation of the sounds of a performance or of other sounds, or of a representation of sounds, other than in the form of a fixation incorporated in a cinematographic or other audiovisual work.' Art 3(b) of the Rome Convention defines a phonogram as 'any exclusively aural fixation of sounds of a performance or of other sounds.'

[3] The terms 'fixation', 'broadcasting' and 'communication to the public' are discussed in ch 4. In brief, a fixation is an embodiment of sounds and or images that exists in a stable and permanent form that enables those sounds and images to be perceived; broadcasting involves the transmission of sounds and images by wireless means; communication to the public involves transmission by wired means.

of a performance covers a wider range of activities than exploitation. As well as the fixation, broadcast and public communication of a performance, the term includes making the necessary preliminary arrangements for the making of a performance, as well as its subsequent exploitation.

In its simplest form, the problem that performers face is one of control. In the millennia before the advent of phonograms, cinematographic films, broadcasting and means of communicating performances to the public, performers had complete control of the exploitation of their performances.[4] If a performer appeared before an audience and performed, there was a performance; if he or she did not perform, then there was no performance. The simple concept of 'no pay—no play', and its equally simple counterpart, 'no play—no pay', was sufficient to determine the limits of a performer's rights in a performance. The loss of the control that performers previously had over their performances was lamented by a representative of the International Federation of Actors ('FIA') in the following terms:

> It was indisputable that it was the mechanical means of reproduction and transmission (recordings, radio and television) which had, in the space of a few years, transformed the actor, who, until then, had been master of his own performance and his own talent, into a supplier for a chain of industries which reproduced and used his talent unrestrictedly.[5]

With the advent of sophisticated means of making audio and audiovisual fixations, of broadcasting and of communication to the public, performances have become commodities. While a thriving market for performances existed before those developments, the production and exploitation of performances now form an integral part of a global entertainment industry that has revenues measured in hundreds of billions of dollars.[6] A performance no longer belongs to a performer alone.

It would be naïve to label technology as the villain. If technology were truly the problem, the answer would be simple—ban the technology. But that would be neither practicable nor desirable. The problem lies not in the technology itself, but in the uses to which it is put. Ideally for performers, they should be granted rights that would return control of their performances to them. But this proposition begs two questions: first, does merely being at risk because of the advance of technology entitle performers to protection; and second, does the

[4] The term 'cinematographic work' is also discussed and defined in ch 4. In brief, a cinematographic work is a recorded sequence of images and sounds.

[5] The quotation is from the opening speech of the representative of FIA to the Rome Diplomatic Conference that concluded the Rome Convention: 'Summary Records of the Proceedings', *Records of the Diplomatic Conference on the International Protection of Performers, Producers of Phonograms and Broadcasting Organisations* (ILO, UNESCO and BIRPI, Geneva, 1968) [165.51].

[6] According to Vogel, entertainment generates annual revenues exceeding $100 billion in the United States. HL Vogel, *Entertainment Industry Economics: A Guide for Financial Analysis* 4th edn, (Cambridge University Press, Cambridge, 1998) 27.

law already provide adequate protection, or in other words, does the means of exerting legal control already lie at hand? Both questions are considered in later chapters.[7] Suffice to say, at this point, that the international community has effectively answered 'Yes' to the first question and 'No' to the second. Performers are right holders in a relatively new branch of intellectual property law. Those rights, which have become known as 'performers' rights', reflect the modes of exploitation of performances and the ongoing development of technology.

Initially, performers sought protection from the use of technology that enabled others to make unauthorised fixations of their unfixed performances, and protection from the use of performances embodied in fixations in ways that restricted their employment prospects. The expansion of the means of broadcasting and of communication to the public meant that the concern of performers was centred on obtaining remuneration for 'secondary uses' of their performances.[8] With the arrival of digital technology, performers have become concerned with issues such as controlling the exploitation of their performances on the Internet. Performers whose performances are exploited in fixations, in broadcasts and public communication and on the Internet are often, although not exclusively, engaged in the entertainment industry. It is dangerous, however, to assume that the entertainment industry is the only source of performances. Although this industry is the most important in terms of revenue generated, there are other important sources of performances including, for example, religious rituals.

The nature of the technology that enabled performances to be exploited also meant that the problem of controlling the use of performances was not confined by political borders. Technology, such as satellite broadcasting, has overcome the barriers of distance and geography. While an individual state can provide for the protection of performances made by its nationals within its territory, it is more difficult to arrange for the protection of those performances when they are transmitted outside the territory in electronic form or when fixations embodying those performances are physically transported to another state. The international nature of the problem, together with the recognition that legal norms regulating the use of performances were needed at both national and international level, were prime factors in generating an international response to this problem.[9]

Essentially, there are three ways in which a state can ensure that performers who are its nationals are protected in other states: (i) it can enter into bilateral agreements; (ii) it can enter into regional agreements; or (iii) it can enter into multilateral agreements that are intended to have broad international effect. This book is concerned with the three international instruments that, taken

[7] As to the justification for performers' rights, see ch 3. As to existing protection, see ch 5.

[8] 'Secondary uses' are discussed in ch 4. The term refers to the use of fixations of performances in broadcasting or communication to the public.

[9] 'Summary Records of the Proceedings', above n 5, [4.11].

together, have established an international system of performers' rights that sets out the rights and obligations to be incorporated into the national law of contracting states. The International Convention for the Protection of Performers, Producers of Phonograms and Broadcasting Organisations done at Rome on 26 October 1961 ('the Rome Convention'), was the first of the three international instruments that confirmed the place of performers' rights in the law of intellectual property. The other two instruments are the Agreement on Trade-Related Aspects of Intellectual Property Rights, Annex 1C to the Agreement Establishing the World Trade Organisation, done at Marrakesh on 15 April 1994 ('TRIPS') and the WIPO Performances and Phonograms Treaty ('WPPT') adopted on 20 December 1996. (WIPO is an anagram for World Intellectual Property Organisation.)[10]

There is another international instrument that has played a significant role in the development of performers' rights. Performers initially looked for protection to the Berne Convention for the Protection of Literary and Artistic Works ('the Berne Convention') which was concluded on 9 September 1886. Although performers were refused protection under this Convention, the influence of the copyright regime should not be underestimated. Because of the long-standing connection performers have to this instrument, references to matters of international copyright in this book are restricted to the Berne Convention and, unless otherwise stated, to the Paris Act, 1971.

II FORMULATING THE QUESTIONS

This book was written to fill a gap in the literature of performers' rights. That literature takes the form either of an analysis of the provisions of individual instruments or an analysis of the performers' rights provisions in national legislation.[11] By contrast, this book views performers' rights in the round, reflects

[10] The Rome Convention came into force on 18 May 1964. TRIPS came into force on 1 January 1995. The WPPT entered into force 20 May 2002. An attempt to negotiate an instrument that would have extended protection, comparable to the levels of protection in the WPPT, to audiovisual performances attempt failed, see ch 13. Performers' rights are also referred to in the Preamble and Article 7(1) of the Convention for the Protection of Producers of Phonograms Against Unauthorized Duplication of Their Phonograms done at Geneva on 21 May 1971, and also in the Preamble and Article 6 of the Convention Relating to the Distribution of Programme-Carrying Signals Transmitted by Satellite done at Brussels on 29 October 1974. However, neither Convention confers rights on performers.

[11] Important examples of the former include the commentaries of Masouye and Ulmer on the Rome Convention and of Gervais on TRIPS: C Masouye (W Wallace trans), *Guide to the Rome Convention and to the Phonograms Convention* (World Intellectual Property Organisation, Geneva, 1981); E Ulmer, 'The Rome Convention for the Protection of Performers, Producers of Phonograms and Broadcasting Organizations. Part I' (1963) 10 *Bulletin Copyright Society of the U.S.A.* 90; E Ulmer, 'The Rome Convention on Neighboring Rights. Part II'(1963) *10 Bulletin. Copyright Society of the U.S.A.* 165; E Ulmer, 'The Rome Convention for the Protection of Performers, Producers of Phonograms and Broadcasting Organizations. Part III' (1963) 10 *Bulletin Copyright Society of the U.S.A.* 219; D Gervais, *The TRIPS Agreement: Drafting History and Analysis* (Sweet &

on the issues that should be considered when formulating performers' rights and analyses those issues in the context of the three international instruments. Although the international system of performers' rights is firmly established, it should not be regarded as a holy cow that is protected from questions and challenges. After all, the subject of the present study is an international system of intellectual property rights that imposes obligations on a large proportion of the world's states.

The underlying purpose of this book is to determine whether the protection afforded to foreign performers under the three international instruments constitutes an appropriate system of protection. It would make the task that much easier if there were generally accepted criteria of appropriateness that had been proven and could be applied in an exercise of this kind. There are, however, no such generally accepted criteria. In their absence, appropriateness can be determined by identifying the fundamental building blocks that form the foundations on which performers' rights are built, by analysing the applicable provisions within the international instruments and by assessing how issues surrounding those building blocks have been handled.

The starting point for this study is to be found in two propositions: (i) performers have a problem and they need protection; (ii) a solution has been identified in the form of a regime of intellectual property rights. From there, the first step in determining appropriateness is to ask a series of simple questions—who, what, where, when, why and so on? Those questions, which are addressed in Part II, have been formulated as follows:

— What is the subject matter of protection?
— Why should performers be protected?
— From whom or from what do performers need protection?
— How should performers be protected?
— Where should protection be available?
— How long should protection last?
— Are other forms of protection adequate?
— Who should be protected?

A complicating factor in the analysis of the treaty provisions in Part III is that there is more than one beneficiary in each of the international instruments. Besides performers, the Rome Convention and TRIPS provide protection for producers of phonograms and for broadcasting organisations, and the WPPT provides protection for producers of phonograms. The content of the present

Maxwell, London, 1998). Commentaries on the WPPT tend to be part of commentaries on the WCT, for example: M Ficsor, 'The Spring 1997 Horace S Manges Lecture—Copyright for the Digital Era: The WIPO "Internet' Treaties" (1997) 21 *Columbia-VLA Journal of Law & the Arts* 197. Arnold's work on performers' rights legislation in the United Kingdom is comprehensive: R Arnold, *Performers' Rights* 2nd edn (Sweet & Maxwell, London, 1997).

discussion is restricted, however, to performers' rights; issues relating to other right holders are referred to, if at all, only in passing.

The protection of performers and the other beneficiaries under the international instruments depends on the incorporation of the provisions of the instruments into national law according to the constitutional law of the contracting states. Although the content of this book is concerned with the international protection of performers, the national legislation of the United Kingdom and Australia—as leading examples of common law states with statutory performers' rights regimes—is referred to, where appropriate. Examples and case law are drawn from those jurisdictions as well as from the federal and state jurisdictions in the United States.

III OUTLINE OF THE CONTENT

This opening chapter has briefly described the nature of the problem that confronts performers. This problem is taken up in more detail in the succeeding chapters.

Chapter 2 addresses the first question posed above: what is the subject matter of protection? That chapter undertakes the task of formulating a principled definition of a performance. It should be obvious that the subject matter of protection needs to be correctly identified, but this cannot be done unless there is a principled definition of that subject matter. Chapter 3 then addresses the question: why should performers be protected? It considers the arguments that can be put forward to justify performers' rights, on the basis that protection for performers and their performances should be granted only if there are good reasons for doing so.

The discussion turns, in chapter 4, to answer the question—from whom or from what do performers need protection? The technology of exploitation that has wrought great changes to the environment of performing is described in a more detailed fashion than the preliminary comments made in this opening chapter. Chapter 4 then discusses the implications of the next three questions: how should performers be protected; where should protection be available; and how long should protection last? The issues of the protection that should be available to performers and the duration of that protection are issues that come up again in other questions and in succeeding chapters. The answer to the question of where protection should be available is non-controversial: the objective of an international system of rights is to protect right holders in foreign states. The means adopted to meet this objective may, however, lead to controversy.

The remaining chapters in Part II address other significant issues that should be borne in mind when a system of performers' rights is being established. Chapter 5 considers whether other forms of protection are adequate. Even if performers can show good reasons why their performances should be protected, it may be that protection is already in place, although the key issue is that protection should be available to foreigners equally with the nationals of a state. Chapter 6, the final chapter in Part II, goes on to consider the question of who should be protected. In that chapter, issues relating to the ownership of performers' rights are examined, the basal theme being that the correct person should be the right holder.

Part III, begins with an 'Historical Interlude' that describes the background to the international instruments and which acts as a link between the issues of principle in Part II and the detailed analysis which is undertaken of the substantive provisions of the three international instruments in Part III. The order in which those provisions are analysed largely follows the order in which they appear in the Rome Convention. Chapter 7 analyses the national treatment provisions and the criteria of eligibility for protection. Chapter 8 evaluates the definition of 'performers', which is an important factor to be considered in determining an individual's eligibility for protection. That chapter also considers the subject matter of protection and the transfer of rights. Chapters 9 and 10 examine the provisions that set out the substantive rights that are protected. Limitations, exceptions and reservations to those rights are considered in chapter 11. In chapter 12, a further limitation, the duration of those rights, is discussed.

The final chapter in Part III is not concerned with the three international instruments. For the sake of completeness, this chapter describes the attempt that was made to conclude a fourth international instrument that would have completed the regime of performers' rights. Chapter 13 describes the background to the proposed audiovisual performances instrument and analyses the transfer provisions that were the cause of its failure.

In Part IV, chapter 14 discusses the conclusions that can be drawn from the discussion in Part II of the questions posed above, together with the conclusions that can be drawn from the analysis of the international instruments in Part III. Finally, the study is drawn together with an answer to the overriding question of the appropriateness of the protection offered by those instruments.

Part II

Developing the Answers

2

Defining a Performance

I INTRODUCTION

THE ANSWER TO the question—what is the subject matter of protection under a regime of performers' rights?—is deceptively simple. The subject matter of protection is a performance. The term 'performance' therefore has the important function of setting boundary markers; it identifies the performative activities that fall inside those markers and implicitly it identifies those that fall outside. The use of those activities that fall within the markers is subject to the system of performers' rights, and the use of those that fall outside is not subject to that regulation. There will be grey areas. A performative activity, whether it falls within the markers or outside, may also be subject to the legal regimes discussed in chapter 5.

The more difficult question is: what is a performance? In any legal regime, a performance is what the law says it is. A performance can be defined widely or narrowly; it can also be defined wisely or injudiciously. It is especially important to get the definition of a performance correct in the context of the protection of foreign performers. International agreements intended to protect foreign performers should be drafted in a way that is sensitive to differences in understandings of what constitutes a performance. It may be that an activity that is recognised as a performance in the culture of State A is not recognised as a performance in the culture of State B. If the point, however, is to protect foreign performers and their performances, then the definition of a performance should be wide enough to encompass the performance of the performer from State A, and therefore to protect it in all contracting states.[1]

The purpose of this chapter is to formulate a definition of a performance that is based on first principles. The exercise has a number of parts: several definitions of a performance need to be analysed; the constituent elements of a performance need to be determined; and then a principled definition of a performance can be developed.

[1] The issue is one of particular importance to performers of expressions of folklore, which are often not covered by definitions that centre on the European performing arts.

II TOWARDS A PRINCIPLED DEFINITION

A hybrid approach is adopted in this chapter that draws on both performance theory and legal studies. The first step is to examine the definition of a performance that currently prevails. That task begs the question amongst whom does the definition prevail? A performance can be defined in many ways for different purposes. How a particular definition is formulated will depend on whether one is, in language used by Goldstein about copyright lawyers, an optimist or a pessimist.[2] An optimist favours granting performers a wide range of rights while a pessimist would restrict those rights to the minimum. Naturally, a person who believes that the class of performances that should be protected is wide will have a different perspective from a person who believes that it should be kept narrow. In this section, three definitions of a performance are considered; each has been chosen for the insights that it provides into the definition of a performance that should be adopted. The first to be considered is the common understanding of a performance. Next, examples of legal definitions are discussed. The third definition is one taken from the discipline of performance theory.

A Common Understanding of a Performance

It is prudent to analyse the common understanding of a performance because that is the understanding that the public and the users of a performance have of a performance. A dictionary definition is a convenient starting point. The relevant entry in the *New Shorter Oxford Dictionary* states:

> **performance** . . . 3 The action of performing a play, a part in a play, a piece of music, etc.; an instance of this, a public exhibition or production of a play, piece of music, etc. . . . A ceremony, a rite.

The common understanding is probably both narrower and wider than this dictionary definition. It is narrower in that most people's view of what constitutes a performance would not include a ceremony or a rite, but would include most of the other concepts in the dictionary definition. The common understanding is wider than the emphasis the dictionary gives to the performing arts, to participation in a play and to the production of music. There are a number of performers who do not participate in a play or who are not musicians who could legitimately claim that the majority of the public, on reflection, would regard their activities as performances. Those claimants would include actors in cinematographic films and television, professional sportspersons, stand-up

[2] P Goldstein, *Copyright's Highway—The Law and Lore of Copyright from Gutenberg to the Celestial Jukebox* (Hill and Wang, New York, 1994) 15 ff.

comedians and performers of various kinds in the fringes of the entertainment industry.

B Legal Definition

While the common understanding of the elements of a performance is interesting, for present purposes the meaning that the public gives to the term is subordinate to the specific legal meaning given to it by the law.

1 *Definition of a Performance at an International Level*

At an international level, there has been little discussion of the elements of a legal definition of a performance. This is probably a consequence of the way in which the Rome Convention is drafted. The Hague Draft, the document that formed the basis for discussion at the Rome Diplomatic Conference, contained a definition of a 'performance' rather than a definition of a 'performer', but for the Rome Convention itself the delegates to the Diplomatic Conference settled on a definition of 'performers'.[3] In the context of international arrangements, particularly those sponsored by WIPO, it is therefore necessary to look to a definition of 'performers' to make out the meaning of a 'performance'.[4] Article 3(a) of the Rome Convention is the classic definition of 'performers.'[5] It states:

> For the purposes of this Convention: (a) 'performers' means actors, singers, musicians, dancers and other persons who act, sing, deliver, declaim, play in, or otherwise perform literary or artistic works.

If one accepts that a performance is the activity of a performer in his or her capacity as a performer, then it follows from this definition that a performance is a performance of a literary or artistic work.[6] This is the approach taken in the

[3] Art 7 of the Hague Draft states: 'For the purposes of this Convention, "performance" means the recitation, presentation or performance of a literary or artistic work. It shall be a matter for national laws and regulations to extend the protection to artistes who do not perform literary or artistic works.' TRIPS does not contain a definition of 'performance' or 'performers'. Art 2(a) of the WPPT defines 'performers'.

[4] Apart from Art 2(a) of the WPPT, see s 1 of the Model Law concerning the Protection of Authors, Performers, Producers of Phonograms and Broadcasting Organisations ('Model Law'): The Intergovernmental Committee of the International Convention for the Protection of Performers, Producers of Phonograms and Broadcasting Organisations done at Rome in 1961, *Model Law Concerning the Protection of Performers, Producers of Phonograms and Broadcasting Organisations with a Commentary on it* (ILO, UNESCO, WIPO; Geneva and Paris, 1974), and 'Annotated Principles of Protection of Authors, Performers, Producers of Phonograms and Broadcasting Organisations in Connection with the Distribution of Programs by Cable' (1984) *Copyright* 131 [106]–[113].

[5] It forms the basis for the definition in Art 2(a) of the WPPT and in s 1 of the Model Law.

[6] It is generally agreed that under Art 3(a) performers must perform literary or artistic works. See the discussion below in ch 8, n 4, and accompanying text.

WIPO Glossary of Terms of the Law of Copyright and Neighbouring Rights. The definition of 'performance of a work' states:

> Generally understood as meaning the presentation of a work to a group of listeners or spectators in their presence, by action such as playing, reciting, singing, dancing or by means of such technical devices as microphones, radio or television receiving sets, record players, or projecting. [sic] Performance of expressions of folklore is consistent with the common understanding of the term 'performances of literary and artistic works' as used in the Rome Convention. Performance, however, may also consist of presentations other than performing such works, for example in the case of performances of variety artists.[7]

There is something comforting about classifying performances as protectable or not according to the concept of a literary or artistic work. First of all, the problem of deciding whether an activity is a performance is shifted from performers' rights to copyright. If the activity involves a literary or artistic work then it is probably a performance, and it is certainly not a performance if it doesn't involve such a work. Secondly, and consequentially, the approach narrows the definition satisfactorily, particularly for users of performances such as broadcasters. Thirdly, it satisfies authors, for it reinforces the view that performances are derivative of literary and artistic works, and are less valuable than those works.

But there is a downside to classifying performances in this way in that it is inevitable that under this approach there will be classes of performances that are left unprotected. Formulating a definition of a performance should entail more than deciding which performances, over and above performances of literary or artistic works, should be protected: it should be possible to construct a legal definition of a performance that is based on principle.

2 *Definition of a Performance at National Level*

Although this work is concerned with the international system of performers' rights, it is worth noting that a number of states within the Commonwealth of Nations have included definitions of 'performance', rather than 'performer', in their performers' rights legislation.[8] The definition in Part XIA of the Copyright Act 1968 (Cth), provides a particularly useful example because it differentiates between performances of works (including parts of works), performances that do not require works and performances that are explicitly excluded from protection. Section 248A(1) states:

[7] The meaning of the term 'expressions of folklore' is discussed below, ch 3, n 45 and accompanying text.

[8] See s 180(2) of the Copyright, Designs and Patents Act 1988 (UK); s 248A(1) of the Copyright Act 1968 (Cth); s 169 of the Copyright Act 1994 (NZ); s 2 of the Copyright Act (RS 1985, C–42, Can).

'performance' means:

(a) a performance (including an improvisation) of a dramatic work, or part of such work, including such a performance given with the use of puppets;

(b) a performance (including an improvisation) of a musical work or part of such a work;

(c) the reading, recitation or delivery of a literary work, or part of such a work, or the recitation or delivery of an improvised literary work;

(d) a performance of a dance; or

(e) a performance of a circus act or a variety act or any similar presentation or show;

being a live performance given in Australia or by one or more qualified persons, whether in the presence of an audience or otherwise.

The first category of performances that is protected, those in paragraphs (a) to (c), comprises performances of dramatic, musical or literary works or of parts of those works. The concept of an improvisation is included in the meaning of those performances. The second category of performances, those in paragraphs (d) and (e), are not defined by reference to activities involving works. It may be that they are activities that, in fact, present or communicate works, but works are not essential to those performances.

Paragraph (d) simply states 'a performance of a dance'. A dance is normally regarded, in copyright terms, as a dramatic work and, as such, a dance, whether improvised or not, would be protected under paragraph (a).[9] However, a work is not required for paragraph (d), nor is there any particular meaning attached to the word 'dance' in that Part of the Copyright Act. A reasonable conclusion is that the provisions of Part XIA protect anything that can be classed as a dance and one should look for the natural meaning of the word among performers of dance. Paragraph (e) is a catch-all provision protecting diverse forms of performances. The plain words of paragraph (e) make it clear that any performance that one might expect to see at a circus or in a music hall will be protected. The common feature of these performances covered in paragraph (e) is that they are not necessarily performances of works.

Apart from defining performances that are protected, section 248A deems certain performances not to be performances for the purposes of Part XIA.[10] The logic behind some of these exclusions is obscure: for example, excluding performances from protection because they are performed in an educational

[9] In the Australian legislation, the definition of 'dramatic work' includes 'a choreographic work', s 10 of the Copyright Act 1968 (Cth); in the United Kingdom legislation, it includes 'a work of dance', s 3 of the Copyright, Designs and Patents Act 1988 (UK).

[10] There are no exclusions from the definition of a performance in the United Kingdom legislation.

environment does not add to the understanding of a performance.[11] The performances that are excluded are, however, listed here as an example of drafting practice; the point is that the legislature has explicitly excluded certain performances. Section 248A(2) states the exclusions:

> [**Not performances**] The following shall be taken not to be performances for the purposes of this Part:
>
> (a) a performance referred to in subsection 28(1);
>
> (b) a reading, recital or delivery of any item of news and information;
>
> (c) a performance of a sporting activity; or
>
> (d) a participation in a performance as a member of an audience.

The thread that runs consistently through the various definitions of a performance that have been considered so far is that a performance is first and foremost a performance of a literary or artistic work, as those words are understood in the Berne Convention.[12] The importance of the Australian legislation is that performances are acknowledged to extend further than the limitations imposed by literary or artistic works. However, there is no suggestion in the legislation of accepting the proposition that all performances should be protected; that approach has been firmly rejected.

C Performance Theory

1 Introduction

In the formulation of a principled legal definition, it must be accepted that there are concepts and issues outside the law that impact on the way in which the law views an issue. The analysis of performances is not the sole or even the primary province of lawyers.

> [T]he law, through its particular historical evolution, has constructed the concepts of performance and performer, and therefore of performers' rights, in particular ways which may not accord with the ways that acting and performance theory have constructed these terms through their own historical evolutions.[13]

[11] This comment is directed at s 248A(2)(a) which provides that 'a performance referred to in sub-s 28(1)' is deemed not to be a performance. Sub-s 28(1) deems certain performances of literary, dramatic or musical works not to be performances in public.

[12] The term 'literary and artistic works' is defined in Art 2(1) of the Berne Convention.

[13] P Auslander, 'Legally Live Performance In/Of the Law' (1997) 41 (2) *TDR The Drama Review* 9, 16. Note that Auslander is not using the term 'performers' rights' to refer to rights granted to performers by international treaty or by legislation, but rather to the general rights a performer may have in a performance.

There has been little discussion in legal circles, or among those concerned with drafting performers' rights provisions at an international level, of the essential elements of a performance. In contrast, within the discipline of performance theory there has been a ferment of thought and writing. One can look upon the performance theorist as the keeper of the realities of a performance and performance theory as pointing the way to the development of a principled legal definition. It is not the complete answer: one performance theorist will not necessarily agree with another, just as a legal theorist will not necessarily agree with another.

The works of theorists such as Auslander, Kirby, Phelan and Schechner are accessible to the ordinary reader and they can be discussed without one having an in-depth familiarity with performance theory. One can only take those materials at their face value and assess their worth for legal analysis. Some theorists adopt a narrow approach, not incompatible with the classic definition of 'performers' in Article 3(a) of the Rome Convention, and discuss and define a performance solely in terms of the theatre.[14] Others have a more expansive approach:

> Performance is an inclusive term. Theater is only one node on a continuum that reaches from the ritualizations of animals (including humans) through performances in everyday life—greetings, displays of emotions, family scenes, professional roles, and so on—through to play, sports, theater, dance, ceremonies, rites and performances of great magnitude.[15]

There are still others who warn of the dangers of using the term 'performance', let alone attempting a definition: '[The word performance] has been appropriated rather than coined and has therefore already been honed down by its users to accommodate what they wish it to mean.'[16] There is a lesson here for those considering the adoption of an inflexible approach to the definition of a performance—others will place their own interpretation on the term, which may not be the interpretation intended by the draftsman.

2 *Definition of a Performance in Performance Theory*

The next section analyses a definition taken from performance theory. That definition states:

[14] Kirby prefers to discuss performance in terms of the theatre alone while recognising that there are other performances. 'There are numerous performances that do not use acting. Many, but by no means all, dance pieces would fit into this category.' See M Kirby, *A Formalist Theatre* (Univ of Pennsylvania Press, Philadelphia, 1987) 3.

[15] R Schechner, *Performance Theory* (Routledge, New York, 1988) xiii.

[16] B Barber, 'Indexing: Conditionalism and its Heretical Equivalents' in AA Bronson and P Gale (eds), *Performance by Artists* (Art Metropole, Toronto, 1979) 191. See P Auslander, *Presence and Resistance—Postmodernism and Cultural Politics in Contemporary American Performance* (Univ of Michigan Press, Ann Arbor, 1994) 185, n 19 where he makes a very similar statement.

> A performance is an activity done by an individual or group in the presence of and for another individual or group.[17]

There are four constituent elements to this definition, which will be referred to as 'Schechner's definition'. Whereas the definitions discussed earlier focused on classes of activities, Schechner's definition is theoretical in its approach and all-encompassing in its coverage.

(a) An Activity An activity is seen or heard, or it is seen and heard. In order to be a performance, an activity must be capable of being perceived by an individual other than the performer; it cannot exist in a vacuum. The requirement that an activity be perceptible to another individual means that the objective characteristics of an activity alone do not make it a performance. For example, reading a play aloud for personal enjoyment does not make the act of reading a performance even though the act of reading aloud might well be a performance in certain circumstances. (It might be performed by an actor in a play.) The bare act lacks something that distinguishes it from everyday activity. It needs to be a performative activity to be considered to be a performance. Schechner's definition implies this essential ingredient which it takes from the other elements to a performance. This ingredient should be made explicit in a legal definition.

An activity can often be identified according to the context in which it occurs.[18] In the context of the entertainment industry, or in any other industry, it would be impossibly unwieldy to apply this approach, that is, to identify each performance. It is obviously necessary to apply one or more limiting factors, or to group performances into classes.

(b) Done by an Individual or Group A performative activity must be performed by a natural person or a group of natural persons. There are two important points in this element. The first and most important is that animals (that is, non-human animals) or inanimate objects (such as robots or cartoons) are excluded from consideration. This follows from the proposition that a performance is an expression of the intellect of the performer, something that is impossible for an animal or an inanimate object to achieve. The second point of note here is that Schechner's definition allows for performances by groups. This is something that the definition shares with the common understanding of a performance, which would include the performative activities of more than one individual.

[17] Schechner, above n 15, 30 n 10.

[18] In *Barnes v Jarvis* [1953] 1 All ER 1061, the question was whether a variety act was 'musical entertainment' under the Public Health Amendment Act 1890 (UK). S 5 defined musical entertainment as 'a concert or similar entertainment consisting of performances of music, with or without singing or recitation'. The Court of Appeal held that the performance could not be characterised as musical entertainment, as claimed by the respondent, merely because there was somebody on the stage playing the piano while the respondent was giving a 'comic turn'. The Court ordered that the case go back to the justices with a direction to convict the respondent.

Extending the definition of a performance to include group activities poses difficulties for the law. The question of a performance involving a group of performers is one of coherence. Does a performance consist of a coherent whole comprised of a number of parts performed by a number of individuals; or does the performance consist of the activity performed by each individual, (in which case each 'part' is a performance)?[19] This is an important issue for the law, because it involves the allocation of rights and the exercise of those rights. If a performance is to be regarded as the sum of the activities of all the individual performers, then the rights in a single performance can be granted to the various individuals jointly and severally. This could lead to problems with the exploitation of the performance, particularly with obtaining the consent of all the performers to the exploitation of individual parts and of the performance as a whole.

As an alternative to joint and several ownership, all the rights could belong to the principal performer or performers. Concentrating ownership of rights in this way would reduce the scope of the problems, but it would deprive minor performers of the right to control the use of their part of the performance. Another alternative is to recognise the person who made the arrangements for the performance as the first owner of the rights.[20]

The best approach is to acknowledge that the performative activity of an individual constitutes a separate and unique performance and that rights attach to each performance independently of every other performance. The justification for this approach can be found in the natural right theory that a performance is an embodiment of an individual's personality.[21] To theorise that there is a group performance would involve merging an individual's personality in some group personality.

(c) In the Presence of and for Another Individual or Group There are two issues here, one concerning the performer and his or her relationship with the audience; and one concerning the audience. The first issue is that Schechner's definition implies that a performance must be performed in the flesh, that is, in the presence of other individuals who can see or at least hear the performer or performers; this overlaps to some extent with the earlier discussion of 'an activity'. There are, however, numerous activities that do not have an audience in the sense of someone whose primary function is to be an involved spectator at the same time, if not necessarily the same place as the activity. Those performances

[19] The Australian legislation includes in the definition of a performance, which was considered above, the qualification that it is 'a live performance given by one or more qualified persons': s 248A(1) of the Copyright Act 1968 (Cth). The United Kingdom legislation defines a performance as 'a live performance given by one or more individuals': s 180(2) of the Copyright, Designs and Patents Act 1988 (UK).

[20] Questions of ownership of rights in a performance are discussed below in ch 6.

[21] The natural right theory is discussed extensively below in ch 3.

are embodied in fixations, they are broadcast and communicated to the public. Once they are fixed, they can be replayed at the whim of the consumer. The prime example is in the popular music industry, where the performance fixed in a phonogram is often more important than the unfixed performance that replicates the former. The unfixed performance is often used as a marketing tool for the fixed performance.[22] Commentators on this industry also suggest that a fixed performance is the real performance.

> [S]tudio reproduction has reversed the conceptual expectation of 'realism' as it applies to 'recorded' and 'live' music. That is to say that whereas initially the 'recording' was expected to be a faithful representation of the original 'live' performance, now it is the 'recording' of the studio performance which is deemed to be the 'original' and the live performance is merely a substandard albeit visually complete copy.[23]

It is not practical or desirable to restrict the protection of the law only to performances that are performed in the physical presence of an audience. It is no longer true to say that performances exist momentarily in space and time and are then lost. Performances that are made with the intention that they are to be embodied in fixations or broadcasts should not be regarded as being outside the boundary markers of a performance. Under a regime of performers' rights, the physical presence of the audience should therefore not be required.[24]

The second issue concerns the nature of the audience. The presence of a group of spectators is not determinative, as crowds gather to watch and participate in all sorts of things—burning buildings and riots are just two examples. What of the person who accidentally witnesses an activity? Does the presence of the casual spectator validate the activity as a performance? The answer is to be found in the performer's intent, which is discussed below. 'Eavesdropping and voyeurism are not theatre because the perceived activity is not intended for an audience.'[25] This comment is as true of other forms of performance as it is of theatre and rules out a role for the casual spectator.

Just as the presence of a casual spectator does not make an activity a 'performance', the absence of an audience does not invalidate a performative activity:

> Even where audiences do not exist as such—some happenings, rituals and play—the function of the audience persists: part of the performing group watches—is meant to

[22] The tours by popular performers, either global or national, are primarily intended to promote sales of their albums and other licensed merchandise, although the profits on these tours can be substantial: HL Vogel, *Entertainment Industry Economics—A Guide for Financial Analysis* 4th edn (Cambridge University Press, Cambridge, 1998) 143.

[23] AL White, 'Introduction' in AL White (ed), *Lost in Music: Culture, Style and the Musical Event* (Routledge and Kegan Paul, London, 1987) 4. See also D Harker, *One for the Money: The Politics of Popular Song* (Hutchinson, London, 1980) 35.

[24] An audience is not required in the Australian legislation: s 248A(1) of the Copyright Act 1968 (Cth) refers to performances 'whether in the presence of an audience or otherwise'. The United Kingdom legislation does not have a similar provision.

[25] Kirby above n 14, x.

> watch—other parts of the performing group; or, as in some rituals, the implied audience is God, or some transcendent Other(s).[26]

Spectators have another more theoretical function which it is important to consider. There are theorists who deny that a performance can be reproduced:

> Stockhausen's music, like Wilson's theatre, can be neither scored nor repeated. The only memory which one can preserve is that of the spectator's more or less distracted perception . . . The work, once performed, disappears forever.[27]

For such theorists, the only authentic version of a performance is one that is given in the flesh before an audience present in time and space. A performance that is fixed, or is otherwise exploited, becomes something else.[28] The audience has a specific function. As the performance (once given) can never be reproduced without the aid of technology, it continues to exist only in the spectator's memory. The presence of spectators is therefore critical to ensure the enduring validity of the performance.

(d) Done For Another Individual or Group A performance done for another individual is one done with intent to affect that individual.[29] Intention is, of course, a subjective requirement but it can be proved by observation and analysis. The intention that transforms an activity into a performance is that of the performer. Within the context of the commercial exploitation of a performance, for example, there will usually be little doubt that the performers intended to engage in performative activity. Ordinary behaviour becomes performative only if the individual involved agrees to its use as a performance and he or she has the intention to affect others.

There can be a number of reasons to engage in an activity and it would be unreasonable to require that an intention to affect or interact with an audience must be the sole or even the primary motive of the performer. This can be illustrated by reference to competitive activities.[30] The intention of competitors can be interpreted in a number of ways, including the desire to win the event, to entertain the spectators, to obtain a commercial return and to enjoy themselves. It would be impossible to determine with certainty the presence or absence of any of these elements of intent.

Intent to affect an audience does not imply that the activity must be immediately perceived by another. The intention relates to making the performance

[26] Schechner above n 15, 30 note 10.

[27] P Pavis (L Kruger trans), *Theatre at the Crossroads of other Culture* (Routledge, London, New York, 1992) 67.

[28] P Phelan, *Unmarked: The Politics of Performance* (Routledge, London, New York, 1993) 146. P Auslander, 'Legally Live Performance In/Of the Law' (1997) 41 *TDR The Drama Review* 9, 16.

[29] Kirby offers a similar comment, although he is speaking of the theatre alone: 'People make something that develops and changes in time—a performance—with the intent of having it affect an audience'. Kirby, above n 14, x.

[30] See the discussion in Kirby, *ibid* xi-xii.

available to an audience at some time. Rather, the audience can comprise of any number of individuals who need not be specially selected. This conclusion ties in with the discussion of the words 'in the presence of' in the previous section. Thus to qualify as a performance, an activity must be done with the intention of providing an audience with access to the activity in any form, unfixed or fixed.

D Characteristics of a Performance

The foregoing, albeit brief, analysis of the representative definitions of a performance provides a simple but worthwhile lesson, namely, that there are various ways of defining a performance. From those definitions, it is possible to identify a number of characteristics that are present in the wide range of different activities that can be described as performances:

(i) A natural person must perform the activity. This requirement excludes computer-generated performances and contributions made by other animals or inanimate objects.
(ii) The activity must be a performative activity. This may be identified restrictively, as in the performing arts, or it may have a wide compass.
(iii) The presence of other individuals is essential. They may be present in the same time and space as that in which the performance is made or they may be able to witness the performance by means of some media. Activities undertaken solely for personal satisfaction are excluded. Casual observers do not constitute an audience.
(iv) The performer must have the intention to have an effect on other individuals. Behaviour that lacks the element of intent to perform cannot be a performance.

There are a number of other features that can arguably be identified by personal observation or by further analysis as being characteristic of performances, but that have been deliberately excluded from the group of key features listed above on the basis that they should not be essential elements of a principled definition of a performance. Some have been excluded on the ground that they are not characteristic of all performances or even of the vast majority of performances. As an example of this, the notion that a performance must be something done for commercial purpose has been excluded. On the other hand, some features may be acknowledged to be present in all performances, but they have been excluded here because they should not form part of an international system of rights. They may be appropriate in national law. The question of the quality or merits of the performance falls into this category. Some of the excluded features, and the reasons for excluding them, are discussed below:

(i) A performance should not be judged against any qualitative criteria, aesthetic or otherwise. A performance that meets a particular aesthetic criterion, for example, should not be entitled to greater rights than a performance that does not meet that criterion.
(ii) The context of a performance is not determinative. It does not have to be a public performance, nor does it have to be made for financial gain. Either requirement would introduce undesirable complications.
(iii) The performer need not be professionally qualified in any sense of the word. Performances by amateurs, qualified or unqualified, should be granted the same level of protection as those of professional performers.
(iv) Performances should not be restricted to a particular form of cultural activity. A performance can and should be defined to include more than the European performing arts, which is the consistent theme of the first two definitions that were considered (those of the *New Shorter Oxford Dictionary* and the Rome Convention). 'Performance, of course, includes "the arts" but goes beyond them. Performance is a broad spectrum of entertainments, arts, rituals, politics, economics, and person-to-person interactions. This broad spectrum enacted multiculturally and interculturally can do much to enhance human life.'[31]

III A PRINCIPLED DEFINITION

This section embarks on the important task of formulating a principled definition of a performance. It begins by considering which of two approaches to the formulation of the definition should be adopted.

A Two Possible Approaches to Formulating a Definition of a Performance

When formulating a definition of a performance, it is important to bear in mind the problem that led to the development of performers' rights. It will be recalled that the problem was identified as one of the control, or more specifically, the lack of control that a performer can exert over the uses that are made of his or her performances. It will also be recalled that this problem stems from the development of the technology that enabled producers and others to exploit performances. Always assuming that the solution to the problem lies in the implementation of a system of performers' rights, the next step is to ask: which performances are open to exploitation?

[31] R Schechner, 'A New Paradigm for Theatre in the Academy' (1992) 36 (4) *TDR The Drama Review* 7, 9.

The answer is that all performances, however defined or classified, are open to exploitation. The technology that enables performances to be exploited in many different ways does not distinguish between performances that are exploited and performances that are not exploited. Producers, broadcasters, bootleggers and pirates make that distinction. The decision to exploit a performance is made for a number of reasons, the most obvious of which is to obtain a financial return. But there are many other reasons for exploiting a performance, including philanthropy, cultural awareness, religious proselytising and political propaganda. The likelihood of exploitation is not a good reason for distinguishing between performances that should be protected and ones that should not be protected. Accordingly, the proper basis for formulating a definition of a performance is to assume that all performances are open to exploitation. This can be characterised as a broad approach.

There is another, narrower way. This is to adopt an incremental approach that starts from a restricted definition and extends protection to new classes of performances on an ad hoc basis. This is the approach taken by the international community. At the Rome Diplomatic Conference, a 'performance', as the activity of a performer, was limited to a performance of literary and artistic works by virtue of the definition of 'performers' in Article 3(a) of the Rome Convention. In spite of that restriction, the recognition that another class of performances could be added had already begun at Rome. Article 9 of the Rome Convention permits but does not oblige Contracting States to 'extend the protection provided for in this Convention to artistes who do not perform literary and artistic works.' (The delegates to the Rome Diplomatic Conference had variety artistes in mind.[32]) Another class of performances has recently received international recognition: the definition of 'performers' in the WPPT was extended to include performers who perform expressions of folklore.[33] The subject matter protected by that Treaty therefore includes performances of expressions of folklore.

B A New Definition of a Performance

The evolution of the legal understanding of the nature of a performance has stalled. A change of approach is required. The classification of performances as protectable only if they are either performances of literary or artistic works or if they are performances of expressions of folklore should be abandoned. It may be possible to come up with a definition that defines the activities included or

[32] 'Report of the Rapporteur-General' *Records of the Diplomatic Conference on the International Protection of Performers, Producers of Phonograms and Broadcasting Organisations* (ILO, UNESCO and BIRPI, Geneva, 1968) 46.

[33] Art 2(a) of the WPPT.

excluded in a way that ensures that the boundaries are clear and sharp.[34] However, the approach that is preferred below is to formulate a definition that leaves those edges blurred. It is suggested that definitions with sharp edges are not appropriate to a discipline that regulates individuals at their most 'creative'. Performances are not like manufactured articles: they incorporate the personality of performers and the range of performances is as varied as the range of performers.[35]

What then are the requirements of a new definition of a performance? It is desirable to have certainty in the law; but absolute certainty, in the form either of protection for all performances or of protection for none, has been rejected herein in favour of a more flexible approach. The legal definition of a performance is located on a continuum between the extremes of complete protection and an absence of protection, but it is closer to complete protection than has been provided for in previous definitions. The definition can now be placed with some certainty and in a principled manner. The requirements of the definition of a performance are as follows: (i) It should encompass the performances that are at risk; (ii) It should be comprehensible to national legislators and be reasonably easy to translate into national law; (iii) It should be technology neutral; (iv) It should leave policy issues, such as the protection of the performing arts, to national law.

A performance should be defined as follows:

> A performance is the transitory activity of a human individual that can be perceived without the aid of technology and that is intended as a form of communication to others for the purpose of entertainment, education or ritual.

This definition incorporates the important elements of a performance. They are:

Transitory nature: Until a performance has been enhanced or augmented in some way by technology that enables the performance to be fixed, either temporarily or permanently, a performance is transitory. It exists past the instant that it is made, if it can be said to exist at all, only in the memories of the spectators who witnessed its creation.

Individual human activity: A performance must be made by a human individual. It must also be something that can be perceived by another: it must be able

[34] The task may be more difficult than it appears. For example, ballroom dancing is an example of a dance that is included, as was noted above, in the definition of a performance in the Australian legislation. However, that same legislation specifically excludes sporting activities. If ballroom dancing is included as a sport in the Olympics are those dancers protected or not under the legislation? (The International DanceSport Federation has been granted recognition as a recognised federation pursuant to Rule 29 of the Olympic Charter: International DanceSport Federation IDSF, 'IDSF and DanceSport now fully Recognised by IOC,' <http://www.idsf.net/press97/idsfp172.htm>.) See above n 8 and accompanying discussion.

[35] See the discussion of the natural right theory in ch 3.

to seen or heard, or seen and heard. The form of words used does not allow for a performance to be the activity of a group of individuals.

Perceived without the aid of technology: A performance is something that can be perceived directly without the aid or presence of intervening technology. It is important that the terminology used in the definition is technology neutral to ensure that the definition remains effective in the face of technological advances. 'Broadcasting', 'communication to the public', 'fixation' and 'reproduction', as those terms are understood in the regime of performers' rights, all affect or enhance a performance. If performances are affected by technology in some way then they should be described in a way that indicates those effects. Such performances should be described as unfixed performances or fixed performances, as in the broadcast of an unfixed performance.

Intended: The element of intention to influence an audience by a performative activity is essential to a performance. Communication at the level of a conversation, for example, is excluded.

As a form of communication: Communication embodies two important aspects of a performance. On the one hand, a performance cannot exist until it is embodied in an activity. On the other hand, the activity must communicate in the form of entertainment, education or ritual.

To others: An audience is essential to a performance. It is not essential, however, that the audience be present spatially and temporally at the making of the performance, provided the element of intention to communicate with an audience is present.

Entertainment, education, ritual: It is suggested that these are the fundamental forms of communication that identify performative activity.[36]

The law performs its work blindly. A performance that falls within the boundary markers proposed above should therefore be protected irrespective of issues such as the content of the performance, the context and purpose for which it is made (that is, it shouldn't have to be made in the entertainment industry) or the quality or merits of the performance. The law, at least at the level of international agreements, should not recognise such differences between performances.

C Assessment

To complete the task of formulating a new definition, there should be an assessment. There are two measures that can be applied.

[36] Schechner includes 'healing' in his 'four great realms of performance': Schechner, 'A New Paradigm for Theatre in the Academy' above n 31, 9.

The first is that the new definition must contain the four characteristics that were identified earlier in this chapter as being present in a wide range of performances. (They are: a natural person; a performative activity; the presence of other individuals; the performer's intention.) Judged by this measure, the new definition successfully achieves its aims as it addresses each of these characteristics directly. It explicitly requires that a performance be the act of an individual human; that it be a performative act of communicating for certain purposes; that there be an audience; and that there be an intention to affect others. It is therefore at least as effective as the other definitions that were reviewed.

The second measure is framed in negative terms. It comprises the four requirements that were identified in this analysis for a new definition of a performance. (They are: absence of qualitative criteria; context is not determinative; performers need not be professionally qualified; performances are not restricted to particular cultural activity.) Again, the new definition is successful. (i) It is based on the premise that all performances are open to exploitation. (ii) The context of the performance is not important. (iii) The performer does not have to be qualified in any sense. (iv) It is neutral in the sense that it does not favour any position or policy decision.

It is probably impossible to arrive at a definition of a performance that contains every performative activity within its boundaries.[37] There will always be activities that slip through. It is submitted, however, that the new definition of a performance that is proposed in this chapter is a major step forward in the evolution of a complete definition. Several features justify special mention. First, it acknowledges that the development of the technology of exploitation has had consequences for all performances, not just for some. It is technology neutral. Second, it is also based on an understanding of the nature of a performance derived from performance theory and legal studies. It is couched in language that should be understood by legislators, users of performances and their legal advisers. Third, the necessary elements of a performance are stated explicitly. Finally, the definition avoids the trap of placing the protectable subject matter into classes.

[37] Certainly, the delegates to the Rome Diplomatic Conference found the 'practical difficulties' too great, 'Report of the Rapporteur-General', above n 32, 46.

3

The Arguments for Performers' Rights

I INTRODUCTION

IN THE GLOBAL economy, rights in the nature of property rights increasingly govern the exploitation of products of the mind. Most economic problems can be solved, at least to the satisfaction of the injured parties, by throwing some rights at the problem. (Becker suggests that 'public expressions of admiration' in the form of honours and awards can be a plausible alternative to property rights.[1]) For the wider public, however, the provision of intellectual property rights means that they are restricted from accessing the products of the mind, the subject matter of protection, without the consent of the right holders.

One of the questions posed in the opening chapter was: why should performers be protected? That is another way of asking the question, does the mere advance of technology entitle performers to protection? Performers should be able to justify a system of rights that protects their interests in their performances. It is not suggested that the arguments must be definitive. There are usually two sides to any debate. Further, there are factors that are important to the performers' arguments that cannot be demonstrated. Although the unique sound and appearance of a performer can be identified, how can one empirically prove that a performance bears the imprint of the personality of a particular performer? However, it should be required of performers that they must be able to point to strong arguments in favour of their position, relative to the counter-arguments.

This chapter identifies the arguments in favour of a regime of intellectual property rights that protects performers and their performances and then examines the most important arguments in detail. There are at least two reasons for analysing these arguments: (i) The grant of a right to control all or some of the uses of a performance, including the right to equitable remuneration for those uses (as that term is used in the language of performers' rights[2]), should be based on something more than a bare assertion of the strength of the case for

[1] LC Becker, 'Deserving to Own Intellectual Property' (1993) 68 *Chicago-Kent Law Review* 609, 622. See also: EC Hettinger, 'Justifying Intellectual Property' (1989) 18 *Philosophy and Public Affairs* 31, 41.

[2] One of the primary rights provided for performers under the Rome Convention and the WPPT, but not under TRIPS, is a right to equitable remuneration. See the discussion below in ch 9.

these rights.[3] If performers cannot justify the establishment of a system of performers' rights then, surely, that system must be called into question; (ii) An analysis of the arguments will provide an insight into the nature of the rights that should be granted.

The arguments that are reviewed relate, in the main, to performances made in the entertainment industry. However, it is an underlying theme of this book that performances should be defined widely and that the protection of performers' rights, where it is available, should not be restricted to performances of literary and artistic works. Nor should the protection of those rights be restricted to performances within the commonly understood boundaries of the entertainment industry.[4] It must therefore be borne in mind when reviewing the arguments raised in favour of performers' rights that performers and performances outside the twin constraints of literary and artistic works and the entertainment industry should be protected.

II INTRODUCING THE ARGUMENTS

The arguments in favour of performers' rights were usefully summarised by the minority of the Copyright Law Review Committee ('CLRC') which reported in 1987 on the need for the legislative protection of performers in Australia.[5] The main arguments include the following:

(i) The justification for works of copyright applies to performances.[6] Performers' contributions easily meet the standard of originality required by copyright.[7]

[3] Arnold comments a number of times on the strength of the arguments in favour of performers' rights but he never really explains those arguments: R Arnold, *Performers' Rights* 2nd edn (Sweet & Maxwell, London, 1997) [1.15] and [1.16].

[4] Of course, it all depends on how entertainment is defined. Simensky refers to five major branches of the entertainment industry: 'movies, television, live theatre, music and print publishing'. M Simensky, 'Defining Entertainment Law' (1986) *The Entertainment and Sports Lawyer* 13, 13. Vogel includes those elements but extends his coverage to include new media, toys and games, gaming and wagering, sports, performing arts and culture, amusement/theme parks: HL Vogel, *Entertainment Industry Economics: A Guide for Financial Analysis* 4th edn (Cambridge University Press, Cambridge, 1998).

[5] The report produced by this committee is one of the most significant government sponsored reports on performers' rights in the common law world: Copyright Law Review Committee, Commonwealth of Australia, *Report on Performers' Protection* (Canberra, Australian Government Publishing Service, May 1987) [120–181]. Those arguments have been reiterated in other Australian commentaries on the subject, for example: Australian Copyright Council, *Performers' Copyright* (Australian Copyright Council, Redfern, Sydney; 1996); D Gruzauskas, 'Performers' Rights; The Right of Personality and the Possibility of a Proprietary Right' (1995) 6 *Australian Intellectual Property Journal* 92.

[6] Copyright Law Review Committee, above n 5, [126]–[134], Australian Copyright Council above n 5, [3.1].

[7] Copyright Law Review Committee, above n 5, [135]–[137].

(ii) The advent of technology that enabled performances to be fixed, broadcast, communicated to the public and re-used justifies the provision of copyright protection.[8] This argument has gained force with the continuing changes in technology associated with the entertainment and leisure industry and with the increasing re-use of performances.[9]

(iii) The system of industrial awards is not an adequate alternative to copyright protection. Although industrial awards ensure the payment of fees, it is not clear whether those fees reflect the proper reward for future use. The system also places the burden of paying for future use on the producer, rather than on the end user.[10]

(iv) The introduction or extension of performers' rights would not be 'inappropriate' given the international recognition of those rights.[11]

(v) A number of organisations, including those representing traditional copyright owners and broadcasters, support performers' rights.[12]

(vi) Performers should have access to compensation schemes and receive a share of the income generated from the use of recorded performances.[13]

It is worth considering in more detail one of the earliest arguments that was made in support of granting performers the right to control the use of their performances. This argument concerned the effect that technology had on performers' employment prospects. (It was, of course, an argument that only performers seeking employment could make.) In their quest for international protection, performers sought the assistance of the International Labour Organisation ('ILO'). For the ILO, performers' rights constituted a 'social and economic' problem.[14] It adopted a 'work protection' approach, addressing the problem as one of providing performers with the means to combat technological unemployment. Work protection was reflected in the proposals for the rights that performers should be granted which included: exclusive economic rights; the right to equitable remuneration; moral rights; and measures to provide increased employment opportunities.[15] The ILO's collectivist approach was gradually abandoned after the Second World War in favour of the 'intellectual

[8] *Ibid* [123]–[125].

[9] Australian Copyright Council, above n 5, [3.2.2].

[10] Copyright Law Review Committee, above n 5, [138]–[147].

[11] *Ibid* [148]–[167], Australian Copyright Council above n 5, [3.3].

[12] Copyright Law Review Committee, above n 5, [168]–[172], Australian Copyright Council above n 5, [3.5].

[13] Australian Copyright Council, above n 5, [3.4].

[14] 'Summary Records of the Proceedings', *Records of the Diplomatic Conference on the International Protection of Performers, Producers of Phonograms and Broadcasting Organisations* (ILO, UNESCO and BIRPI, Geneva, 1968) [4.2].

[15] International Labour Organisation, 'Rights of Performers in Broadcasting, Television and the Mechanical Reproduction of Sound' in *Report III of the ILO Advisory Committee on Salaried Employees and Professional Workers Second Session* (International Labour Office, Geneva, 1951) 80–85.

rights' approach favoured by UNESCO and the Berne Union, bodies that were accustomed to thinking in terms of copyright and individual rights.[16]

> Organizations of performing artists, especially the International Federation of Musicians (FIM), still regret that this collaboration led to a protection conceived in the form of individual rights and that it excluded any system of social guarantees.[17]

Performers' fears of mass unemployment have not been realised. The threat of technological unemployment, while it still exists, is no longer a serious argument in favour of performers' rights. It is true that the possibility of digital acting, the use of digital technology to generate 'virtual' performers, would appear to put the employment prospects of 'real' performers under some pressure. However, it is indicative that the powerful Screen Actors Guild in the United States has adopted a positive approach and has pointed out that there are real opportunities available within the digital environment.[18] The concern is more for the unauthorised digital manipulation of performers' images.[19]

There is a wide range of arguments that performers should have rights to enable them to prevent the unauthorised use of their performances and to enable them to secure equitable remuneration for authorised use. They are matched by counter-arguments that are at least as convincing.[20] It has been suggested, for example, that by the simple act of appearing before a microphone a performer accepts that a performance can be exploited by others.[21] This suggestion ignores the possibility of a contractual term to the contrary but it does

[16] R Rembe, 'Time for a Performers' Convention' (1991) 25 (4) *Copyright Bulletin* 25, 25–26. Rembe, a former Secretary General of the FIA, suggests that the reasons for this shift were twofold: that performers could no longer argue that fixed performances were merely an addition to an unfixed performance, and producers of phonograms could not stop the use of phonograms by broadcasters.

[17] Chesnais, another former Secretary General of FIA, made this comment. In that capacity, he was an observer at the Rome Diplomatic Conference. P Chesnais, 'The Rome Convention: Twenty-five Years Later' (1986) 20 (4) *Copyright Bulletin* 8, 11.

[18] C Koseluk, 'Digital Acting' <http://www.sag.com/dgtlacting.html>. Max Headroom, a computer generated television pitchman-personality that was popular in the early 1980s, has since faded into obscurity. More recently, the first virtual newscaster went on-line at <http://www.ananova.com/>.

[19] The first cinematographic film to use computer generated images was 'Tron' in 1982. Fully digital productions such as 'Final Fantasy: The Spirits Within', which was released in 2001, take the use of digital characters much further: R Lyman, 'Movie Stars Fear Inroads by Upstart Digital Actors' The New York Times (New York, United States of America), 7 July 2001, <http://www.nytimes.com/2001/07/08/technology/08FANT.html> .

[20] Arnold lists ten of the counter-arguments that have been advanced: the contribution of performers is subsidiary to that of authors; performers' rights may prejudice the rights of authors; performers' rights should be settled by collective bargaining; granting rights to all performers is impracticable; performances are transitory, works of copyright have permanent form; free copying of performances enhances performers' reputations; performers' rights are anti-competitive; requiring performers' consent may inhibit exploitation of performances; granting rights to performers may lead others to demand rights; performers' rights are not required under a state's international obligations. Arnold, above n 3, [1.15].

[21] C Masouye (W Wallace trans), *Guide to the Rome Convention and to the Phonograms Convention* (World Intellectual Property Organisation, Geneva, 1981) [XVI].

make the useful point that the performer has an option whether or not to perform. However, even with legally enforceable rights and the ability to walk away from a performance, performers as performers are seldom in a position to prevent or control the exploitation of their performances. It is futile to suggest that without performances there will be no phonograms, cinematographic films or television—the financial power represented by the producer is far greater than that of the individual performer.[22] The average performer who wants to work, to perform, must do so on terms established by the producer.

III THE COPYRIGHT APPROACH

The minority members of the CLRC were in favour of granting performers copyright in their performances 'for all the usual reasons'.

> The minority believes that for all the usual, although varying, reasons given as justification for copyright protection for those works which are presently protected, performances should be similarly protected.[23]

The rationale for copyright protection provides a useful framework for a discussion of the principles underlying performers' rights, for the following reasons. First, there are strong similarities between the making of a performance and the making of a literary or artistic work. Both a performance and a literary or artistic work are the products of intellectual effort—and the skills of the performer and of the author contribute to the success of the performance and of the work.[24] Secondly, both a performance and a literary or artistic work are vulnerable to unauthorised exploitation by a number of groups. While industrial property tends to establish two-way linkages between the right holder and the user, copyright supports a three-way relationship between (i) the right holder, (ii) the entrepreneur and (iii) the user.[25] Performers' rights also support a three-way relationship and, to the extent that the interests of a performer and an author are complementary, there is a useful analogy with copyright. Thirdly, performers' rights are characterised as neighbouring rights; they are recognised as being rights that are similar to copyright. It should not be surprising, therefore, that the arguments in favour of copyright are applicable to performers' rights.

There are two fundamental approaches to the justification of a system of copyright protection, and all the various arguments raised in the literature can

[22] Lucas appears to suggest this. A Lucas, 'Summary of the Proceedings of the Symposium' (Paper presented at the WIPO Worldwide Symposium of the Future of Copyright and Neighbouring Rights Paris, France, June 1–3, 1994) 269, 277.

[23] Copyright Law Review Committee, above n 5, [126].

[24] S Globerman and MP Rothman, *An Economic Analysis of a Performers' Right* (Consumer and Corporate Affairs Canada, Ottawa, 1981) 15.

[25] WR Cornish, *Intellectual Property: Patents, Copyright, Trade Marks and Allied Rights* 4th edn (Sweet & Maxwell, London, 1999) [9–42] and [12–01].

be seen as falling within these two approaches. The common law system is based on the grant of copyright as a form of economic inducement for works to be created and disseminated to the public. The author's right system, however, is based on the belief that the author is entitled to control the output of his or her labour that constitutes the reflection of his or her personality. These two approaches, which are referred to below as the 'economic incentive' theory and the 'natural right' theory will be applied in the following sections to the justification of performers' rights.

A The Economic Incentive Theory

As applied to literary and artistic works, the economic incentive theory assumes that the provision of exclusive rights encourages authors to create and publish those works.[26] Applied to the production of performances, it assumes that the prospect of the economic benefits assured by those rights will function as an inducement to the performer, as the right holder, for the production and exploitation of performances. The inducements may take the form of returns from the sale of performances, either as services, as in the theatre, or as goods, as in phonograms. In fact, performers are encouraged to perform for reasons that are varied and complex. There are different incentives for different categories of performers, some are monetary and others are non-monetary. A continuum would range at one end from the predominantly financial rewards of performing as a member of a professional orchestra, to the predominantly spiritual rewards of participating in a religious festival at the other end.[27]

A theory based on the need to provide an economic inducement for the production of performances presumes that a market exists for those performances and that resources are scarce. There is no doubt that there are a number of markets for performers and for performances; an important issue, therefore, is whether resources for the production of performances are scarce. In the developed countries, there is an excess of people anxious to perform. Performers in general are not a scarce resource.[28] If performers are not in short supply, then the incentive theory suggests that performers' rights should be regarded as an incentive to the production and exploitation of selected performances or to the

[26] Hettinger has suggested that the incentive theory is a paradoxical approach in that: 'It establishes a right to restrict the current availability and use of intellectual products for the purpose of increasing the production and thus future availability and use of future intellectual products.' See Hettinger, above n 1, 48.

[27] As to the position of a member of an orchestra, see C Flesch, 'The Orchestra Violinist' in G Seltzer (ed), *The Professional Symphony Orchestra in the United States* (The Scarecrow Press, Meutchen, NJ, 1975) 189.

[28] In respect of the United States, Australia, and Canada respectively, see: Screen Actors Guild, 'So You Wannabe an Actor?' <http://www.sag.com/wannabe.html>; D Throsby and B Thompson, *But What Do You Do for a Living? A New Economic Study of Australian Artists* (Australia Council, Strawberry Hill, NSW, 1994) 19; Globerman and Rothman, above n 24, 19–20.

making of performances in general that will at least return the costs of production. If this presumption is correct, it places a question mark over the economic incentive theory, for it is argued in this chapter that performers, as performers, do not initiate the production of performances and that they do not provide the economic investment for the production and exploitation of performances.

1 *The Decision to Invest in a Performance*

Whether or not a performance is made depends on a number of factors, and the existence of the protection of performers' rights may or may not be relevant. If performers' rights are to function as an incentive to the production of a performance, they must reward the person who is in the best position to exploit the performance by making it available to the public. But this is not the performer; the entrepreneur in the entertainment industry, who must meet high risks and high costs, is a much more likely candidate. In the popular music industry, for example, profits from 10 per cent of releases must cover the losses from the many unsuccessful products. In the cinematographic film industry, seven out of ten projects are losses.[29] Producers will naturally seek to produce performances that provide an adequate, or better than adequate, level of return. 'Producers produce what consumers will pay for, in the case of intellectual goods no less than in the case of breakfast cereals and automobiles.'[30] Similar arguments can be applied to the realms of education and ritual. There, performers are unlikely to be the ones making the decision as to whether performances will occur; rather, they are likely to perform at the behest of their superiors.[31]

It is outside the capacity of a performer, as a performer, to make the arrangements necessary for a performance. In situations where a performer is in the position to make the arrangements for a performance, the performer functions as a producer, not as a performer.[32] Performances are not made in a vacuum: they are intended to be performed for an audience. The traditional role of a producer is to arrange the financing; to select the performers and the director and participate in the creative decisions; to make choices as to the venue and the material to be performed; and also to set the price of the admission, an important determinant in the success of the production.[33] There are other arrangements to be made. Performances are usually augmented by the technology of

[29] See Vogel, above, n 4, 147 and 314. This proportion is confirmed by the Recording Industry Association of America in respect of CDs: Recording Industry Association of America, 'The Cost of a CD' <http://www.riaa.com/MD-US-7.ctm>.
[30] P Goldstein, *Copyright's Highway—The Law and Lore of Copyright from Gutenberg to the Celestial Jukebox* (Hill and Wang, New York, 1994) 178.
[31] It was suggested in the discussion of 'A New Definition of a Performance' in ch 2 that entertainment, education and ritual are the fundamental forms of communication that identify performative activity.
[32] In ch 6 a performer is defined as: 'a natural person who has performed an activity defined as a performance.'
[33] Globerman and Rothman above, n 24, 51.

broadcasting or communication to the public and arrangements need to be made for this technology. Performances may be performed in a purpose-built venue, such as a theatre, or 'on location' anywhere in the world.

These arrangements all require a range of support staff. Large productions will have the input of 'creative' people such as the music composer, the author of the script, the director and the choreographer. Other people who have input include lighting designers and costume designers and so on. The value of the performance in the market place is often determined by the contributions of people other than the performer. The result is that the performer is subordinate to the producer and is dependent on an invitation to perform. However much he or she may wish to perform, the performer does not make the decision as to whether a performance will go ahead and as to who will fill various roles. Even the decision to withhold his or her services, and not perform, does not determine whether or not the performance occurs. Nobody is irreplaceable. Yet it is precisely in his or her character as a performer that the performer is rewarded by the grant of rights in a performance to which many others have made substantial contributions.

As Cornish notes: 'The first purpose of the protection is to allow recoupment for the initiative of creating the material and the investment risked in producing and marketing it.'[34] Cornish was here talking about copyright, and the nature of copyright is such that it allows for this recoupment. Although the author of the work is usually the first owner, the requisite rights can be transferred to the publisher or to the other person involved in the exploitation of the work. Copyright therefore provides an incentive to the staging of performances of works by protecting the rights of the person who makes the financial investment, provided of course that the relevant rights have been transferred to that person. Performers' rights are a different and separate category of rights to be negotiated over. Unless performers' rights are as transferable as copyright, the danger is that instead of being an incentive they will be a disincentive to the person who takes the initiative in making the arrangements for a performance—that is, the producer.[35]

2 *The Nature of the Decision to Perform*

The notion of an incentive to perform suggests that a performer weighs the costs or difficulties of appearing in a performance against the benefits that will

[34] Cornish, above n 25, [9–46].

[35] Globerman and Rothman, above n 24, 94. This view is challenged by Rembe, who points out that the author's right to control the use of a work has not been a problem and claims that there is no reason to believe that performers are less capable of dealing with such rights in a responsible manner: R Rembe, 'Authors and Performers: Equal Contribution: Equal Protection' (1986) 20(4) *Copyright Bulletin* 30, 31. Rembe ignores two things: the importance of the transferability of copyright rights and the fact that performers' rights form another layer of rights on top of copyright that producers must secure.

accrue from the exploitation of the performance.[36] There are a number of obvious costs and benefits that must be considered. The costs may include special training, being away from home, long hours and losing income through forgoing other employment; the obvious benefits include the remuneration, the recognition and the opportunity for further employment. It seems unlikely that, when a producer has confirmed that a performance will be staged, the existence of performers' rights will act as an incentive in the form of the promise of future financial benefit for the performer to accept the opportunity.

At best, the right to control the uses that are made of a performance will strengthen the performer's bargaining position in negotiating the terms of employment. The knowledge that a regime of rights protects a performer's basic position as to first fixation or first broadcast of a performance, for example, may enable a performer to extract better terms and conditions from a producer and may therefore induce him or her to perform. If performers' rights are necessary to ensure basic financial rewards for performers, then performers deserve the protection of those rights. Yet, the performer should negotiate in the knowledge that threatening to use those rights unreasonably could prevent him or her from being chosen to perform.

A performer performs for two basic reasons. The first, which is not necessarily the most important, is the monetary reward that may be derived from several sources, including the enhancement of employment prospects in the future. Performers' rights support the performer's bargaining position; if a producer wants a performer's consent to the exploitation of a performance then the producer must pay. Some performers are attracted by the lure of future success, ultimately as a 'star', that offers the prospect of significant monetary benefits. The prospect of future employment, rather than the actual remuneration for the present performance, will often determine a performer's decision.[37] The second reason involves non-monetary benefits: public recognition, fame, glamour and the other elements of the star system can be as important as, or more important than, the monetary benefits to which they are closely related. '[Authors and artists] are not motivated primarily by monetary interests; many are impelled to create as part of their personality, creation being in their nature.'[38] Other non-monetary benefits include the person's pride in achievement and the enjoyment of the nature of the employment.[39]

[36] The minority members of the CLRC were prepared to widen the view taken of risk and investment in a performance to include the cost to the performer of a lost employment opportunity represented by a fixed performance. This assumes that the performer would have been employed in the place of the fixation, something that is extremely difficult to show: see Copyright Law Review Committee, above n 5 [128].

[37] Globerman and Rothman, above n 24, 50.

[38] G Davies, *Copyright and the Public Interest* (Wiley-VCH, Weinheim, 1994) 142. See the discussion in A Plant, 'The economic aspects of copyright in books' in A Plant, *Selected Economic Essays and Addresses* (Routledge Kegan Paul, London, Boston, 1974) 58–59.

[39] Globerman and Rothman, above n 24, 36. These commentators also suggest that modest changes in the level of income are unlikely to produce a significant increase in the number of performances.

3 *Performances of Special Cultural Significance*

Certain performances are regarded as being of special cultural significance to the state. Are there circumstances in which protection in the form of performers' rights could act as an incentive to the production of those performances?

There is a strong belief that certain performances, particularly in the performing arts, are an important part of the culture of the state and are a stimulus to learning and creativity. Four general benefits are said to flow from the performing arts: (i) the prestige conferred on a nation; (ii) economic benefits to businesses in the vicinity; (iii) provision for future generations; (iv) educational contribution to the community.[40] Performers have maintained a sense of their importance, a particular view of the value of creative endeavours associated with the performing arts. This has been expressed by a former Secretary General of the FIA in the following words: 'The ultimate purpose of legislation to protect authors and performers is to stimulate artistic creativity, in the interests of the public and the development of culture.'[41]

The view that a specific regime of intellectual property rights can act as an incentive to the making of such a narrow category of performances presents difficulties. Performances are not homogeneous. If the protection of those rights is restricted to performances of literary and artistic works, a number of categories of performances that are generally considered as making a valuable contribution to the culture of the state will be excluded.[42] Moreover, within the category of literary and artistic works, there are numerous performances that some critics would not recognise as contributing to the culture of the state, even performances of 'high culture' such as opera, let alone the excesses of popular culture.[43] One view is that the law should reward successful productions for their contributions to the economy of the state. The performing arts are not reliable sources of successful performances when measured against the criterion of popular success.[44] Popular music, cinematographic films and sport are the dominant forms of performance in modern culture.

Performances of expressions of folklore are also regarded as having special cultural significance. Although the term 'expressions of folklore' is used throughout this book, there is little agreement on how to define 'folklore', and the term is not used in the Rome Convention on TRIPS nor is it used in the Berne

[40] W Baumol and WG Bowen, 'On the Rationale of Public Support' in R Towse (ed), *Baumol's Cost Disease The Arts and other Victims* (Edward Elgar, Cheltenham, UK, 1997) 256–259.

[41] Rembe, 'Authors and Performers: Equal Contribution Equal Protection', above n 35, 30.

[42] The most notable are performances of expressions of folklore and performances of variety acts.

[43] 'Three Tenors concerts are artistic disasters because they are helpless captives of their audiences. Their listenership knows exactly what it wants to hear down to the song or the aria. These wildly profitable concerts thrive on the premise that curiosity makes people uncomfortable.' B Holland, 'Composers' Whys Affect the Whats' *The New York Times* (New York, United States of America), 11 August 1996, s 2 p 24.

[44] This is a point that is made in a number of the contributions to Part II and Part III of Towse, above n 40.

Convention. It is not defined in Article 2(a) of the WPPT. The closest that there is to an internationally accepted definition can be found in the 'Model Provisions for National Laws on the Protection of Expressions of Folklore against Illicit Exploitation and other Prejudicial Actions' that were adopted in 1982 following a series of meetings convened by WIPO and UNESCO.[45] Those understandings do not define folklore; instead they use the term 'expressions of folklore' to mean 'productions' of the characteristic elements of a community's artistic heritage.

As a means of protecting expressions of folklore under the intellectual property umbrella, copyright is not generally useful.[46] If copyright subsisted in the underlying material, which is often doubtful, the duration of copyright protection will usually have expired. But in the absence of copyright protection for the underlying works, performers' rights may provide a limited form of protection. Whether this protection actually functions as an incentive to the production of performances is unclear. The first owner of rights in a performance is usually the performer. For spiritual or cultural reasons, it may be important that the right to control the exploitation of a performance belongs to the community and not to the performer.[47] Performers' rights may therefore be a problem for the community group claiming ownership of the folklore. Where this is an issue, the simplest response would be for the community to refuse permission for a performance to take place; this demonstrates that performers' rights are potentially a disincentive to performances of expressions of folklore.

It can be seen that performers' rights are not the best way to ensure that performances of special cultural significance take place. A better way of increasing the number of those performances is to fund them directly.

[45] 'Report of the Committee of Governmental Experts on the Intellectual Property Aspects of the Protection of Expressions of Folklore', (1982) *Copyright* 278. The Model Provisions are Annex I to the report. They were followed by the preparation in 1984 of the Draft Treaty for the Protection of Expressions of Folklore Against Illicit Exploitation and Other Prejudicial Actions. Report of the Group of Experts on the International Protection of Expressions of Folklore by Intellectual Property, (1985) *Copyright*, 40, 47.

[46] World Intellectual Property Organisation (ed), *Introduction to Intellectual Property Theory and Practice* (World Intellectual Property Organisation, London, Boston, 1997) [8.120]–[8.123]. Article 15(4) of the Berne Convention is intended to protect works of folklore, C Masouye (W Wallace trans,) *Guide to the Berne Convention for the Protection of Literary and Artistic Works (Paris Act, 1971)* (World Intellectual Property Organisation, Geneva, 1978) (1978) [15.9].

[47] This possibility has recently received judicial recognition in the Australian case, *Milpurrurru v Indofurn Pty Ltd* (1995) 30 IPR 210, 214 per von Doussa J: 'Notions of responsibility under Aboriginal law differ from those of the English common law. If permission has been given by the traditional owners to a particular artist to create a picture of the dreaming, and that artwork is later inappropriately used or reproduced by a third party, the artist is held responsible for the breach which has occurred.' Certain waiata or songs of the Maori, the indigenous people of New Zealand, are not readily shared with people outside certain members of the tribal hierarchy. Ownership of the knowledge contained in such oral records is regarded as a form of caretakership. See M McLean, *Maori Music* (Auckland University Press, Auckland, 1996) 212–216.

> Common to [cultural] activities is the fact that their production at a socially optimal level cannot be wholly ensured by the market. Consequently, the state or other 'patrons' step in to support them.[48]

This is often achieved by imposing minimum local content requirements on local broadcasting and by the funding of performances by the state or other sponsors.[49] Hettinger has suggested that intellectual works stimulated by state funding could become public property without restrictions on their availability or use and outside the confines of an intellectual property regime.[50] This is an interesting suggestion but one that runs contrary to the arguments in favour of a regime of performers' rights that vests rights in individual performers.

B The Natural Right Theory

Under the natural right theory, works that spring from the intellect of the artist are seen as the expression or projection of the artist's personality.[51] On this basis, the artist has a natural right to control the use to which the work is put. It is appealing to apply this theory to performers and performances:

> The economic and moral rights of the performer in his performance, incorporated as it is in the film he made or the disc he recorded, do not arise from the fact that he has performed the work of another but rather from the fact that he has imprinted part of his personality and his art on a carrier, thereby allowing it to be exploited.[52]

The fact that sometimes a performer is the conduit for another's personal interpretation, (for example, as a player in an orchestra), or the fact that the performer usually interprets an author's work, does not detract from the

[48] B Casey, R Dunlop and S Selwood, *Culture as Commodity—The Economics of the Arts and Built Heritage in the UK* (Policy Studies Institute, London, 1996) xviii.

[49] The overarching theme of the United Kingdom Government support for culture and creativity is 'to free the creative potential of individuals through radical new initiatives'—Great Britain Department for Culture, Media and Sport, *Culture and Creativity: The Next Ten Years* (Department for Culture, Media and Sport, London, 2001) available at <http://www.culture.gov.uk/role/creative_next10.html>. Support for public funding of the performing arts is justified on three grounds: it provides opportunities for talented individuals from non-affluent backgrounds; it has an educational benefit; and arts are public goods that benefit society. See Vogel, above n 4, 288. On the arguments for and against public support for the performing arts, see 'Panel Discussion: Public Support for the Arts' in Towse, above n 40, 261.

[50] Hettinger above n 1.

[51] HC Jehoram, 'The Relationship between Copyright and Neighbouring Rights' (1990) 144 *Revue Internationale du Droit D'Auteur* 81, 87; D Gaudel, 'The Eternally Excommunicated—The Situation of Performers in France' (1980) 103 *Revue Internationale du Droit D'Auteur* 92, 128. In a well known statement written on behalf of the majority of the Supreme Court, Holmes J acknowledged the personal nature of an artist's work. 'Personality always contains something unique. It expresses its singularity even in handwriting, and a very modest grade of art has in it something irreducible, which is one man's alone.' *Bleistein v Donaldson Lithographing Company* 47 L Ed 460, 462.

[52] A Mille (WIPO trans), 'Performers' Rights: A New Independent Institution of Intellectual Property Law' (1984) *Copyright* 289, 290.

performer's relationship with his or her performance.[53] It is implicit in the natural right theory that all performances should be protected.

Performers' rights protect the unique sound and appearance of a performance, the constituent components that identify the performer. A performance always contains a recognisable physical representation of the performer. When a performance is made in the presence of an audience or fixed or a performance is broadcast or communicated to the public in audiovisual media, the appearance of the performer is there for all to see, although it may be camouflaged in a group performance. Even a performance that is made available on a purely audio level, by a masked performer or through a sound recording or a radio broadcast, carries an indelible mark by which the performer can be identified. Many individuals are familiar with the sound of particular vocalists or musicians and can easily detect a cover version of one of their performances as opposed to an original. At a more sophisticated level the listener may have access to equipment that can 'voice-print' the performance and identify the performer's voice. The connection between a performance and the performer is therefore manifest. (By contrast, an author can conceal his or her connection with a work simply by writing under a pseudonym.)

The appeal of the natural right theory is, however, somewhat blunted by the wide variety of performances that can be performed and by the varying standards of those performances. Nevertheless, it has already been noted that the law performs its work blindly. If a performance meets the criteria of a performance that are set in the law, then the performance will be protected irrespective of its content or its standard. Unless a level of personal expression is defined and rigidly enforced—and this would lead to difficulties in deciding the necessary level of expression and the choice of arbiter of these levels—it must be accepted that all performances bear the imprint of the performers who made them. Even if a 'personality ratio' measuring a performer's contribution to a performance could be devised and was widely accepted, the problem would still remain that an individual with a low ratio might imbue a performance with a personal interpretation beyond that of an individual with a higher ratio.[54]

[53] There was considerable opposition from authors to the grant of performers' rights. On a theoretical level, this opposition was based on the proposition that there was no room for exclusive rights in addition to those of authors. As set out in the work of Piola Caselli, as discussed in: W Nordemann, K Vinck, PW Hertin, (English version by G Meyer based on the translation by R Livingston), *International Copyright and Neighboring Rights Law: commentary with special emphasis on the European Community* (VCH Publishers, New York, 1990) 342 and E Ulmer 'The Rome Convention on Neighboring Rights. Part II' (1963) *10 Bulletin. Copyright Society of the U.S.A.* 165, 166.

[54] For an example of a 'personality ratio', see A Bertrand, 'The Moral Rights of Performers: French Law, International Law and Comparative Law' [1994] 4 *Entertainment Law Review* 114, 121. The problem of finding reliable indicia for personality that justifies a stake in property rights is discussed in J Hughes 'The Philosophy of Intellectual Property' (1988) 77 *The Georgetown Law Journal* 287, 339.

Copyright has overcome this obstacle by requiring a level of originality, however small that might be in practice, and by requiring that works and other subject matter must be fixed in order to be protected. It is inappropriate, however, to apply the copyright test of originality to performances and performers' rights. This can be illustrated by considering copying. Literary or artistic works that are copies of another work will not normally meet the requirement of originality. No performance can ever be the same as another performance (excluding performances reproduced in audio or audiovisual fixations). Each performance is a physically and psychically unique activity even if the performer deliberately sets out to mimic another performance. Nor is there a place for the fixation requirement that is common in copyright legislation. Performances do not have to be fixed in order to be exploited. Indeed, the earliest demand made by performers was for protection for their unfixed performances. It follows, therefore, that rights should subsist in each and every performance by virtue of the imprint of the performer's personality on each performance.

There are two elements to a performer's natural right in a performance. The first is the right to protect the embodiment of his or her self-expression:

> [t]he essentially moral right . . . which should enable a performer to compel respect for the integrity of his performance, to have his name attached to his performances, and to be able to conduct his career in accordance with his essential choices.[55]

The second is the performer's purely economic interest in the use of the performance: the performer is accorded the right to profit from the uses to which the performance is put, including the right to object to the performance being used for a different use from that to which consent was originally given. These two elements are not entirely distinct. It is also difficult to separate (i) the arguments in favour of performers' rights based on an economic incentive from (ii) the arguments based on the economic element of a performer's natural right to control the uses to which a performance may be put. A performer's natural right, however, justifies a wider level of protection than the protection justified by an incentive to increase financial returns.

There is an inherent problem associated with justifying a regime of performers' rights on the basis that a performance expresses the personality of the performer. This problem arises with the need to exploit the performance. A producer will normally require that all the economic rights in a performance be gathered under his control. However, can a performer part with rights that he or she has justified on the basis that the performance those rights protect is an expression of his or her self? If the performer agrees to transfer the rights, that is tantamount to transferring control over an aspect of his or her personality and denying the link that justified the award of rights in the first place.[56]

[55] Gaudel, above n 51, 128.

[56] There is an interesting discussion of this issue in the context of copyright in Hughes, above n 54, 345–350.

1 *Protection of the Performer's Self-Expression*

A performer should be able to object to uses that exploit a performance in ways that show the performer in a bad light. In the first place, a performance reflects a person's personality and an injury done to a performance will therefore strike at the performer's personality and at the performer's opinion of himself or herself as a person. In the second place, showing a performer in a bad light will affect his or her reputation prejudicially and therefore could lead to the loss of opportunities to perform.[57] These observations are subject to the qualification that the so-called prejudicial use may be apparent only to the performer, who is unlikely to be a detached and objective observer.[58]

The means of protection in these circumstances are two-fold: by moral rights or by other means. A system of performers' rights founded on the natural right theory should, however, provide explicit protection for a performer's self-expression in the form of moral rights. It is worth noting, however, that the existence of inalienable moral rights could result in the performer having the right to control the aesthetic content of the performance as it is finally distributed to the public. This is potentially another disincentive to the production of performances.[59]

2 *The Economic Element*

There are two desirable outcomes that could flow from an award of economic rights to performers: (i) The income of performers as a group would be increased. (This is desirable only if performers are underpaid; if they are not, then consumers will be called on to meet the increased costs of performances.) (ii) The level of resources devoted to the production of performances that are deemed culturally valuable would be increased. Unfortunately, neither outcome is likely. Any measures that achieve an increase in income and a redistribution of income amongst performers are likely to be accompanied by a

[57] This consequence has received judicial recognition in a number of English cases, including *Marbe v George Edwardes (Daly's Theatre) Ltd* [1928] 1 KB 269 and *Tolnay v Criterion Film Productions Ltd* [1936] 2 All ER 1625.

[58] *Shostakovich v Twentieth Century Fox Film Corp* 80 NYS 2d 575 illustrates the problem, especially if relief is sought in a state that is unlikely to be sympathetic to the performer's views. The case concerned composers who were Soviet citizens suing in a United States court. They sought a permanent injunction to prevent the use of their names and music in a cinematographic film that had an anti-Communist theme. The plaintiffs were unsuccessful in showing wilful injury or invasion of a moral right.

[59] The prospect that performers could prevent the exploitation of works was considered at the Diplomatic Conference that concluded the Rome Convention: see the discussion in Masouye, *Guide to the Rome Convention* above n 21.[1.4]–[1.10].

reduction of income to producers and a consequent reduction in the number of performances.[60]

Although the state has an interest in the production and exploitation of performances for the benefits that they provide to citizens in general, it can be argued that a performer holds the economic rights to control the use of those performances on the basis that he or she is special, that he or she deserves those rights.[61] There is a cross–over at this point with the economic incentive theory, for it can be said that those rights are granted as a reward and therefore that they act as an incentive to the performer. The argument is that performers, as the people who make performances, are morally deserving and therefore it is appropriate to reward them as a matter of policy. The problem with this argument is the validity of the assertion that performers are deserving people. Waldron has pointed out that it is all too easy to fall into the trap of arguing that it is appropriate to reward performers and to punish or constrain free-riders, and that therefore performers must be morally deserving. The steps in this process are to argue: (i) If a creative person such as a performer is morally deserving, then it is appropriate to reward that person. (ii) If it is appropriate to reward a person, then he or she must be morally deserving. (This is a fallacious inference.) (iii) It is appropriate to reward performers. (iv) Performers are morally deserving.[62] Another problem concerns the difficult value judgement as to which performances, and therefore which performers, are deserving. In all the circumstances, the better conclusion is that all performances should be protected.

Assuming that performers are indeed morally deserving and that they should be rewarded, an important subsidiary argument needs to be examined. It is sometimes said that performers should have the same rights as authors, because it is fair that they should.[63] In terms of the present discussion, fairness has several dimensions. (i) It is fair that performers should be able to profit from their performances and that others should not be able to take the benefit of those performances without the performer's consent and without paying an equitable sum. (ii) Performers as a group cannot be expected to look after themselves, but they are worthy individuals and therefore deserve rights to enable them to bargain on equal terms with producers. (iii) It is fair that performers should have the same rights as authors because they are all creative people and should therefore be dealt with in a similar fashion.

[60] Globerman and Rothman, above n 28, 7; Paper prepared by the Bureau of Transport and Communications for the Department of Communications and the Arts, *Economic Effects of Extended Performers' Rights* (Department of Communications and the Arts, Canberra, 1996) 11.

[61] For a discussion of 'copyright and the deserving author', see SE Sterk, 'Rhetoric and Reality in Copyright Law' (1996) 94 *Michigan Law Review* 1197, 1227–1244.

[62] J Waldron, 'From Authors to Copiers: Individual Rights and Social Values in Intellectual Property' (1993) 68 *Chicago-Kent Law Review* 841, 851–852.

[63] As to fairness generally, see Globerman and Rothman, above n 24, 8–16. See also Mr Justice Laddie, 'Copyright: Over-strength, Over-regulated, Over-rated?' [1996] *European Intellectual Property Review* 253.

However, it is very difficult to establish an objective standard of fairness. The Courts have recognised that fairness alone is an unsatisfactory and open-ended ground for the grant of a legal right and is not a substitute for legal principle.[64]

C Is Bootlegging a Special Case?

One of the earliest complaints of performers was that the new technology enabled their unfixed performances to be fixed without their consent and without providing them with any economic return. The broad category of bootlegging covers this activity. It has been defined as:

> [T]he creation of unauthorized recordings not from pre-existing ones, but from unauthorized taping of live performances or radio and TV broadcasts, or utilization of stolen tapes from unreleased studio sessions.[65]

Bootlegging illustrates some of the issues that arise when intellectual property rights are granted. Perhaps the most important is that the grant of performers' rights must recognise the interests of the individual performers, the interests of the state, the interests of the users who are constrained by the particular rights, and the interests of the members of the public who are also constrained.

If performers' rights are intended to promote the production and exploitation of performances, protected performances should be made available to the widest possible audience. Those rights can, however, be used to restrict access to the very performances for which they are intended to act as an incentive. When a performer deliberately restricts the public's access to a performance—an example being the refusal by a performer and his or her recording company to make and release a performance embodied in a phonogram—then the performer should be able to justify this decision. (A performer's failure to make a fixation of a performance available to the public is a frequent complaint of bootleggers.[66]) The public has an interest in having access to the performance as both an unfixed performance and as a fixed performance. If performers exercise their rights to restrict the public's access to unfixed forms of performances, the public and the bootlegger are worse off for the grant of those rights. The performer should be required to demonstrate that the restriction is for legitimate commercial reasons, perhaps in order to maximise the impact of the fixed

[64] *King v Mister Maestro, Inc* 224 F Supp 101, 105; *Moorgate Tobacco Co Ltd v Philip Morris Ltd (No 2)* (1985) 59 ALJR 77, 88.

[65] T Schultheiss, 'Everything You Always Wanted to Know About Bootlegs, But Were Too Busy Collecting Them to Ask: A Treatise on the Wages of Sinning for Sound' in C Reinhart (ed), *You Can't Do That! : Beatles, Bootlegs and Novelty Records, 1963–80* (Pierian Press, Ann Arbor, 1981) 396. Bootlegs were given their rather colourful name by the journal *Variety* in 1929.

[66] C Heylin, *Bootleg—The Secret History of the Other Recording Industry* (New York, St Martins Press, 1994) 382–390.

version that he or she has authorised, if and when that is released. The question is whether there is a proper balance between the interests of the parties. The bootlegger, purportedly arguing on behalf of the public interest, would answer that question in the negative.

Bootleggers make several other claims: (i) Bootleg sound recordings do not cause financial loss to the record companies and to the performer because those entities never intended to make a commercial release of phonograms embodying the performances in question.[67] (ii) The actual value of bootlegs is small compared to the overall value of the music industry.[68] (iii) Bootlegs may be in the public interest in that they are the only means of preserving historical performances.[69] (iv) Bootleg buyers will already have bought all the available recordings of the performer.[70]

Essentially, there are three arguments against bootlegs: (i) A performer may feel that a bootleg version does not accurately reflect his or her personal artistic or imaginative talents. This argument encompasses issues of quality of recording, packaging and the like.[71] (ii) The producer may have plans to release a legitimate fixed version of the same performance, in which case the bootleg would pre-empt this release to the detriment of the producer, the performer and the public. (iii) The bootlegger is free-riding on the investment of others, whether the phonogram is for commercial distribution or personal enjoyment.[72]

IV THE ARGUMENTS REVIEWED

In this section, the two major arguments in favour of performers' rights discussed above—the economic incentive theory and the natural right theory—are reviewed to determine whether either justifies the implementation of a system

[67] C Heylin, *Bootleg—The Secret History of the Other Recording Industry* (New York, St Martins Press, 1994) 382–390.

[68] In 2000, the value of retail sales of recorded music in the United Kingdom was £2,0474 million. In the same period, the estimated retail value of bootlegs was £1.1 million. The corresponding figures for 1995 were retail sales: £1,6303 million and £15.5 million, British Phonographic Industry Ltd, *BPI Statistical Handbook 2001* (BPI, London, 2001) 56 and 85.

[69] The first bootleg recordings, which were made of the 1901–1903 seasons of the New York Metropolitan Opera House, are now regarded as valuable historical objects: Heylin, above n 66, 28.

[70] Schultheiss, above n 65, 405–406.

[71] The argument of inferior quality did not impress the Court in *Sony Music Productions Pty Ltd v Tansing (t/a Apple Music House)* 27 IPR 640. That case involved an unsuccessful attempt by Michael Jackson and his exclusive licensee in Australia to obtain an injunction to prevent the marketing of a number of CDs containing performances by Jackson. In an action under s 52 of the Trade Practices Act 1974 (Cth), it was argued that Jackson's reputation would be damaged by the inferior quality of the recordings. Einfeld J rejected this argument because the respondent had prominently labelled the product 'unauthorised' or 'not authorised' and the public therefore had the choice between high-quality authorised products and possibly inferior unauthorised products.

[72] D Schwartz, 'Strange Fixation: Bootleg Sound Recordings Enjoy the Benefits of Improving Technology' (1995) 47 *Federal Communications Law Journal* 611, 614.

of performers' rights. This section also considers whether performers have a special status that justifies those rights.

The extension of intellectual property rights into new fields should be a cautious exercise. It takes only a little effort, particularly for a performer, to come to either or both of the following conclusions: (i) that a performance should not be fixed or broadcast without the performer's consent, and (ii) that there should be equitable remuneration for the uses made of the performance. To a large extent, however, these issues can be dealt with on a contractual basis between the performer and the producer. The performer can decide whether or not to be involved and to perform. The terms on which the performance takes place are a matter for negotiation and will be subject to the parties' relative bargaining power. (Performers' advocates might well respond that exclusive rights are required precisely because of the need to redress the bargaining imbalance, and this may be the strongest argument in favour of a regime of performers' rights.) The performer also has recourse, in appropriate circumstances, to copyright and to causes of action that protect reputation.[73]

A Do the Arguments Justify a System of Performers' Rights?

The argument for performers' rights as an economic incentive to the production and exploitation of performances is unconvincing, primarily because the first right holder, the performer, is seldom able to initiate the production of a performance. The extensive level of copyright protection provided in most states also reduces the potential incentive value of performers' rights. Once a performance is fixed or broadcast, there will usually be protection for the interests of the producer and initiator of the performance as the person making the arrangements for the cinematographic film, broadcast or other subject matter in which the performance is embodied. The producer may also have taken an assignment of the copyright in the underlying work. Performers' rights are not an incentive to the producer; in fact they may function as a disincentive if they are used by performers as a weapon in the bargaining process. Even if performers' rights are transferable to the producer, this does not reward the producer who already has adequate protection under copyright. Thus, the transferability of performers' rights does not provide a benefit; it merely removes an obstacle, the possibility that a performer could withhold the performance. Performers' rights are thereby reduced to something to be bargained over and, as moral rights, to a means of ensuring that performances are not dealt with in ways that offend the performer's personal sensibilities.

Apart from the potential to act as a disincentive, the downside of an extensive performers' rights regime is that it will result in a number of costs. There are

[73] Ch 5 discusses the protection that is available to performers under several causes of action.

potential costs associated with establishing mechanisms to administer the collection and distribution of payments for the various uses of the performances. For countries that are net importers of performances there will be an outflow of royalties. A less obvious cost will arise if the performers' rights cannot be transferred or made subject to a compulsory licence, or, in the case of moral rights, if they cannot be waived. If performers' rights are inalienable, a performer will be in a position to disrupt the exploitation of the performance. The award of economic rights and moral rights is therefore unlikely to lead to the desirable end result of greater numbers of those performances that the state deems to be of especial value, particularly if those performances are likely to result in a net financial loss to the producer.

However, legal rights are not always grounded on sound economic reasoning. The strongest argument for performers' rights is the one that is hardest to test, namely that performers invest performances with aspects of their personality and that they are morally deserving of legal rights to control the uses made of the performance. The natural right theory rests upon an intuitive, unanalysed feeling that a performance belongs to a performer.[74] The theory is open to criticism, particularly the criticism that the personal interests of performers do not justify the award of legal rights, but it is still the strongest argument in favour of performers' rights.[75] If arguments based on economic efficiency do not stand up to scrutiny, then theories based loosely on cultural policy must take their place.

> The work of artists is the foundation on which much of what we regard as our distinctive culture is built and through which we come as a nation to some sort of cultural awareness.[76]

The implementation or the extension of performers' rights should therefore be acknowledged as being based on the recognition of the performer as an individual deserving of special rights not accorded to other workers. This may be difficult to accept, of course, for those who regard authors as the only artists deserving of personal protection, or for those who do not accept that artists are special individuals.

The legal analysis of issues that cross over into the social and human sciences is always fraught with difficulty.

[74] In his seminal work on the justification for a copyright system for books, Breyer described the natural rights theory as resting upon 'an intuitive, unanalyzed feeling that an author's book is his "property"': S Breyer, 'The Uneasy Case for Copyright: A Study of Copyright in Books, Photocopies, and Computer Programs' (1970) 84 *Harvard Law Review* 281, 288.

[75] The theory that a performance is an expression of a performer's self is not universally recognised. Auslander has described the theory as 'a highly problematic position from the perspective of acting and performance theory.' P Auslander, 'Legally Live Performance In/Of the Law' (1997) 41 *TDR The Drama Review* 9, 16.

[76] Throsby and Thompson, above n 28, 54. In this study, artists are defined as including performers.

> [T]he debates about popular music, plunder and 'theft' in popular culture, and the concepts of legality and illegality, have taken place . . . against the backcloth of controversy in the social and human sciences generally.[77]

If there is controversy in the social and human sciences then legal analysis is that much more difficult. In answer to the question posed at the beginning of this chapter, that of why performers should be protected, the issues raised in the discussion of the arguments for performers' rights do raise doubts about the grant of those rights. To justify those rights there is one possible conclusion: that it is in the public interest that performers and performances are protected as part of 'the Romantic myth that creative people are heroes of almost divine status.'[78]

B Are Performers Special?

Intellectual property rights should not be granted unless the recipients deserve those rights. If performers are to be the beneficiaries of valuable rights in the nature of property rights, it presumably follows that there must be something special about performers that marks them out from other workers and from other so-called creative people who are not similarly privileged. The concept that performers are special is a relatively recent one. Adam Smith gave 'players, buffoons, musicians, opera-singers, opera dancers' as examples of unproductive labour.[79] That attitude no longer prevails, but it is worth remembering that the categories of performers mentioned did not always hold the respected position that some, at least, do in modern society. By the time that performers approached the Berne Union requesting recognition for performances as a species of works, they did so from the stance that they were the equal of authors.

At any time, amongst all those people who can be described as performers, there will always be outstanding individuals. The problem is to identify those individuals and to agree that they are special. The identification of outstanding performers usually depends on the formulation of criteria and on gaining sufficient agreement on the criteria.[80] These may be fruitless tasks. Is it possible to develop criteria that identify outstanding street performers as well as outstanding opera singers, not to mention outstanding performers of expressions of

[77] S Redhead, *Unpopular Cultures—The Birth of Law and Popular Culture* (Manchester University Press, Manchester, 1995) 57.

[78] T Zeldin, 'The Value of Creativity' (1997) *International Arts Manager* 21, 23. See also J Boyle, 'The Search for an Author: Shakespeare and the Framers' (1988) *The American University Law Review* 625.

[79] Smith's comment has been cited by a number of commentators, for example: E Thompson, 'Twenty Years of the Rome Convention' *Copyright* (1981) 270, 274, and SM Stewart, *International Copyright and Neighbouring Rights* 2nd edn (Butterworths, London, 1989) [7.16].

[80] Note the reference to a personality ratio: see above n 54 and accompanying text.

folklore? Who will set the criteria and who will judge the candidates for protection? It is probably better to rely on a 'gut reaction' to decide whether a performer is outstanding and deserves to be described and treated as special.[81]

If it is impossible to agree on criteria that makes individual performers special and that entitle them to demand protection for their performative activities, the question arises: are performers as a group special? Performative activities are the product of intellectual endeavour. Some, at least, of these activities are deemed to be valuable as part of the culture of society. These activities are open to exploitation without the consent of performers. As a group, performers lack bargaining power when negotiating with producers. They also lack the ability to constrain the activities of third parties. They therefore need help. If performers are special, therefore, it is for those reasons. However, those reasons do not demonstrate that performers should have rights and that others should not. The issue as to whether others, such as directors and editors, who are involved in the production of performances and who are currently unprotected should have rights is outside the bounds of the present discussion.

The performers' perspective is simple and clear.

> In crude practical terms, the principle must be that each presentation of a performance must be paid for, whether it be live or in front of a (paying) audience, in a cinema, a department store or a private home—wherever it is and transmitted by whatever means.[82]

Technological developments resulted in performers losing control of their performances. A system of performers' rights can return that control. As deserving individuals, performers should have the right to control the uses that are made of a performance. They should also be able to transfer that right to another person. Apart from the right to determine whether a performance is to be exploited at all, control includes the right to determine the form of the exploitation, and the time and the place at which the performance will be made available.

[81] See the discussion of excellence in Becker, above n 1, 621.
[82] Rembe, above n 16, 29.

4

Technology and the Development of Performers' Rights

I INTRODUCTION

TWO IMPORTANT QUESTIONS are addressed in this chapter: from whom or from what do performers need to be protected; and, how should performers be protected? In discussing the second question, two other questions are addressed: where should protection be available; and how long should it last?

In answering those questions, this chapter is partly descriptive and partly prescriptive. In the first place, it expands on the inability of performers to control the uses that are made of their performances. The problem of control, or rather the lack of control, was identified in previous chapters as a significant consequence of the advance of technology. This chapter describes aspects of the relevant technology and also identifies the entities that decide how the technology is applied. The description of the technology of exploitation provides a sense of context and makes it clear that, for performers, the issue of control of their performances is not a minor problem. In the second place, this chapter builds on the descriptive material and explores issues relating to the rights that should be granted performers. As with copyright, the law of performers' rights is a child of technology.[1] Rights that are intended to restrict the uses that are made of a performance should respond to the modes of use to which technology has given rise. The prime consideration here is that performances are exploited without regard to geographical or political boundaries.

II TECHNOLOGY AND PERFORMANCES

In the context of the exploitation of performances, the function of technology is to provide the public with access to those performances. As noted in the opening chapter, performances that are unaffected by technology share two features.

[1] Goldstein has said that, 'Copyright was technology's child from the start.' P Goldstein, *Copyright's Highway—The Law and Lore of Copyright from Gutenberg to the Celestial Jukebox* (Hill and Wang, New York, 1994) 27.

They are transitory; and they are accessible only to those people present at the time and place of the performance. Technology has addressed those issues of accessibility in time and space to make performances permanent and transportable. They can now be embodied in audio or audiovisual fixations or both, and copies can be made of those fixations. Unfixed or fixed, performances can also be distributed in a variety of ways to a variety of audiences around the world.

A Categories of Technology

The simplest methods of making a performance available to a larger audience are to increase the size of the venue, to increase the volume of sound and to make the performance more visible. Relatively simple technology, such as a public-address system, enables a performer to reach large audiences, sometimes tens of thousands in very large auditoriums. The steps by which a performance reaches an audience of billions require more advanced technology such as phonograms, satellite broadcasting and digital technology.

For the purpose of the present discussion, it is useful to divide technology into two strands. One strand is directed to the fixation and reproduction of performances and another is directed to the broadcasting or communication of performances to the public. In practical terms, of course, this division is somewhat artificial for both strands are employed together in the exploitation of performances. Further, the development of technology is not a finite process; as new ways of exploiting performances are developed, performers will face new challenges.

1 *Fixation and Reproduction of a Performance*

The development of technology allowing performances to be permanently fixed was enormously significant because it meant that performances could no longer be regarded as merely transitory activities. It is accepted that a fixation requires sufficient stability of form for the performance to be perceived, reproduced or otherwise communicated by an appropriate device.[2] Once performances were

[2] M Ficsor, 'The Spring 1997 Horace S Manges Lecture—Copyright for the Digital Era: The WIPO "Internet" Treaties' (1997) 21 *Columbia-VLA Journal of Law & the Arts* 197, 205. Fixation is defined in Art 2(c) of the WPPT as: 'the embodiment of sounds, or of the representations thereof, from which they can be perceived, reproduced or communicated through a device'. This follows the definition of 'Fixation (First—) of sounds' in the *WIPO Glossary of Terms of the Law of Copyright and Neighbouring Rights*: 'The original embodiment of sounds of a live performance, or of any other sounds not taken from another existing fixation, in some enduring material form such as tapes, records or other appropriate device permitting them to be perceived, reproduced or otherwise repeatedly communicated.' An audiovisual fixation is defined in the same source as: 'The simultaneous sound and visual recording of scenes from life or a live performance or recitation of a work in any appropriate durable material form permitting them to be made perceptible.'

embodied in audio or audiovisual fixations it meant that they had been transformed into commodities—things to be traded, broadcast and re-broadcast, re-recorded, played and replayed.

Apart from ensuring that a particular performance can be reproduced at any time and in any place, the embodiment of a performance in an audio or audiovisual fixation has had a number other consequences that must be considered when a system of rights is framed:

(i) Copies of the first fixation can be easily and cheaply made and they can also be easily distributed around the globe. Further, each copy can be dealt with in the same manner as the first fixation. The development of digital technology has meant that those copies are as good as and sometimes better than the originals.[3] The two main components of the technology of fixation—phonograms and cinematographic films—are familiar throughout the world.[4] From the perspective of the law, the most important recent development in the technology of fixation has been the popularisation of cheap, efficient and simple means of fixing audio and audiovisual performances. The difficulty of policing the private use of the audiocassette player—recorder and then the video camera and the video cassette recorder meant not only that the performer had lost the ability to control the exploitation of a performance, but also that control had escaped from the hands of the recording and broadcasting industries.[5] This loss of control has continued with the Internet and the use of programs such as Napster and Aimster.[6]

For the purposes of the following discussion, reproduction is understood to mean 'the making of a copy or copies of a fixation,' as defined in Art 3(e) of the Rome Convention.

[3] For example, phonograms made with analog technology are often digitally remastered.

[4] The *WIPO Glossary of Terms of the Law of Copyright and Neighbouring Rights* defines 'Cinematographic work' as: 'Any sequence of images recorded successively on an appropriate sensitive material, mostly accompanied by sound, for the purpose of being shown as a moving picture. The classic form of cinematographic work is the cinematographic film to be projected on a screen.'

[5] It has been suggested that private use is becoming 'the usual and soon possibly even the only exploitation mode'. A Lucas, 'Summary of the Proceedings of the Symposium' (Paper presented at the WIPO Worldwide Symposium of the Future of Copyright and Neighbouring Rights, Paris, France, 1–3 June 1994) 269, 277–278.

[6] 'Napster is an application that gives individuals access to one another's MP3 files by creating a unique file-sharing system via the Internet. Napster lets users view and download the contents of MP3 directories from other users' hard drives. Type in the artist and/or song to receive a list, compiled by Napster's servers, of all the files currently available. Double click on a song to download from user's hard drive. Because Napster searches individual's hard drives, the number and variety of MP3 files vary. Not all Napster users are online at the same time; therefore, what you may not find one day, may, in fact, be there the next.' *Webopaedia Online Dictionary and Search Engine* <http://www.pcwebopaedia.com/TERM/N/Napster.html>. For a judicial discussion of Napster see: *A & M Records, Inc. v Napster, Inc* 114 F Supp 2d 896; and on appeal, *A & M Records, Inc. v Napster, Inc* 239 F 3d 1004. Aimster is described on its website in the following terms: 'Aimster allows you to find new buddies and to share with buddies. Aimster is safe and private. With Aimster you can add people to your buddy list, and share files in a protected environment. Aimster provides a secure private network where you are in control of your buddy list and control access to your files.

(ii) Fixations of performances in the form of phonograms and cinematographic films have become essential to the broadcasting industries. While broadcasts of unfixed performances are not uncommon, a glance at the television and radio listings will show that fixations of performances predominate.

(iii) A performance embodied in a fixation is open to manipulation and editing in ways performers may take exception to. 'Sampling' and 'morphing' are two examples.[7]

2 *Broadcasting and Communication to the Public*

The development of broadcasting was another important step in the transformation of performances into commodities. Broadcasting is defined in the WPPT as: 'the transmission by wireless means for public reception of sounds or of images and sounds or of the representations thereof: such transmission by satellite is also "broadcasting".'[8] While it is often associated with communication to the public, in the language of performers' rights broadcasting is distinct from communication to the public. The feature that distinguishes broadcasting is that it involves transmission of images or sounds or images and sounds by wireless means. By contrast, communication to the public means making a performance available to the public by wire, such as cable television; it excludes transmission by wireless means.[9]

As with the technology of fixation, the development of broadcasting and of forms of communication to the public had significant consequences:

(i) It is no longer necessary for a spectator to be physically near to a performer to enjoy a performance. Performances can now be transmitted

Aimster allows you to be in control without complex overhead or controls. It can be as closed and private as you need.' 'What is Aimster?' <http://www.aimster.com/whatis.phtml>.

[7] In *Jarvis v A & M Records* 827 F Supp 282 the defendants moved for summary judgment in a claim for copyright infringement involving sampling. The Court held partly for the defendant and partly for the plaintiff. At 286, sampling was described in simple terms as being 'similar to taping the original composition and reusing it in another context.' The Court also cited a more sophisticated definition of digital sampling: 'The conversion of analog sound waves into a digital code. The digital code that describes the sampled music . . . can then be reused, manipulated or combined with other digitalized or recorded sounds using a machine with digital data processing capabilities, such as . . . computerised synthesiser.' JG Finell, 'How a Musicologist Views Digital Sampling' (1992) *New York Law Journal* 5 n 3. Morphing is defined as: 'The animated transformation of one image into another by gradually distorting the first image so as to move certain chosen points to the position of corresponding points in the second image': *Free On-Line Dictionary of Computing* <http://www.nightflight.com/foldoc/>

In a recent example of 'morphing', Oliver Reed, the actor, died during the filming of the cinematographic film 'Gladiator', and to solve the problem, three separate head shots of Reed were taken from previous scenes and superimposed on the body of a stunt double.

[8] Art 2(f) of the WPPT.

[9] '"Communication to the public" of a performance or of a phonogram means the transmission to the public by any medium otherwise than by broadcasting,' Art 2(g) of the WPPT.

over distances, great or small. They can be transmitted globally, or they can be communicated within an auditorium. This technology has dramatically increased the number of people who have access to a performance. The availability of the necessary technology, rather than the availability of a performer, governs that access. Performers have lost the ability to control the number of spectators who view a performance and they no longer dictate where those people are physically located.

(ii) Performers have no effective means of controlling the making of fixations of their performances from a broadcast or a communication to the public. Although encoding devices are used in pay-to-view television and encryption devices are used on the Internet, performers seldom control them.

(iii) As with performances embodied in fixations, performances that are broadcast or communicated to the public are open to editing or manipulation, and performers may see these changes as distortions, mutilations or modifications that are prejudicial to their honour or reputation.[10] Even public-address systems in stadiums are usually equipped with controls that can be used to vary the volume and tone of the sound communicated to the audience. The content of the audiovisual element, conveyed through the television screens now common at rock concerts, religious revival meetings, sports events and other performances, will be determined by a director.

(iv) Broadcasting and communication to the public are more flexible forms of technology than fixations in the sense that they are capable of transmitting either fixed or unfixed performances. However, as noted above, fixed performances predominate.

3 *The Current Situation*

Compared with the printing press that eventually led to the law of copyright, the evolution of the new entertainment-oriented technology was rapid. The development of the phonogram industry was soon followed by the cinematographic film industry and then by various forms of broadcasting and communication to the public.

While Edison's invention of the phonograph dates to 1877, it was not until the development of the 78 rpm shellac disc, around 1896, that the recording industry became truly viable.[11] Phonograms are still hugely popular and hugely

[10] *Gilliam v American Broadcasting Corporation* 538 F2d 14 is an interesting example. This case involved a claim by the members of Monty Python against a broadcaster who had cut elements from their shows. It is discussed in ch 5 at n 33 and accompanying text.

[11] The shellac disc made mass production possible on an international scale. It was easier to manufacture and gave a better sound quality than the cylinders originally introduced by Edison. Important landmarks were soon reached. The sale of a million copies of a phonogram is still regarded as

profitable.[12] Audiovisual technology was slower to develop. Although devices for showing moving images were in use as early as the late eighteenth century, the first demonstration of the '*Cinematographe*' by the Lumière brothers on 28 December 1895 marks the beginning of the history of the cinema.[13] The cinema is now an important part of social and cultural life, bringing performances to billions of people every year.[14]

In the decades following the First World War, radio made both fixed and unfixed performances available to huge numbers of people all over the globe. More recently, television has become the prime entertainment tool of the developed world. The choice of the Marconi-EMI standard for the London Television Service in February 1937 was the beginning of modern television broadcasting.[15] After television became established, cable television was launched in the United States in the early 1950s although its penetration of the market was slow in the face of sustained opposition from the television networks. The range of television broadcasting was greatly extended with the introduction of commercial satellites. Television is now a huge, global industry capable of reaching billions of people simultaneously with broadcasts of performances.[16]

The recent development of digital technology has raised new issues, including the ability to produce virtually flawless pirate copies of fixations of performances and to distribute those copies easily, cheaply and quickly to any point on the globe. The development of digital technology has also extended the means of transmitting performances to include the Internet in which the

an important achievement in the music industry. As early as 1904, the opera star, Enrico Caruso, became the first recording artist to make a recording, 'Vesti la Giubba', that sold a million copies: M Chanan, *Repeated Takes—A Short History of Recording and its Effects on Music* (Verson, London, 1995) 5.

[12] Vogel reports that manufacturing costs for CDs in 1995 were US 60 cents as against a wholesale price of US$8.00. HL Vogel, *Entertainment Industry Economics: A Guide for Financial Analysis* 4th edn (Cambridge University Press, Cambridge, 1998) 146. The global music market was estimated to be worth US$36.9 billion in 2000. 'Recording Industry World Sales 2000: CD albums up, overall unit sales down 1.2%' <http://www.ifpi.org/site-content/statistics/worldsales.html>.

[13] S Robinson, *The History of World Cinema* (Stein and Day, New York, 1981) 1. The first feature film of over an hour's duration was 'The Story of the Kelly Gang' produced in Australia in 1906: R Vasey, 'The World-Wide Spread of Cinema' in G Nowell-Smith (ed), *The Oxford History of World Cinema* (Oxford University Press, Oxford, 1996)53. By the late 1920s 'talkies' had been developed. 'The Jazz Singer' with Al Jolson appeared in 1927 and the first all-dialogue feature film, 'The Lights of New York', was released in 1928, see Robinson, 163.

[14] It is claimed that the most viewed feature film of all time is 'Jesus', which had been seen by more than 1.5 billion people between 1979 and 1998: S Lee, 'Jesus Draws' (10 August 1998) 162 *Forbes Magazine* 58.

[15] Although the German Post Office offered a television service in 1935 it was not successful: A Abramson, 'The Invention of Television' in A Smith (ed) *Television An International History* (Oxford University Press, Oxford, 1995) 29–30. Notable performances that were televised in the early days of television included the Berlin Olympic Games in 1936 and Neville Chamberlain's 'Peace in Our Time' speech in 1938.

[16] An important development was the launch of the first commercial communications satellite, Intelsat I, on 6 April 1965.

convergence of technology has reached a new height. Consumers can now access, from their own computers, audio and audiovisual material embodying performances.

The continuing development of technology has therefore profoundly altered the status of a performance. The commodification of performances is most clearly seen in the entertainment industries. There is a symbiotic relationship between those industries and the performances that they exploit. Without phonograms, cinematographic films, broadcasting and the Internet, performances would obviously not be so widely distributed. Without a steady supply of popular performances, both fixed and unfixed, the profitability of those industries would be fundamentally undermined. The challenge for the law is to decide how to meet the issues raised by technology.

B Who Uses the Technology?

If technology is not in itself a threat or a problem for performers, then one must ask: who uses the technology? If performers' rights are implemented, against whom will those rights be exercised? It is not possible to describe the cycle of production, exploitation and reception of performances in a manner that applies across the board. While all performances, not just those made in the entertainment industry, are open to commodification, nevertheless, that cycle cannot easily be described in the same terms that apply to the production and distribution of tangible products.[17] It is true that elements within the entertainment industry respond to the same marketing and distribution imperatives that can be identified in other industries, but it is a mistake to view the entertainment industry as the only source of performances. It is also a mistake to regard the entertainment industry as sufficiently homogeneous to provide an example of a basic structure that can be applied to performances in general. Any attempt to devise a structure that is universally applicable to the making of performances will be frustrated by the sheer variety that exists in the entertainment industry alone, where the concept of a performance encompasses activities as diverse as busking, rock festivals, grand opera, sport in all its manifestations, expressions of folklore and circus entertainment. In turn, that variety demands a corresponding diversity of arrangements.

The short answer to the questions posed above is that there are two broad groups who use technology to exploit performances: those who exploit a

[17] Lovering has pointed out that, contrary to the dictates of economics textbooks, investment decisions in the music industry are based as much on subjective assessments as objective considerations: J Lovering, 'The Global Music Industry Contradictions in the Commodification of the Sublime' in A Leyshon, D Matless and G Revill (eds), *The Place of Music* (The Guildford Press, New York, 1998) 33.

performance with the performer's consent and those who exploit a performance without that consent.

1 *The Performer-Producer Relationship*

Four functions are essential to a performance: the producer, the performer, the author and the spectator. One individual may perform more than one of these functions. For instance, one individual may be both performer and author. It has even been suggested that all four roles may be conflated in the same individual.[18]

The relationship between performer and producer is at the heart of the production and exploitation of a performance. A performer is an individual who performs an activity that meets the definition of a performance.[19] The decision to exploit a performance by the use of technology will be a decision for the producer. 'Producer' has a more varied meaning. However, unless the term has a specific application in the text, for example—producers of phonograms, a producer is a person (including a legal person) who makes the arrangements for a performance and for its exploitation. Producer therefore encompasses such varied examples as the traditional producer in the entertainment industry, the person who makes the arrangements for the broadcast of a performance, the person who makes the arrangements for a lecture, the person who makes the arrangements for a religious service and everyone in between who makes the arrangements for a performance.[20] A producer will be the person responsible for the diverse arrangements associated with the exploitation of a rock concert at a stadium, which would conceivably include: the communication of the concert to the audience in the stadium, the broadcast of the concert on television and the making of a phonogram or an audiovisual fixation of the event.

It is in the interests of both the performer and the producer to ensure, first, that no use is made of the performances that they have made available to the public without their consent and, second, that the economic returns on the exploitation of the performances are maximised. This level of co-operation does not always extend to their dealings with each other where personal interests over the division of remuneration are likely to create tension. In many situations, the performer will be at a disadvantage in negotiating with the producer, who will usually be able to call on greater financial resources and greater experience. However, this is not always the case: the decline in the profitability of the

[18] J Dolan, J Roach, R Schechner, PB Zarilli and WB Worthen, 'Responses to WB Worthen's "Disciplines of the Text/Sites of Performance"' (1995) 39 (1) *TDR The Drama Review* 28, 36–37.

[19] In ch 6, a performer is defined as: 'A performer is a natural person who has performed an activity that is defined as a performance.'

[20] The *WIPO Glossary of Terms of the Law of Copyright and Neighbouring Rights* defines a 'producer' as: 'Generally understood as meaning the person who organises or finances and organises stage performances, the production of cinematographic works, the broadcasting of radiophonic works or the production of phonograms.' This is too narrow for present purposes.

phonogram industry during the 1970s has been attributed to excessive royalty bidding by major companies for popular artists.[21]

2 *Secondary Uses*

The secondary uses of fixations, particularly phonograms, illustrate the difficulties that performers have in controlling the use of a performance once it has been embodied in a fixation.[22] The expression 'secondary uses' is understood to mean the use of audio or audiovisual fixations in broadcasting or communication to the public.[23] The primary use of a phonogram, according to phonogram producers, is in the home. Any other use should be subject to a payment.[24] The use of phonograms in public places, in broadcasts and over the Internet has led performers and phonogram producers to seek remuneration for their consent to the use of the performances embodied in the phonograms. The broadcasters have argued that they are instrumental in promoting phonograms for the benefit of both performers and producers and that therefore they should not be obliged to pay for the use of those recordings.[25] In reply, the main argument of the performers and phonogram producers has been that since broadcasters could not function without phonograms they should pay a reasonable price for using them.

3 *Other Users of a Performance*

New technology is often accompanied by the swift emergence of people prepared to take advantage of opportunities for unlawful exploitation. In this category fall bootleggers and pirates.

Two general points are worth noting about bootlegs: (i) they are made from unfixed performances and (ii) they are not necessarily made for commercial purposes.[26] The loss to performers from bootlegging is said to come about because the sale of a bootleg means that the consumer will not buy an authorised copy of a performance and may not attend a performance in person.

[21] Vogel, above n 12, 145.

[22] The difficulty of controlling such use by way of contract is discussed below in ch 5.

[23] At the Rome Diplomatic Conference it was restricted to the use of phonograms: 'Report of the Rapporteur-General', *Records of the Diplomatic Conference on the International Protection of Performers, Producers of Phonograms and Broadcasting Organisations* (ILO, UNESCO and BIRPI, Geneva, 1968) 48.

[24] G Davies, 'The Rome Convention 1961—A Brief Summary of its Developments and Prospects' (1979) *European Intellectual Property Review* 154, 155; SM Stewart, *International Copyright and Neighbouring Rights* 2nd edn (Butterworths, London, 1989) [8.26].

[25] C Masouye (W Wallace trans), *Guide to the Rome Convention and to the Phonograms Convention* (World Intellectual Property Organisation, Geneva, 1981) [12.24]. Davies emphatically rejects this argument, Davies above n 24, 155.

[26] The non-commercial nature of the bootleggers' transactions was accepted by the Court in *Helliwell v Piggott-Sims* [1980] FSR 582. In that case the Court held that phonograms made for disposal by barter were not made for 'private and domestic use'.

Bootlegging is distinguished from piracy in that the latter involves the unauthorised copying for commercial purposes of materials that have been commercially produced with the performer's consent. Pirates usually seek to pass off the unauthorised or 'counterfeit' copy as an original. Apologists for bootleggers attempt to take the distinction further by claiming that: 'The notion that a bootleg exists in direct competition to the product peddled by legitimate record companies is absurd.'[27] They suggest that: 'An essential element of creativity separates bootleggers from their piratical cousins.'[28] They also suggest that: 'The distinction between bootlegs and pirate albums should be clear-cut: bootlegs are primarily designed to be collectors' items.'[29]

There may be a philosophical distinction to be made between bootleggers and pirates, but in terms of the present discussion there is no distinction. Both are categories of people who use increasingly sophisticated technology to make unauthorised fixations of performances and to make unauthorised copies of those fixations.

As well as bootleggers and pirates, a producer is the other person who may use a performance in a manner that has not been not authorised by the performer. There are circumstances when the use that a producer makes of a performance is outside the terms of the consent given by the performer. This may occur for a number of reasons including an error or oversight by the producer as to the limits of the consent;[30] a deliberate act by the producer;[31] or the exploitation of a performance by technology that was not yet developed when the performer gave his or her consent to other forms of exploitation.[32] The point is that performers may need rights to protect themselves against the producer.

C The Consequences for Performers

So long as performances remained unaffected by technology, answers to questions, such as when, where and how often would a performance be repeated, depended on the performer. When their physical presence was no longer necessary for the further enjoyment of performances, performers lost control of

[27] C Heylin, *Bootleg—The Secret History of the Other Recording Industry* (St Martins Press, New York, 1994) 7.
[28] *Ibid* 8.
[29] *Ibid.*
[30] *Ekland v Scripglow Limited* [1982] FSR 431. An actress consented to appear in a performance fixed in a video cassette. This consent did not include consent to fixation of the performance in a cinematographic film.
[31] *Reformation Publishing Co Ltd v Chrysalis Records Ltd* (Unreported, Court of Appeal, Oliver and Nourse LJJ, 15 November 1985). The marketing of a rock group's performances on television was held to be part of industry practice.
[32] *Ettore v Philco Broadcasting Corporation* 229 F 2d 481. The plaintiff's consent to the making of a cinematographic film of a prize fight did not include consent to the film being broadcast, some years later, on television.

the use of their performances with consequences for them that are, primarily, economic.

The immediate consequence, so performers asserted, was one of technological unemployment, a term used to describe the effect on employment that significant technological change has for the workers in an affected industry. Performers claimed that they had been placed in the position of competing with phonograms embodying their performances in dance halls, restaurants and theatres.[33] Another variant of this assertion was that television was devouring the raw material of variety artists or circus performers who had spent years perfecting their acts. The suggestion is that people who see the performance on television will not pay to see it performed in person.[34] Performers have pointed to other consequences of the development of technology. Bootlegging and piracy are said to have led to a loss of remuneration in the form of royalties and ticket sales to concerts. Currently, and most importantly, the claim is that absence of control has meant that performers have found it harder to negotiate a share in the profits made from the secondary uses of their performances.[35]

There are difficulties with these arguments. A claim based on the loss of an opportunity to perform assumes that there was such an opportunity in the first place. Similarly, a claim based on a share of royalties or profits assumes that the claimant is entitled to that share in the first place. The other major flaw in these arguments is that technology has been as much a benefit and a challenge to performers as a reason for economic loss. It has provided opportunities for employment and rewards for successful performers that were far greater than had previously been available.[36]

[33] E Thompson, 'International Protection of Performers' Rights: Some Current Problems' (1973) 107 *International Labour Review* 303, 304; Copyright Law Review Committee, Commonwealth of Australia, *Report on Performers' Protection* (Australian Government Publishing Service, Canberra, May 1987) [125].

[34] Thompson, above n 33, 308. The issue has come before the United States Supreme Court in *Zacchini v Scripps-Howard Broadcasting Company* 53 L Ed 2d 965. In that case, an unauthorised recording of a human cannonball act was later broadcast on the news of a local television station. The Court found for the plaintiff-performer.

[35] However, negotiations can provide performers with a high level of protection. The 2001 negotiations in the United States between the Screen Actors Guild and the American Federation of Television and Radio Artists on the one hand and the Alliance of Motion Picture and Television Producers on the other hand resulted in a three year theatrical motion picture and television production agreement. Highlights of the agreement include: significant increases in basic cable residuals and new provisions for the Internet. Details of the agreement are available at: <http://www.sag.com>; <http://www.aftra.org>; <http://www.amptp.org>. A similar two year agreement was also reached in 2001 between the Canadian Film and Television Producers Association and the Alliance of Canadian Cinema, Television and Radio Artists: <http://www.actra.ca>

[36] 'Explosive technology has been responsible for long-term growth in all sectors of the industry except live performing arts. Although millions of jobs have been created, employment growth has been selective, generally creating jobs for performers and other above-the-line personnel while eliminating jobs for technicians and skilled craft workers.' LS Gray and RL Seeber, 'The Industry and the Unions: An Overview' in LS Gray and RL Seeber (eds), *Under the Stars Essays on Labor Relations in Arts and Entertainment* (ILR Press, Ithaca, 1996) 42. Elsewhere, Gray and Seeber point out, at 17, that performing arts benefit from new markets created by technology.

Performers have also had to face the reality that performances can now be easily edited and manipulated. This places not only their economic but also their moral interests at risk. A performance in a cinematographic film can be altered or deleted with the consequence that the performer may lose a future employment opportunity because he or she is not seen as prominently or as favourably or is not seen at all. The other effect relates to the connection a performer retains with his or her performance, an activity that a performer may regard as an act of self-expression. A performer may also regard editing as distorting or mutilating his or her performance in a way that is prejudicial to his or her honour or reputation.

III THE PROTECTION OF PERFORMERS

In certain respects, the application of technology to the twin issues of the transitory nature of a performance and a spectator's limited access to a performance did not change anything. It was and is open to a performer to negotiate controls with the producer, and with anybody else, over the use that is a made of a performance.[37] In addition, it is always an option for a performer to refuse to perform, although withholding one's services is not a solution to the problem of unauthorised use once a performance is made. But in the absence of a sufficient demand for their services that can be translated into bargaining power, if performers are to retain control of the exploitation of their performances then they must be able to rely on a system of rights that responds to the differing modes of exploitation.[38] Looked at this way, performers' economic and moral rights have a dual function: (i) as a set of rules that protects them against the superior bargaining power of producers; and (ii) as a means of controlling the use of performances by third parties.

The first of these two functions proved to be influential with the majority of the Copyright Law Review Committee ('CLRC') that reported in 1987 on performers' protection in Australia.

> It seems to the majority that what is in substance sought by those representing performers is not a 'copy-right' at all, but rather a convenient basis upon which a system of enforceable collective bargaining can be superimposed upon the arbitration system. The issue, in a very real sense, is an industrial issue rather than a copyright issue.[39]

The minority of the CLRC, in a section headed 'The Inadequacy of the Industrial System', took issue with this approach. While acknowledging that

[37] The benefits and problems for performers of contract as a means of protection are considered in ch 5.
[38] The possibility of a performer seeking protection under contract, copyright and unfair competition is considered in ch 5.
[39] Copyright Law Review Committee, above n 33, [118].

performers could be protected by various means, it argued that they should have the right to control the use of a performance, together with a right of remuneration.[40]

Over time, the view espoused by the minority of the CLRC has prevailed. The place of performers' rights as a species of intellectual property rights is now unchallenged.[41] Such debate as there is has concerned whether performers should be entitled to copyright or whether they should be restricted to neighbouring rights (or 'related rights' as in Part II of TRIPS).[42] For present purposes, it is sufficient to acknowledge that performances meet the basic requirements of protection under an intellectual property rights regime. They are the products of intellectual effort, not only of performers but also of authors, producers and any other who contribute to the making of performances. They also meet the requirement for some degree of originality, in that each performance is a unique activity.[43]

A An International System of Rights

As noted in the previous chapter, the production and exploitation of performances is not limited by national boundaries and the international character of these phenomena is at the centre of the present study. The problems that performers face are on two fronts: first, there is the issue of obtaining protection in their state of origin; second, there is the issue of obtaining protection in other states. The technology is the same and the consequences for performers of the exploitation of their performances are the same in each state. An effective system of performers' rights should therefore be international in application and should ensure that performers of one state are protected in other states in which they are foreigners. The protection accorded foreign performers in a particular state should also be of the same level and character as that accorded to the performers who are nationals of that state.

[40] *Ibid* [180].

[41] Art 2(viii) of the Convention Establishing the World Intellectual Property Organisation 1967 states that: '"intellectual property" shall include the rights relating to: . . . performances of performing artists'. Performers' rights received wide international recognition by being included in Art 14 of TRIPS.

[42] For example, see: R Arnold, *Performers' Rights* 2nd edn (Sweet & Maxwell, London, 1997) [1.13]; Australian Copyright Council, *Performers' Copyright* (Australian Copyright Council, Redfern, Sydney; 1996); Copyright Law Review Committee, above n 33 [120]–[181].

[43] For a judicial perspective, see the comments of Stern J on performers' creativity in *Waring v WDAS Broadcasting Station, Inc* 327 Pa. 433, 440–441, a case decided by the Supreme Court of Pennsylvania.

B Scope of Protection

The question of the proper scope of protection to be afforded by performers' rights will be determined by whether one is an optimist or a pessimist.[44] Optimists are those who believe that performers' rights are rooted in the natural rights theory and that performers are therefore entitled to a range of rights that covers all the uses that are made of performances. Pessimists are those who think that performers' rights should be restricted to the minimum necessary to induce the making of performances. Clearly, optimists are in the performers' camp and pessimists are in the producers' camp.[45]

1 *The Problem of Method*

Lucas has suggested that there are two approaches to the implementation of economic rights in response to new technology. He calls the choice of approaches 'the problem of method'.[46] The first approach is a broad one that limits the number of economic rights to one or two, such as the right of reproduction and the right of communication. In the second approach, the specific rights, which are essentially components within the general rights, are spelt out as separate rights. For example, under the first approach, a right of first fixation would be included as part of the right of reproduction, but under the second approach it would be listed as a separate right.

Both approaches have advantages and drawbacks. The advantages of the general approach are that it is simple and, importantly, that it is technology neutral. Rights should relate to the technology that is currently used to exploit the subject matter of protection and, where at all possible, to the technology that will be used in the future. Provided the rights are drawn broadly enough, there can be reasonable certainty that all infringing activities will be covered, although it will be up to the performer to demonstrate that this is so. Lucas comments that the general approach 'is more intellectually satisfying, but it does sometimes suggest that groping in the dark which the practitioners so rightly fear.'[47] The second approach can claim the advantage of certainty. If a particular activity is listed then it is subject to a particular right. If that activity is not mentioned then users will argue, of course, that the right does not extend to that particular field of activity. Under this approach, whenever the law confronts new technology there is a choice to be made. Either the system of rights is expanded by the introduction of a separate right or the right is withheld and there are no

[44] It was noted in ch 2 that Goldstein categorises copyright lawyers as optimists or pessimists.
[45] See also the discussion in PE Geller, 'Must Copyright be Forever Caught Between Marketplace and Authorship Norms' in B Sherman and A Strowel (eds) *Of Authors and Origins* (Clarendon Press, Oxford, 1994) 176.
[46] Lucas, above n 5, 278.
[47] *Ibid.*

further constraints on the use of performances. Technology is developing with such speed and sophistication that it is impossible to predict developments. In such an environment, the general, technology neutral approach is to be preferred.

2 *Economic Rights*

Economic rights can exist at various levels in a performance. This becomes apparent as a performance is taken further away from its origin as an activity performed by a performer. At the preliminary level, a performance may exist only as a description in a work or in the mind of a producer. There can be no performers' rights in a performance until it assumes the form of an activity performed by a performer and spectators have been granted access to that activity:

(i) On the primary level of protection, rights should protect an unfixed performance against exploitation that is not authorised by the performer. An unfixed performance may be exploited by fixation, by broadcasting, or by communication to the public.

(ii) On the second level, performances that have been broadcast or communicated to the public, but have not been embodied in a fixation, should be protected from being exploited further without the performer's consent. A good example would be the right to make a fixation of a performance that is communicated to the public—in other words, the right to prohibit a form of bootlegging.

(iii) On the next level, there may be rights that protect fixations of a performance in the same way, *mutatis mutandis*, as an unfixed performance is protected. Thus, a performer may have the right to control the communication to the public of a fixation of a performance. Although in principle there should be no distinction between the protection afforded an audio fixation and an audiovisual fixation, such a distinction is made in the three international instruments.[48]

(iv) The final level of protection relates to derivatives of the performance. A derivative may take one of two forms. First, it may involve the making of a fixation of a performance in which the fixed performance is altered in some way. For example, a performer may appear to say or to do something different, or he or she may appear to perform in an entirely new context, that is, his or her performance is morphed. In most instances, a right of reproduction will cover this form of derivative exploitation, as the new fixation will include a substantial part of the original fixation. The second form of derivation is one in which another performer has copied, in a new

[48] The distinction that is made will be clarified in Part III in the discussion of the scope of protection provided by the international instruments.

> performance, the gestures, voice, appearance or other indicia that were embodied in the performance of the original performer. Currently, there is no protection at an international level for this form of adaptation.

In line with the general approach advocated above, it is proposed that there are two basic economic rights that are directly linked to the ways in which performances are exploited which, in turn, are linked to the technology employed. They are therefore the two economic rights that should be granted to performers. Those two rights are the right of making available and the right of reproduction.

The right of making available has a broad compass. The exploitation of a performance flows from its initial presentation: unless a performance has been made, there is nothing to exploit. Performers hold within themselves the ability to control the initial presentation. It is those acts of exploitation that make the performance available to a wider audience that they need to control. The right of making available encompasses: (i) the right to authorise the broadcasting and communication to the public of an unfixed performance; (ii) the right to authorise the broadcasting and communication to the public of a fixed performance; (iii) the right to authorise the rebroadcasting of a fixed or unfixed performance; and recently, (iv) the right to authorise the making available of a fixed or unfixed performance in an interactive system. (The last right may also be said to be included in the right of reproduction.) The right of making available includes the right to authorise access to intangible representations of a performance, such as those embodied in audio or audiovisual broadcasts. In the words of one commentator, these are 'non-copy-related rights': they cover acts by which performances are made available for direct rather than deferred use, which means that the performance is perceived at the time it is made available.[49]

The right of reproduction is of similarly broad compass. It can also be seen to flow from the act of making a performance available. The right of reproduction protects a performer's interests in fixations of a performance. It encompasses: (i) the right to authorise the first fixation of a performance; (ii) the right to authorise the reproduction of a fixation of a performance; (iii) the right to authorise the distribution of a fixation of a performance; (iv) the right to authorise the rental of a fixation of a performance; and, (v) the right to authorise the lending of a fixation of a performance.[50] These are 'copy-related rights'; they cover acts by which copies of performances are made available to consumers for deferred use, in that the act by which the copy is made available is separate in time from the perception by the consumer of the copy.[51]

[49] Ficsor, above n 2, 207–208.
[50] For an analysis of the elements of the right of reproduction, see C Masouye (W Wallace trans,) *Guide to the Berne Convention for the Protection of Literary and Artistic Works (Paris Act, 1971)* (World Intellectual Property Organisation, Geneva, 1978) [9.2]–[9.5].
[51] Ficsor, above n 2, 207–208.

Optimists and pessimists will argue over the proper scope of performers' rights. An optimist will argue that a wide interpretation should be given to the basic economic rights, that they should be interpreted in terms of the purpose that they are intended to achieve. The right of making available would, under this interpretation, include the right of making available in the digital environment. A pessimist will argue that the economic rights should be interpreted descriptively and therefore narrowly. Thus, the right of making available would be restricted to the right to prevent unauthorised fixation of an unfixed performance.

3 *Moral Rights*

The provision of moral rights can be justified on the basis that a performance is a reflection of a performer's personality.[52] The moral rights that are relevant to the performer are the right to be identified as the performer of a performance ('the right of attribution') and the right to object to distortion, mutilation or other modification of his or her performance ('the right of integrity').

The right of attribution translates easily into the context of performers' rights from industry practice in the entertainment industry. Custom and contract have, for a long time, demanded that the names of at least the principal performers be provided for performances both fixed and unfixed. In the entertainment industry, performers are dependent on their reputation to obtain engagements so it is important that their role in a production be acknowledged. However, the right to be identified should always be subject to practicalities; it is unlikely that all the performers on phonograms broadcast on radio, for example, could or should be identified.[53]

The right to object to injury done to a performance because that performance is an expression of a performer's personality is more contentious. The right of integrity threatens the producer's control of the form of the finished product. A producer will usually want this control so that the finished product can be exploited in the manner that the producer has determined, although a producer may surrender creative control to a performer who has sufficient bargaining power.[54]

Apart from moral rights, the level and nature of exploitation is something that can be dealt with by contract between performer and producer prior to

[52] The natural right theory is discussed at length in ch 3.

[53] Contrast, for example, the screen credits that list performers in a cinematographic film and the lack of credit given to members of an orchestra on the jacket of a phonogram.

[54] Performers in the popular music industry are more likely to be granted artistic control than performers in the cinematographic film industry. It has been suggested by a proponent of moral rights for performers that performers should waive moral rights over the final cut of a cinematographic film: N Steer, 'Moral Rights for Performers' (1994) 12 (1) *Copyright Reporter* 19, 21.

the performance itself, although this is always subject to the extent of the performer's bargaining power. Where contractual rights are inadequate because of third party use, various causes of action, such as defamation and passing off, are available to the performer against third parties whose actions in respect of a performance might injure the performer's honour or reputation.

C Duration

A discussion of technology and performers' rights must always carefully consider the duration of those rights, that is the term of protection. The duration of any intellectual property rights is affected by a number of factors including the juridical basis for granting those rights and the public interest in access to the intellectual property that is protected. The technology that is applied to the exploitation of performances is constantly being upgraded, and in practical terms, this means that performances are open to exploitation for increasingly longer periods. In other words, technology has extended the economic life of a performance. While not the sole determinant of the duration of rights, the advance of technology is therefore a factor to be considered.

The duration of performers' rights should be set as a reasonable period of time within which the right holder has the ability to protect fixations of a performance against unauthorised use having regard to technological developments and to the public interest in the wide dissemination of performances. Within these constraints it is possible to decide on a term of protection that is not entirely arbitrary. There are three main options:

(i) The term of protection could be linked to the life of the performer. This option reflects the argument that performers' rights can be justified as protecting an expression of the performer's personality. Rights, both economic rights and moral rights, should therefore terminate on the death of the performer.

(ii) The rights could last in perpetuity. A perpetual term is arguably oppressive in that it takes no account of the public interest in ensuring the widest possible dissemination of performances.

(iii) The third option is to link the rights to the economic life of the performance on the basis that the protection of a performance secures economic advantages to the performer from the exploitation of the performance. If performers' rights are justified on the basis of their economic benefits to the performer, then logically, this is the most attractive proposition. Why should performances be protected past their 'use-by-date', their economic life? The interests of performers and producers will have been served. The difficulty with linking rights to the economic life of the performance is deciding when that economic life has ended; as already noted, this is something that technology may extend.[55]

D The Question of a Live Performance

The expression 'live performance' has been deliberately avoided up to this point in the discussion because it lacks precision.[56] Nevertheless, it is a term that is often used and the concept needs to be discussed.[57] (The use of the term 'create a performance' has also been avoided; the neutral term 'make a performance' has been preferred to avoid any suggestion that a performer is, or must be, creative.[58])

'Live performance' is usually used in ordinary discourse to refer to a performance that is made at the same time that an audience perceives it. The term includes performances that the audience perceives solely through their senses, that is, without the aid of technology. It also includes performances that are enhanced by technology in a variety of ways. An individual who attends a 'live concert' at a large stadium will hear sounds through the amplification system and will see the performer in close-up on a giant screen. The performance may also include pre-recorded and computerised sounds. Can either the appearance or the sounds of the performance be accurately described as 'live'? The effect of technology is even greater when an individual perceives a 'live broadcast' of a performance. The audience does not perceive the performance as an integral whole; rather, the audience's perception is mediated by the director's decisions as to camera angles and the like.[59] Another difficulty is the transitory nature of a performance, for it exists only in present time and space and immediately moves into the past. Once it is performed, it is gone forever. In the absence of technology, a performance can exist only in the memory of the individual members of the audience physically present in time and space. It is this transitory nature of a performance that the law finds at once difficult to deal with but impossible to ignore.

A distinction is therefore to be made between performances that are unfixed and those that have been fixed. A further distinction can be made between performances that have been exploited by the technology of broadcasting or

[55] Performances that have been recorded in analog phonograms as LPs, for example, can be re-recorded in digital format and re-issued as CDs.

[56] In the Report of the Rapporteur-General to the Rome Diplomatic Conference, it is noted that the Conference agreed not to use the term 'live performance' because of its ambiguity. Several attempts to define the term were unsuccessful. Report of the Rapporteur-General, above n 23, 43–44.

[57] The term is used in the United Kingdom and Australian legislation, see s 180(2) of the Copyright, Designs and Patents Act 1988 (UK) and s 248A(1) of the Copyright Act 1968 (Cth).

[58] The exception is that the use of the term by other commentators has been preserved.

[59] See the discussion of this point in W Benjamin (H Arendt ed, H Zohn trans), *Illuminations* (Fontana, London, 1973) 230.

communication to the public and ones that have not been exploited in this manner. Where it is necessary to refer to a performance and to indicate that the audience's perception of the performance has been enhanced or affected by intervening technology the primary term 'performance' will be qualified. Thus, a performance that is embodied in a fixation will be described as such or as a 'fixed performance', and a performance that is not embodied in a fixation will be described as an 'unfixed performance'. Using this terminology, it can be seen that a 'live performance' is accurately described as 'an unfixed performance', or 'an unfixed performance that has been broadcast or communicated to the public'.

E Performances Exploited in Audiovisual Media

There is obviously a difference between exploiting performances in audiovisual media and exploiting them in audio media. In principle, however, the fact that a performance is fixed, broadcast or communicated to the public by means of audiovisual rather than audio media should not affect the protection that is available for the performer.[60] The implementation of rights for performances exploited in audiovisual media as compared with audio media may lead to problems for producers, but they are certainly not insuperable. Legal devices, some of which are already in place, could overcome the difficulties that cinematographic film producers, particularly those in the United States, would allegedly face. Awards and agreements incorporated in contracts of employment already deal with the rights of performers to share in the rewards from the exploitation of performances embodied in audiovisual media.[61] Another approach is to incorporate in national law provisions enabling the transfer of the economic rights in performances, such as a rebuttable presumption of the transfer of rights from the performer to the producer.[62]

If one is going to provide rights for audiovisual performances at a lower level than those applying to audio performances then the arguments for doing so

[60] No distinction is made in the United Kingdom legislation and, generally, there is no distinction made in the Australian legislation. However, the application of Part XIA of the Copyright Act 1968 (Cth) to World Trade Organisation countries is restricted to sound recordings, sound broadcasts and sound transmissions through diffusion services, see Regulation 4B(2) of the Copyright (International Protection) Regulations 1969 (Cth).

[61] See the new agreements referred to above, n 35. For a discussion of copyright and the cinematographic film industry, see N Reber, *Film Copyright, Contracts and Profit Participation* (Wiley-VCH, Weinheim, 2000).

[62] In the United Kingdom legislation, performers' property rights are 'transmissible by assignment, by testamentary disposition or by operation of law', s 191B of the Copyright, Designs and Patents Act 1988 (UK). Art 2(5) of the Council Directive 92/100/EC of November 19, 1992 on rental right and lending right and on certain rights related to copyright in the field of intellectual property provides for a rebuttable presumption of transfer in respect of the rental right. Art 2(7) goes even further and would allow Member States to provide for all kinds of means of transfer including a non rebuttable presumption of transfer and the application of the presumption to other rights of performers.

should be strong. In meetings at WIPO prior to the Diplomatic Conference in 1996, the arguments raised against the extension of protection to include audiovisual performances were as follows: (i) The rights of performers should not be superior to the rights of authors. (ii) There are important differences in the legal, economic and social conditions that apply in the phonogram and audiovisual industries. (iii) The status and conditions of employment of performers in the two industries are quite different. (iv) Any attempt to assimilate the two types of performers will weaken the audiovisual industry. (v) Any 'assimilation' of the rights of performers in the two industries is an industrial relations matter and should not be dealt with in an international instrument concerned with intellectual property rights.[63]

The arguments raised in favour of the extension of the protection of performers were: (i) Technological and commercial developments mean that the question of the rights of performers in audiovisual fixations no longer concerns only film actors. Other forms of performances are frequently embodied in audiovisual fixations and the traditional distinction between audio and audiovisual fixations of performances is no longer realistic; (ii) Performers need more than just copy-related rights, as their performances are increasingly exploited by audiovisual means of broadcasting and communication to the public; (iii) Performers' rights in audiovisual fixations have been included in the national law of some states and they also form part of the EC Directive on rental and lending;[64] (iv) Experience has shown that collective administration can solve the problems of the exercise of rights in audiovisual fixations; (v) The development of new technology means that it is appropriate for performers to have the right to negotiate for payment for all uses of their performances on the basis of exclusive rights; (vi) Collective agreements to make payments are no substitute for statutory rights for two reasons: first, the effectiveness of these agreements depends on the bargaining strength of the organisations representing performers; and second, they are not effective against third parties.[65]

It can be seen that the arguments raised against protection for performances in audiovisual media have more to do with the perceived difficulties for producers than they have to do with the inherent justice of the claims of performers. The arguments in favour of providing rights for audiovisual performers are stronger. However, the practical requirements of the audiovisual industry may be stronger than principle.

[63] The arguments put forward in various sessions of the Committees of Experts that met before the Geneva Diplomatic Conference were summarised by the International Bureau of WIPO: Discussion Paper prepared by the International Bureau of WIPO, 'Questions of the Rights of Performers in Audiovisual Fixations of their Performances', INR/CE/IV/3, (Committee of Experts on a Possible Instrument for the Protection of the Rights of Performers and Producers of Phonograms, Fourth Session, Geneva, September 4 to 8 and 12, 1995) [8].

[64] Council Directive 92/100/EC of 19 November 1992 on rental right and lending right and on certain rights related to copyright in the field of intellectual property.

[65] Discussion Paper prepared by the International Bureau of WIPO, above n 63, [7].

5

Other Protection for Performers

I INTRODUCTION

THE PURPOSE OF the present chapter is to answer the question: does the law already provide adequate protection for performers against the unauthorised use of their performances? In answering that question, various points that were made in the preceding chapters are developed. In chapter 3, the conclusion was reached that there are good arguments in favour of a regime of intellectual property rights. However, the question posed for discussion in the present chapter was foreshadowed in chapter 4 where it was pointed out that performers could, in fact, look to a number of legal regimes to protect their performances. Intellectual property rights, such as performers' rights, are open to the criticism that they are unnecessary or, worse, that they are oppressive. By determining whether other forms of protection are adequate, this chapter also determines whether performers do need the protection of a system of intellectual property rights dedicated to their interests.

To assess whether a system of performers' rights is, in fact, needed, two steps must be taken. The first step is to identify the major forms of protection that exist in national law for performers and their performances. The next step, which takes up the majority of this chapter, is to describe the main features of the various legal regimes, including any shortcomings. An assessment can then be made of the potential of existing legal regimes to meet the needs of performers for protection.

II CATEGORIES OF PROTECTION

Although performers' rights are protected under a number of international instruments, it is valuable to imagine an international legal community in which that system of rights does not exist. In such a world, are the means at hand by which performers can protect their performances against unauthorised use bearing in mind the technology, existing and to be developed, of the twenty-first century? As noted above, the first step is to identify the protection that exists.

A Identifying the Categories of Protection

Although performers have always been able to look to a variety of legal remedies, for present purposes only the three major categories will be considered.[1] One or more of the remedies in those categories will usually be available to performers who want to control the uses made of their performances. The first category is contract, which provides the most direct and, often, the most important form of protection that a performer may require. A step removed from the direct protection of a performance is the second category of copyright. It protects the underlying literary or artistic work from which the performance is derived, and other protected subject matter in which the performance is embodied, or both. Even less directly connected to a performance is the third broad category of unfair competition; in this chapter, the discussion of unfair competition is restricted to acts that involve damage to a performer's reputation.[2]

B The Basis for Analysis

In an imaginary world that has not implemented performers' rights, the continuing development of sophisticated technology will present performers with the problem of controlling the use of their performances, just as it has in the real world. Performers are therefore vulnerable to the possibility that their performances might be used without their consent or without remuneration for that use. They are also left in the position that the use that is made of their performances by producers, bootleggers or broadcasters could damage their honour or reputation.

There are a number of factors that should be considered in determining whether the protection offered by contract, copyright and unfair competition, either separately or together, is adequate for the purposes of performers. It is beyond the reach of this chapter to provide a comprehensive analysis of the principles that apply to those legal regimes. There are, however, four major questions that must be answered in respect of each regime: (i) Who is protected? (ii) What is the term of protection? (iii) Is protection available to performers in states in which they are foreigners? (iv) What is the scope of the protection? The answers to these questions will establish whether there are shortcomings in these other forms of protection for performers. If there are

[1] Masouye suggests that Art 7 of the Rome Convention could be implemented by means of 'any one or more of a number of legal theories: law of employment, of personality, of unfair competition or unjust enrichment, etc—and of course, if they wish, an exclusive right.' C Masouye (W Wallace trans), *Guide to the Rome Convention and to the Phonograms Convention* (World Intellectual Property Organisation, Geneva, 1981) [7.4].

[2] 'Unfair competition' is used in this chapter as a generic term to cover a range of causes of action.

serious shortcomings and they can be met by a regime of performers' rights, it follows that such a regime cannot be dismissed as unnecessary or oppressive.

III CONTRACT

A contract between a performer and a producer will be at the core of the commercial production and exploitation of a performance.[3] It may deal with a single performance or a series of performances. Various commentators have pointed out that the inter-related issues of risk, power and control in the entertainment industry are regulated by contract.[4] The importance of contract is nowhere clearer than in the entertainment industry, although it should be remembered that this industry is just one source of performances. Whether a performer is employed in the entertainment industry or in another, the principles of the law of contract remain the same.

In order to be in a position to enforce contractual rights concerning a performance, a performer must first of all be a party to a contract that establishes the rights, duties and liabilities of the parties in respect of the production and exploitation of that performance. Where the parties have agreed that a performance should be fixed or broadcast or communicated to the public by a producer, the task is then to establish the limits of a performer's control over the exploitation of the performance by the producer. The terms of the contract will depend on a number of factors, including the relative bargaining power of the performer and the application of awards and agreements to the situation.

A Nature of the Protection for a Performer under a Contract

In respect of contracts, the answers to the four fundamental questions that were identified above can all be settled by negotiation between the parties:

(i) The performer, together with the other party, will be the first owner of rights under the contract. It is up to the performer to ensure that he or she has rights to control the uses of the performance or, more typically,

[3] The significance of a contract as a means of establishing rights was emphasised in general discussion by the French delegate to the Diplomatic Conference that concluded the Rome Convention. He stated the reservations of his government concerning the need for a convention, and expressed the view that the aims proposed for the convention could be achieved by contract. 'Summary Records of the Proceedings', *Records of the Diplomatic Conference on the International Protection of Performers, Producers of Phonograms and Broadcasting Organisations* (ILO, UNESCO and BIRPI, Geneva, 1968) [50].

[4] S Greenfield and G Osborn, *Contract and Control in the Entertainment Industry* (Ashgate, Aldershot, 1998); AW Campbell, *Entertainment Law Cases and Materials* 4th edn (Austin and Winfield, San Francisco, 1997).

to receive appropriate remuneration for those uses including profit participation and residuals.

(ii) The duration of the contract is a matter for the parties to decide. The principle of restraint of trade has been applied in circumstances involving the exploitation of performers.[5] However, it would need to be an unusual circumstance for the principle to apply in respect of a particular performance, remembering that it is an individual performance that is the subject matter of protection under performers' rights.

(iii) On first principles, there is nothing to prevent the parties making the terms of the contract, and hence the protection of the performer, apply throughout the world.[6] It is in the interests of a performer to specify the proper law of the contract. If a dispute arises as to the application of the contract in a state in which the performer is a foreigner, the performer then has the comfort of knowing that the contract will be construed in accordance with legal principles with which his or her legal advisers are familiar.

(iv) As to the scope of protection under a contract, performers need to turn their minds to the relevant issues, which, in the context of the protection of performances, include: (a) the performance, which could be defined widely or narrowly; (b) the remuneration for the making of the performance and its subsequent exploitation; (c) the form and timing of the first fixation of a performance and its subsequent reproduction; (d) the distribution of the performance, whether it is to be made available to the public in phonograms or other tangible forms or whether it is to be made available to the public by broadcasting or communication to the public.

Performers who are employees are likely to find that their contracts of employment contain provisions that stipulate that all intellectual property rights belong to their employer. Although such clauses usually refer to copyright, patents and trade secrets, they may be broad enough to cover rights in performances. In jurisdictions where performers are well organised, the bargaining position of employee-performers has been bolstered by industrial awards and collective agreements which are incorporated either expressly or by implication into the contract of employment.[7] An

[5] There have been a number of cases in the popular music industry that have concerned the length of the term to which authors and performers were tied to publishers and producers: *A Schroeder Music Publishing Co Ltd v Macaulay* [1974] 3 All ER 616; *O'Sullivan v Management Agency and Music Ltd* [1985] 3 All ER 351; *Zang Tumb Tuum Records Ltd v Johnson* [1993] EMLR 61; *Silvertone Records Ltd v Mountfield* [1993] EMLR 152.

[6] In a case that is well-known in the cinematographic film industry, *Warner Bros Pictures Inc v Nelson* [1936] 3 KB 160, Warner Bros were able to enforce a restraint of trade provision against the actress Bette Davis. Although the contract was not an English contract and the parties were not British subjects, the contract was enforceable in the English courts.

[7] The International Labour Organisation believes that collective agreements have been an important factor in protecting the rights of performers: International Labour Organisation, *Conditions*

employer may not employ a performer on conditions less favourable than those set out in an award or agreement, although the parties may agree to more favourable terms for the performer.

B Shortcomings of the Protection under a Contract

There are three major problem areas for performers who rely on contracts to protect their performances. They are, however, common to all contractual arrangements and therefore do not represent good reasons, on their own, for rejecting the law of contract as an alternative to a system of performers' rights.

1 *Third Parties*

Subject to statutory provisions to the contrary, contractual rights can be enforced only against parties to a contract.[8] Technology has, however, made a performance open to exploitation by a number of groups that are not party to contracts between performer and producer. The largest group of strangers to that contract will be the members of an audience of a performance.

Members of an audience make unauthorised use of an unfixed performance commonly, if not exclusively, by making bootleg audio or audiovisual fixations of the performance. A performer can attempt to meet the problem by shifting the obligation to the producer to take steps to prevent the unauthorised fixations.[9] (Part of the producer's obligation will be to ensure that if an unfixed performance is broadcast no unauthorised fixation is made of the performance by the broadcaster. Television and radio stations routinely record broadcasts.) In limited circumstances, a performer may assume the responsibilities of a

of Employment and Work of Performers (International Labour Office, Geneva ,1992) 61. Orsattti provides evidence of the influence of the Screen Actors Guild in the United States: K Orsatti, 'The Actor's Road to Empowerment' <http://www.sag.com/rdtoempwrmnt.html>. A significant example is the agreement reached in 2001 between unions and producers in the United States. The Screen Actors Guild and the American Federation of Television and Radio Artists approved a new agreement with the Alliance of Motion Picture and Television Producers. In the United Kingdom an example is the agreement reached between the British Phonographic Industry Ltd and The Musicians' Union: British Phonographic Industry Ltd and The Musicians' Union, *The BPI and the Musicians Union Agreement for the Engagement of Musicians* (August, 1996. This agreement has been updated several times, most recently by the *Third Agreement* in 2001. Examples of awards can be found in Australia. They include the Actors etc (Television) Award 1985; the Musicians (ABC) Award; the Dance Company Award 1987.

[8] *Abernethy v Hutchinson* (1825) 47 ER 1313 is an early authority that involves performances. The plaintiff lectured on surgery; he had not published his lectures and students were aware that notes that they might make were not to be published. The defendant proposed to publish the lectures; he was restrained.

[9] Clause 14(a) of 'Artist's Agreement with a Promoter' included in R Bagehot and N Kannar, *Music Business Agreements* 2nd edn (Sweet & Maxwell, London, 1998) 274, provides: 'The Promoter will ensure that no unauthorised recording (whether audio or audio-visual) will be undertaken in the Venue during the Concert.'

producer and contract directly with members of the audience to prohibit the fixation of a performance. If a member of the audience then makes a fixation of a performance, he or she will be in breach of the contract made with the performer-producer.[10]

Members of the audience may avoid the imposition of conditions on their attendance, including a prohibition against making audio or audiovisual fixations of the performance, if they refuse to be bound by those conditions. It is open to a spectator to argue that conditions, often written in small print on the back of a ticket, were not brought to his or her attention at the time the contract was made and therefore that they do not form part of any contract made either with the performer or the producer.[11]

Another problem arises in situations where access to a performance cannot be controlled or can only be controlled with extreme difficulty, as with open-air performances. A performer will not have entered into a contract with a spectator who attends or views the performance without paying because the essential elements of a contract—such as consideration and intent to enter into legal relations—will be missing. Similarly, there will be no contractual agreement involving members of the audience where access is not subject to any obligation or where payment is voluntary; for example, there is no obligation to pay a street busker.

Performances that are fixed or that are broadcast or communicated widely to the public generate another level of difficulty for a performer seeking to rely on a contract.[12] In the general law of contract, the imposition of liabilities upon strangers is restricted to situations in which a subsequent purchaser is aware of the plaintiff's rights. The purchaser may be bound not to act inconsistently with the obligations assumed by the original contracting party. Case law also requires that the plaintiff has retained a proprietary interest.[13] A performer is unlikely to succeed, therefore, against a broadcaster who is unaware of any arrangements

[10] *Sports and General Press Agency, Ltd v 'Our Dogs' Publishing Company, Ltd* [1917] 2 KB 125, 127. In that case, the assignees of the sole rights to take photographs at a dog show sought an injunction to restrain the production of photographs taken by an independent photographer. The plaintiffs failed. The promoters of the dog show had not made it a condition that parties should not take photographs or make sketches. The plaintiffs could have acquired the rights they claimed by contract, but they had not done so.

[11] *Thornton v Shoe Lane Parking Ltd* [1971] 2 QB 163. Although this well known case does not concern a performer, it illustrates the principle.

[12] In a number of cases in the United States in the 1930s and 1940s, performers and phonogram producers were successful in controlling the use of phonograms by means of labels that warned that the phonograms were not licensed for broadcast. The Courts found that the performers had a common law property right. For example, see *Waring v Dunlea* 26 F Supp 338, 340. Such a common law property right was immaterial, however, in the view of Learned Hand J, stating the opinion of the Court of Appeals, Second Circuit, in *RCA Mfg Co, Inc v Whiteman* 114 F2d 86, 88. He held that even if a common law property right survived the sale of the records, it was difficult to see how a performer or, a fortiori, a manufacturer could impose a valid restriction upon their resale.

[13] *De Mattos v Gibson* (1859) 45 ER 108; *Lord Strathcona SS Co Ltd v Dominion Coal Co* [1926] AC 108; *Swiss Bank Corpn* v *Lloyds Bank Ltd* [1979] 2 All ER 853; *Law Debenture Trust Corporation v Ural Caspian Oil Corporation Ltd* [1993] 1 WLR 138.

between the producer and the performer that restrict the broadcasting of a performance. The principle does, however, seem to fit the limited situation where a performer has a contract with a member of the audience who makes a bootleg fixation of the performance, provided the third party is aware that the recording was made in breach of a contract and the performer has maintained some proprietary interest.[14]

Apart from the broadcaster, members of the audience of a radio or television broadcast may make use of a performance in ways that have not been authorised by the performer, particularly by home-copying. Protecting performances on the Internet presents even greater challenges. However, in digital media, technology may enable the person providing access to a performance to control that access and to impose conditions of use. Contracts and technological measures designed to prevent unauthorised use may prove to be at least as effective as intellectual property rights in protecting those performances.[15] The difficulty for the performer is that the contract is unlikely to be in his or her name and the technological measures are unlikely to be under his or her control.

2 *Terms of the Contract May Not Cover the Circumstances*

A performer must also consider the use that a producer makes of a performance when the producer is the other party to a contract for the production and exploitation of a performance. The issue most commonly litigated is the nature of the consent that a performer has given to the exploitation of a performance.[16] To ensure that it has unrestrained ability to exploit a performance without further reference to a performer, a producer should obtain from the performer all the necessary consents covering all foreseeable contingencies.[17]

[14] The facts of *Abernethy v Hutchinson*, above n 8, would fit the requirement as to knowledge of the restriction.

[15] P Goldstein, 'Copyright and its Substitutes' (1997) *Wisconsin Law Review* 865; JC Ginsburg 'Surveying the Borders of Copyright' (Paper presented at the WIPO Worldwide Symposium on the Future of Copyright and Neighboring Rights, Paris, 1 to 3 June 1994) 221, 224.

[16] A number of well-known performers have become involved in litigation on the issue of consent to the exploitation of their performances, including Britt Ekland, Peter Sellers and Shirley Bassey. See, respectively, *Ekland v Scripglow Ltd* [1982] FSR 431; *Rickless v United Artists Corp* [1988] QB 40; and *Bassey v Icon Entertainment plc* [1995] EMLR 596. In each of these cases, the Courts found for the plaintiff-performers.

[17] An example of a blanket consent provision is to be found in the Consent Form agreed by the British Phonographic Industry Limited and the Musicians' Union. The provision reads, 'I hereby grant to the Record Company in respect of all and any of my performances in respect of the above Title(s) all consents required under Part II of the Copyright, Designs and Patents Act 1988 (as subsequently varied, modified or amended) and all equivalent consents required throughout the world to enable the reproduction and use of all and any of my performances to the extent permitted by this Consent Form and the agreements prevailing at the time of the reproduction and/or use between the Musicians' Union and the British Phonographic Industry Limited.' The Musicians' Union and The British Phonographic Industry Ltd, *The Third Agreement between the Musicians Union and British Phonographic Industry Ltd'* (2000).

The rapid development of the technology of exploitation has required the Courts in a number of jurisdictions to decide whether the parties had a particular form of exploitation in mind when they negotiated their agreement. This situation normally arises when a performance is exploited by technology that was not developed or not readily available when the contract was negotiated. Exploitation of the performance using that technology may result in a windfall profit for the producer. Over time, the technology in question has changed from cinematographic films to television to video cassettes. A number of principles can be extracted from the judgments:[18] (i) The Court must consider the circumstances and particularly whether the parties have turned their mind to the inclusion of a particular medium or form of exploitation;[19] (ii) If the medium in question is not well known then it is unlikely that the parties had it in mind or should have had it in mind;[20] (iii) Depending on the circumstances, terms in the agreement may be interpreted to include other media;[21] (iv) The absence of a reservation in respect of a particular medium should not be read as a consent to exploitation by that medium.[22]

3 *Inequality of Bargaining Power*

The first hurdle that a performer faces in negotiating a contract with a producer is that he or she seldom has equal bargaining power. It is therefore more likely that a contract will favour the interests of the producer. Vogel has commented on the importance of a performer's bargaining power in the entertainment industry:

[18] On a related point, the minority in the Copyright Law Review Committee that reported on performers' rights were firmly of the opinion that consent to the exploitation of a performance in future technology should not form part of a contract. 'It is impossible to contract for use that is not foreseen. Technological development creates new forms of delivery and new markets and the control over these new uses, and the need for payment to performers must be addressed.' Copyright Law Review Committee, Commonwealth of Australia, *Report on Performers' Protection* (Australian Government Publishing Service, Canberra, May 1987) [145]. The issue does not appear to have troubled the majority.

[19] *JC Williamson v Metro-Goldwyn-Mayer Theatres Ltd* (1936) 56 CLR 567. In that case, the High Court held that a reference in an agreement to 'the motion picture film rights' covered 'Sound pictures, as well as silent films'. In another English case, the Court of Appeal held that an agreement in respect of 'cinematograph or moving picture films' entered into in 1919 licensed only the making of silent films: *Board of Governors of the Hospital for Sick Children v Walt Disney Productions, Inc* [1967] 1 All ER 1005.

[20] *Ettore v Philco Television Broadcasting Corporation* 229 F 2d 481. The Court of Appeals, Third Circuit, determined that the plaintiff-boxer's consent to the cinematographic film rights of his prize fight with Joe Louis in 1936 did not extend to the medium of television. The telecast of a film was a new use which was not in commercial existence when the plaintiff made his contract.

[21] *Ventura v Titan Sports, Inc* 65 F 3d 725. The plaintiff was employed to perform commentary for television broadcasts of wrestling matches; the majority of the Court of Appeals, Eighth Circuit, held that the contract did not contemplate a license for videotape distribution.

[22] *Ettore v Philco Television Broadcasting Corporation,* above n 20.

> As in all loosely structured private-market negotiations, bargaining power (in the industry's jargon, 'clout') is the only thing that matters. A new, unknown talent who happens on the scene will have little if any clout with anyone. Top stars, by definition, have enough clout to command the attention of just about everyone.[23]

Although a relatively small number of performers in the entertainment industry are in a position to dictate the terms of their contracts with producers, the majority of performers do not have that luxury and must depend on the safety net of awards and agreements. In this regard, they are no different from employees or self-employed people in other industries. Stars choose to bargain directly from a position of strength. Other performers have varying degrees of bargaining power and some bargain directly, not because they are in a powerful position but because of the nature of the engagement. A range of performers, from pub bands to variety acts, are obliged to arrange their own contracts with producers and with owners of venues.

Negotiating a contract places a performer in the position of having to make difficult commercial decisions. The valuation of the likely commercial success of his or her performance and the assessment of the producer's ability to meet the financial obligations to pay for the exploitation of a performance are just two such decisions. However, these are the sorts of decisions that involvement in the entertainment industry or in any other industry demands of the individual. Of course, a performer is at a disadvantage in that a producer will often have more experience in these matters. The overall inequality that performers find themselves in is therefore another shortcoming that performers face in depending on the law of contract to protect their interests in their performances.

IV COPYRIGHT

There are significant advantages for performers if they are able to rely on copyright as a form of protection for their performances. First ownership, term of protection, international application and the bundle of rights that is copyright all favour the performer. The difficulty is that under the Berne Convention the subject matter of protection of copyright does not include performances. Nonetheless, copyright is potentially valuable to a performer. Many performances are derivative of literary or artistic works; performances also provide the content of other subject matter protected by copyright, such as cinematographic films and phonograms.[24] The relationship between performances and

[23] HL Vogel, *Entertainment Industry Economics: A Guide for Financial Analysis* 4th edn (Cambridge University Press, Cambridge, 1998) 92–93.

[24] Although phonograms are excluded from protection under the Berne Convention, they are often protected under domestic copyright legislation, for example: s 1 of the Copyright, Designs and Patents Act 1988 (UK); s 89 of the Copyright Act 1968 (Cth).

copyright is, however, very definitely an arms-length one: any protection that is afforded to a performance is incidental to the protection that is provided for works of copyright and other subject matter. Does this matter? A pragmatist would answer, 'Of course not!' A sensible performer will grasp any opportunity that the law provides.

A Nature of the Protection for a Performer under Copyright

Of the four questions that are to be asked of each category of protection, the question of ownership of the rights is the most important in the category of copyright. The other three questions are more easily answered.

(i) If copyright is to provide a successful form of protection for a performance, the performer must establish that he or she is the first owner of copyright in a literary or artistic work or in other subject matter such as a phonogram. Performers can establish ownership in a number of ways:

   (a) Performers in the popular music industry are often the authors of the material used in their performances. They will be the first owners of the copyright in literary or artistic works. (Their ownership will be subject to provisions in national law as to the ownership of works of copyright created by employees or by persons under a commission.)
   (b) It has been suggested that 'many performers alter the work performed to such an extent that it is arguable that their contribution should be categorised as adaptation or arrangement rather than "mere" performance, or even as a new work. This has the consequence that the artist may acquire a separate copyright in the adaptation or new work.'[25]
   (c) Improvisation, which is commonplace for performers such as musicians, dancers, singers and comedians, is another way in which a performer may obtain copyright in a work. In its purest form, two features distinguish improvisation: First, the performer creates a work as he or she performs; the performance is not a reproduction of a pre-existing work. (It bears repeating that the copyright subsists in the literary or artistic work performed and not in the performance itself.) Second, unless the performance is fixed in some

[25] R Arnold, *Performers' Rights* 2nd edn (Sweet & Maxwell, London, 1997) [8.03]. In the same paragraph, Arnold gives a number of interesting examples of performers acquiring copyright in adaptations including: a popular musician making a disco version of an existing song, *ZYX Music GMBH v King* [1995] EMLR 281; a classically trained musician embellishing existing pop songs by writing an orchestral arrangement and adding new instrumental passages, *Godfrey v Lees* [1995] EMLR 307.

manner, when the performance is complete there will be no work in which copyright subsists.

(d) If a performer can show that he or she is the owner of the copyright in other subject matter—for example, a phonogram—in which a performance is embodied then the performer will be able to control the use of the performance, as a corollary to the protection afforded to the phonogram. Performers are less likely to be the first owners of copyright in other subject matter than they are to be the first owners of copyright in the traditional categories of literary and artistic works. It is the usual practice under national law that the person who makes the arrangements necessary for the making of a broadcast, phonogram or cinematographic film will be the owner of the copyright.[26] In some circumstances, the performer will be the person who makes the necessary arrangements.[27] However, the person who makes the necessary arrangements, and who is therefore the first owner of copyright is usually another person, a producer or, in a worst-case scenario, a bootlegger.

(ii) Article 7(1) of the Berne Convention sets the minimum term of protection for literary and artistic works as the life of the author plus 50 years. Article 7(2) provides that the term of protection for cinematographic works is 50 years. The term of protection of other subject matter relevant to performers that is protected under national law is commonly 50 years.[28]

(iii) National treatment is one of the fundamental principles underpinning the Berne Convention.[29] Provided that a performer who owns the copyright in a work or other subject matter is a national of a state that has acceded to the Convention, his or her works will be protected in other states that have also acceded to the Convention.

(iv) The bundle of rights that make up copyright is well-known. It is sufficient at this point to note that the two basic rights are the right of reproduction

[26] For example, s 9 and s 11 of the Copyright, Designs and Patents Act 1988 (UK); ss 97–99 of the Copyright Act 1968 (Cth).

[27] *Silly Wizard Limited v Shaughnessy* [1984] FSR 163, 168–9 The issues included the ownership of copyright in the fixation of a performance of works in the public domain. The folk group known as Silly Wizard played and sang traditionally based music from the Highlands of Scotland. They were in the practice of making tape recordings of their performances for the purposes of reviewing the band's music. A tape of a particular concert was made and a record made from that tape. The group successfully sought interdict against the marketing or distribution of the record. On the facts, the group was able to establish that they had made the necessary arrangements for taping the concert.

[28] Ss 13–14 of the Copyright, Designs and Patents Act 1988 (UK); ss 93–95 of the Copyright Act 1968 (Cth).

[29] Art 5(1) of the Berne Convention provides: 'Authors shall enjoy, in respect of the works for which they are protected under this Convention, in countries of the Union other than the country of origin, the rights which their respective laws do now or may hereafter grant to their nationals, as well as the rights specially granted by this Convention.' The principle of national treatment is discussed at length in ch 7.

and the right of performance.[30] If a performer is able to exercise those rights then, although indirectly, he or she will be able to control the exploitation of a performance that is either derived from a literary or artistic work or is embodied in other subject matter protected by copyright. Moral rights will also provide performers with the means to protect uses of performances that are prejudicial to their reputations.[31]

B Shortcomings of the Protection under Copyright

The shortcomings of copyright as a form of protection that enables performers to control the use of their performances can be brought together under two headings.

1 Performances Are Not Directly Protected

It is trite, but nonetheless accurate, to say that if protection is sought under copyright then the requirements of the law of copyright must be met. If a performer cannot point to a work or other subject matter in which copyright subsists, there will be no protection for a performance under copyright. There will be numerous occasions on which a performer performs a work that is not protected by copyright. Performers who make those performances are vulnerable to the unauthorised exploitation of their unfixed performances by bootleggers, for the bootleg fixations will not infringe copyright in the underlying works. Performances of expressions of folklore, variety acts and sporting activities are often not derivative of literary or artistic works. Equally numerous are the occasions on which no arrangements have been made by a performer or a person authorised by him or her for making a phonogram or other subject matter protected by copyright. Improvisational performers are also vulnerable to the activities of bootleggers. It will be the bootleggers who make the arrangements to exploit the performance and hence they will be the owner of copyright in the cinematographic work or other subject matter that results.

A performer must also recognise that the control that he or she is able to exert over the use of a performance is a by-product of the protection that copyright affords to works and other subject matter. The unlawful activity must involve a work or other subject matter or both.

[30] Arts 9 and 11 of the Berne Convention.
[31] Art 6*bis* of the Berne Convention.

2 *Ownership of the Rights*

Ownership is the most important issue that performers face in making use of copyright to protect their performances. A performer's status as a performer does not entitle him or her to the protection of copyright. Effectively, a performer must be able to show that he or she is not just a performer, but is also either the author of a literary or artistic work, or the person who made the arrangements for the making of other subject matter, something that would normally be done by a producer. Apart from taking on the persona of an author or producer, a performer must also be aware of the rules in national law that deem works and other subject matter created by employees and persons working under a commission to be the property of the employer.[32]

When a performance is simultaneously fixed, broadcast or communicated to the public according to arrangements made by a performer and another person, the performer may be forced to compete with that other person. The actions of an employer, bootlegger or broadcaster may entitle that other person to first ownership of copyright in separate examples of subject matter, all of which, like the subject matter made by the performer, are based on the same performance. Copyright will subsist separately in each fixation and broadcast of the performance; however, the performer will own copyright only in the subject matter for which he or she made the necessary arrangements and will therefore be able to exercise control of his or her performance only to the extent that it is embodied in that subject matter.

V UNFAIR COMPETITION—DAMAGE TO REPUTATION

The third and final category of protection to be considered in this chapter comprises causes of action in which the reputation of the performer is a principal factor at issue. Reputation—the fact that a performer is well-known and is a prominent personality—is protectable. A good reputation is crucial to the careers of performers, particularly those in the entertainment industry. This was noted by the Court of Appeals, Second Circuit in a case involving the British performers, Monty Python. 'The subsequent injury to appellants' theatrical reputation would imperil their ability to attract the large audiences necessary to the success of their venture.'[33] The ease with which reputation—'a sensitive,

[32] Probably the best known example is § 201(b) of the Copyright Act 1976 (US) which provides: 'In the case of a work made for hire, the employer or other person for whom the work was prepared is considered the author for purposes of this title, and, unless the parties have expressly agreed otherwise in a written agreement signed by them, owns all of the rights comprised in the copyright.'

[33] *Gilliam v American Broadcasting Corporation* 538 F2d 14, 19. In that case, the ABC had acquired the rights to broadcast the notorious Monty Python shows and proposed to broadcast two 90-minute specials made up of three 30-minute 'programs'. In the broadcast of the first special, 24 minutes of the original 90 minutes were omitted. The Court regarded the ABC's actions as

fragile thing'—can be damaged has also been recognised by the English Courts.[34] A performer may owe his or her reputation to a number of performances presented over a number of years, nevertheless that reputation may enable him or her to control aspects of the use of a specific performance.

There are three principal situations in which the use of a performance will damage a performer's reputation:

(i) A performance may be exploited in ways that suggest that there is a connection in the course of trade between the performer and the person using the performance. Take the example of a video of a couple ballroom dancing: if that video were used, without the couple's consent, as part of an advertisement for a phonogram containing music suitable for ballroom dancing, a remedy would arguably be available.[35] A suitable remedy would take the form of an injunction to prevent the broadcasting or communication to the public of the advertisement;

(ii) A performer may claim that the use of a performance has belittled his or her performance. This use may take various forms including: the implication that the performer endorsed X-rated material;[36] the suggestion that the performer supported a particular political cause;[37] and, the 'mutilation of a performance'.[38] The similarity to the protection under moral rights is marked;[39]

having caused damage to the plaintiffs. On the narrow grounds in the case, the Court recognised that the performers had the right to control the form of their performances that were broadcast to the public.

[34] *Clayton-Greene v De Courville* (1920) 36 TLR 790, 791 per McCardle J. In that case, the plaintiff performer succeeded in an action for breach of contract against a theatrical manager. The performer had been engaged to play a principal part in a play and the Court held that he had rightly refused to play a different part which, after rehearsals had begun, was offered in place of the first part.

[35] This scenario adapts the facts of the leading Australian case *Henderson v Radio Corp Pty Ltd* [1960] SR (NSW) 576. The actual facts of the case, in which the plaintiffs were successful, were that the defendants reproduced a photo of the plaintiffs on the cover of a phonogram. In that case it was said that: 'the wrongful appropriation of another's professional or business reputation is an injury in itself, no less, in our opinion, than the appropriation of his goods or money.' At 595 per Evatt CJ and Myers J.

[36] *Benson v Paul Winley Record Sales Corp* 452 F Supp 516, 518. An album of music was marketed without the approval of the plaintiff-performer. It was entitled 'George Benson, Erotic Moods', and carried the caption 'X rated LP'. A preliminary injunction was granted.

[37] *Shostakovich v Twentieth Century-Fox Film Corp* 80 NYS 2d 575 (1948). A number of Soviet composers unsuccessfully sued in the Supreme Court of New York to prevent the use of their compositions and the placement of their names in the credits in a cinematographic film, 'The Iron Curtain', that showed the Soviet Union in a bad light.

[38] *Gilliam v American Broadcasting Corporation*, above n 33.

[39] Moral rights are part of the international system of performers' rights and they are therefore not discussed in this chapter. For a commentary on moral rights and *Gilliam v American Broadcasting Corporation,* see the numerous articles listed in DE Pinover, 'The Rights of Authors, Artists, and Performers under Section 43(a) of the Lanham Act' (1993) 83 *Trade Mark Reporter* 38, 49 n 50.

(iii) Some performances have become so well-known that they have become identified with the performer and valuable for character merchandising purposes. This has led to the use of sound-alikes or look-alikes—the use of performers to imitate the sound or appearance of other well-known performers and well-known performances.[40] A circumstance in which a sound-alike is found is the commissioning of a performance, usually for advertising purposes, that deliberately copies the essential sound or appearance of another performer or aspects of a performance with the purpose of deceiving the consumer.[41]

In each of the situations described above, the performances will be protected only as an adjunct to a remedy granted, for example, to protect the performer's reputation. Again, it should be asked whether this matters if a performer achieves his or her objective and is able to restrain the use of a performance—that is, the performance being fixed, broadcast, communicated to the public or reproduced. As with copyright, the pragmatist would answer that performers should take their protection wherever they can find it.

A Nature of the Protection for a Performer under Actions that Protect Reputation

The member states of the International Union for the Protection of Industrial Property ('the Paris Union') are obliged to provide the nationals of other member states with effective protection against unfair competition.[42] Article *10bis*(1) of the Paris Convention for the Protection of Industrial Property (as revised at Stockholm in 1967) ('the Paris Convention') provides:

> The countries of the Union are bound to assure to nationals of such countries effective protection against unfair competition.

'Unfair competition' is defined in Article 10*bis*(2) which states:

[40] The Australian actor, Paul Hogan, was closely associated with his role and performance as the principal character in the cinematographic film, 'Crocodile Dundee'. In *Hogan v Pacific Dunlop Limited* (1988) ATPR ¶40–914, he was successful in an action against a company which reproduced elements of a well-known scene from that film in an advertisement. Although the actor in the infringing advertisement was not a look-alike, he was dressed in similar clothes to those worn by the distinctively dressed Crocodile Dundee character.

[41] In an early sound-alike case decided in England, the plaintiff was unsuccessful in an application for an interlocutory injunction on the ground of passing off: *Sim v HJ Heinz Co., Ltd* [1959] 1 All ER 547. The plaintiffs were successful in two cases more recently decided in the United States: *Midler v Ford Motor Co* 849 F 2d 460 and *Waits v Frito-Lay, Inc* 978 F 2d 1093. The actor, Woody Allen, was successful in a look-alike case: *Allen v National Video, Inc* 610 F Supp 612.

[42] The obligation to provide effective protection against unfair competition is extended to Members of the World Trade Organisation by Art 2(1) of TRIPS which requires Members to comply with Arts 1 through 12 and Art 19 of the Paris Convention.

> Any act of competition contrary to honest practices in industrial or commercial matters constitutes an act of unfair competition.

The meaning of 'competition' can be interpreted by member states according to their own laws and customs. The interpretation may be quite broad and include acts that are not competitive in a narrow sense.[43] The obligation to provide effective protection imposed by Article 10*bis*(1) can be met in a number of ways: specific legislation, general tort law including passing off, or a combination of these two approaches.[44] The present discussion will be restricted to passing off and its statutory equivalent which has been developed in Australasia,[45] although at least one other related cause of action has been suggested in the United Kingdom.[46] In respect of passing off and its statutory equivalent, the answers to the four fundamental questions are:

(i) The person to whom the reputation belongs will be entitled to take action to protect that reputation. In the present context, this will normally be the performer.

(ii) The term of protection is linked to the essential requirement of reputation. Actions that depend on the reputation of the performer will be available as long as the reputation lasts.

> 'It must be a question of fact and degree at what point in time a trader who has either temporarily or permanently closed down his business should be treated

[43] GHC Bodenhausen, *Guide to the Application of the Paris Convention for the Protection of Industrial Property As Revised at Stockholm in 1967* (United International Bureaux for the Protection of Intellectual Property, Geneva, 1968) 144.

[44] 'It was admitted at several Revision Conferences that member States are not obliged to introduce *special* legislation to this effect if their existing general legislation—for example, provisions of civil law directed against torts, or principles of common law suffices to assure effective protection against unfair competition.' *Ibid* 143. This is also the view taken by WIPO, see World Intellectual Property Organisation (ed), *Introduction to Intellectual Property Theory and Practice* (World Intellectual Property Organisation, London, Boston, 1997) [12.23]–[12.26]. See the discussion of 'free riding' at [12.103]–[12.107].

[45] The essential elements of the tort of passing off are goodwill, misrepresentation and damage: *Erven Warnink BV v J Townend and Sons (Hull) Ltd* [1979] 2 All ER 927, 932–933. S 52(1) of the Trade Practices Act 1974 (Cth) provides: 'A corporation shall not, in trade or commerce, engage in conduct that is misleading or deceptive or is likely to mislead or deceive.' S 9 of the Fair Trading Act 1986 (NZ), which is based on s 52, provides: 'No person shall, in trade, engage in conduct that is misleading or deceptive or is likely to mislead or deceive.'

[46] In *Shelley v Cunane* [1983] FSR 390, 398: Harman J considered the possibility that performers had a property right in goodwill that was associated with their performances and that 'reputation, goodwill and property' might be damaged by bootlegging. He regarded this as a separate cause of action from passing off, the basis of which would be the production of inferior records. However, the point is moot as the statement of claim bore no relation to such a claim. Another unexplored possibility is an action for defamation. This suggestion is made in D Gruzauskas 'Performers' rights: The Right of Personality and the Possibility of a Proprietary Right' (1995) 6 *Australian Intellectual Property Journal* 92, 111.

> as no longer having any goodwill in that business or in any name attached to it which he is entitled to have protected by law.'[47]

The plaintiff should also have regard to any statutory periods within which action must be commenced.[48]

(iii) National treatment is embodied in Article 2(1) of the Paris Convention and formed part of the original text of 1883.[49] A performer who is a national of a state that is a member of the Paris Union must be accorded the same rights in all the other member states of the Union that those states grant to their own performers.[50] The principles of protection that may assist performers vary from state to state: for example, it is arguable that the English Courts do not recognise the principles enunciated in certain Australian cases; in the United States, the right of publicity is available.[51] A performer will therefore have to look to national law to establish a cause of action in each state.

(iv) 'A passing-off action is a remedy for the invasion of a right of property not in the mark, name or get-up improperly used, but in the business or goodwill likely to be injured by the misrepresentation made by passing off one person's goods as the goods of another.'[52]

Although a plaintiff does not have to show such a proprietary right in order to succeed in an equivalent statutory action, reputation is still an essential element of the action.[53] While it is fair to say that the scope of protection under the common law action and its statutory equivalent is bounded by the commercial value of the performer's reputation, it may be difficult, even when establishing reputation is not a problem, for a

[47] *Ad-Lib Club Ltd v Granville* (1972) RPC 673, 677 per Pennycuick VC, cited with approval by Pincus J in *Elders IXL Ltd v Australian Estates Pty Ltd* (1987) ATPR ¶40–832, 48,978.

[48] The limitation period in passing off is the normal one of six years. S 82(2) of the Trade Practices Act 1974 (Cth) provides that an action for damages may be commenced within six years of the date on which the cause of action accrued. Under s 43(5) of the Fair Trading Act 1986 (NZ), an application for an order may be made within three years from the time the matter giving rise to the application occurred.

[49] Bodenhausen, above n 43, 27.

[50] Art 2(1) provides: 'Nationals of any country of the Union shall, as regards the protection of industrial property, enjoy in all the other countries of the Union the advantages that their respective laws now grant, or may hereafter grant, to nationals; all without prejudice to the rights specially provided for by this Convention. Consequently, they shall have the same rights as the latter, and the same legal remedy against any infringement of their rights, provided that the conditions and formalities imposed upon nationals are complied with.'

[51] Examples of such cases are: *Hogan v Pacific Dunlop Limited* above, n 40 and *Hogan v Koala Dundee Pty Ltd* (1988) ATPR ¶40–902. The English position is discussed in C Wadlow, *The Law of Passing Off* 2nd edn (Sweet & Maxwell, London, 1995) and 1st Supplement (Sweet & Maxwell, London, 1997) [5.40–5.46].

[52] *Star Industrial Co Ltd v Yap Kwee Kor* [1976] FSR 256, 269 (Privy Council) per Lord Diplock. See also similar comments in *Conagra Inc v McCain Foods (Aust) Pty Ltd* 23 IPR 193, 231 per Lockhart J.

[53] *Ibid* 244 per Lockhart J, 266 per Gummow J, 271 per French J.

performer to show the other requisite elements of misrepresentation and damage.[54]

B Shortcomings of the Protection under Actions that Protect Reputation

The shortcomings of protection for performances based on the reputation that a performer has acquired are similar to those discussed in respect of copyright.

1 *Performances Are Not Directly Protected*

As with the protection provided under copyright, performances are not directly protected by passing off and its statutory equivalent.[55] If a performer is able to control the use of a performance—for example, to obtain an injunction against the broadcast of an advertisement—it will only be as a result of action directed to protect the performer's reputation. The consequence is that there will be situations in which a performer will not be able to take action, primarily because he or she has insufficient reputation. The point was well put by a performance theorist:

> [A] performer must be sufficiently famous so that someone else would seek to purchase her identity to enjoy protection of her performance under the publicity paradigm. Even then, that protection is not of the performance as a work, but as an extension of the performer's identity, construed as having value in itself.[56]

As noted above, to succeed in an action for passing off, a performer must also be able to establish that there has been a misrepresentation and damage.

2 *Need for Reputation*

It is important to emphasise that there will be no protection for a performer based on reputation if he or she cannot demonstrate the requisite level of reputation. Passing off and its statutory equivalent have little value, therefore, for performers who are not in the limelight or who have been out of the limelight

[54] In *Harrison and Starkey v Polydor Limited* [1977] FSR 1, two members of the Beatles failed in an action to prevent the release of phonograms containing taped interviews and also some Beatles music. The album clearly identified the source and content of the phonograms. The Court held that any representation as to a connection with the Beatles was justified in the circumstances. On the question of reputation, the Court held, at 5, that the mere distribution of the phonograms could not harm the Beatles professionally.

[55] Cornish has suggested that 'the reputation may lie in the work or performance itself'. If this is so, then the performer has little difficulty: See WR Cornish, *Intellectual Property: Patents, Copyright, Trade Marks and Allied Rights* 4th edn (1999) [16–09]. Unfortunately, Cornish does not expand on this point and the case cited as authority, *Shaw Bros (Hong Kong) Ltd v Golden Harvest (H.K.) Ltd* [1972] RPC 559 concerned the passing off of a film—not a performance in that film.

[56] P Auslander, 'Legally Live Performance in/of the Law' (1997) 41 *TDR The Drama Review* 9, 15.

for some time.[57] A professional performer in the entertainment industry may easily achieve a reputation that is sufficient to found an action in passing off. While causes of action such as passing off are not restricted to professional performers in the entertainment industry, they will be of greater value to those performers. The ability to establish a reputation may be more difficult for an amateur performer. (An 'amateur' performer is considered herein to be an individual who does not expect his or her performances to be commercially exploited, or a person who performs outside the entertainment industry).

VI ASSESSMENT

It is common to find overlapping legal protection: for example, an author may have protection for his or her works under both copyright and contract. This overlap is not necessarily a bad thing. However, the establishment of a regime of exclusive rights should be undertaken only in the full knowledge of the protection that is already available. A system of performers' rights can hardly be regarded as being appropriate if they are unnecessary, oppressive or an obstacle to the exploitation of a performance.

A Positive Findings

The preceding analysis has shown that in a world that does not recognise performers' rights there is comprehensive protection for performers under the regimes of contract, copyright and unfair competition. Performers could conceivably turn to all three legal regimes which, together with technological measures against unauthorised access, would provide them with a variety of protection. A well-known English singer-songwriter could take action against his or her producer in a contractual dispute in the United Kingdom; against a bootlegger under copyright in the United States; against an advertising agency for the use of a confusingly similar sound-alike advertisement under passing off in Australia; and could use technological measures to prevent anybody else from downloading his or her latest performance from the Internet.

Looking beyond that scenario, in certain respects the scope of the protection available under contract, copyright and unfair competition is greater than that available for performers under the international system of performers' rights: (i) Those legal regimes protect all performances, not just performances of literary

[57] *Serville v Constance* [1954] 1 All ER 662. On arrival in England, the undisputed 'welter-weight champion of Trinidad' failed in an action against the defendant, who was well established in England and had styled himself as the welter-weight champion of Trinidad. Harman J pointed out (at 665) that it was a situation of 'the unknown seeking remedies against the known.'

or artistic works or performances of expressions of folklore.[58] (ii) No distinction is drawn, unless the parties agree in the case of a contract, between performances exploited in audio or audiovisual media.[59] (iii) Reproductions of works embodied in performances will be actionable at the suit of a performer who owns the copyright in those works even if those reproductions are not exact copies.[60] (iv) In the event of a breach of contract, a performer has the advantage of knowing the details of the other party, something that may be difficult to discover about a bootlegger.

B Negative Findings

Despite the positive aspects of the protection that exists alongside performers' rights, there are shortcomings. The protection discussed above does not form a coherent framework of protection. It was not designed to meet performers' needs to regain the control over the use of their performances that technology took away. Although the overlap of protection between the three legal regimes can provide a star with wide-ranging protection, that performer has still to consult a range of common law and statutory rights. Protection is therefore clumsy.

As a means of protection for ordinary performers who are not stars, the three legal regimes all have serious shortcomings. Contract, which otherwise provides a performer with all the necessary protection, is effective only between the parties to a contract. It is therefore ineffective against a third party. Success for the performer in the other categories depends on ownership of copyright or ownership of an actionable reputation, matters that may not be easy to establish. The forms of protection canvassed in this chapter also assume that performances have been made in a commercial setting. A contract requires some form of agreement that will normally be absent from a casual, social setting; many performances are fixed for commercial reasons; and the existence of a reputation also suggests a commercial setting. Many performances, however, are made without thought of commercial exploitation.

A problem with looking to contract, copyright or unfair competition for protection is that each regime requires an additional element not required of a system of protection dedicated to performers. The making of a performance is

[58] By virtue of Art 3(a) of the Rome Convention, which is impliedly incorporated into Art 14(1) of TRIPS, protection is restricted to performances of literary or artistic works. Art 2(a) of the WPPT extends this to performances of expressions of folklore. Contracting states are free to extend protection further. These provisions are discussed in ch 8.

[59] Only limited protection is given to performances embodied in audiovisual media in the international instruments concerned with performers' rights. This is made clear below, particularly in chs 9 and 10, which discuss the scope of rights available to performers.

[60] In performers' rights, infringement consists of the direct or indirect use of a performance. Ss 182–184 of the Copyright, Designs and Patents Act 1988; ss 248(G) and 248(J) of the Copyright Act 1968 (Cth).

sufficient to endow a performer with a legal right under a system of performers' rights, subject to issues of ownership that are discussed in the next chapter. Under contract, agreement must be reached, the terms settled and consideration exchanged before a performer has contractual rights in a performance. In respect of copyright, the performer must also, as an author have composed the work from which the performance is derived, or, as a producer, have made the arrangements for the fixation or broadcast of the performance. Passing off and its statutory equivalent require that the performer establish a protectable reputation.

C Determination

The protection available under contract, copyright and unfair competition favours performances created in the expectation of remuneration or enhancement of reputation. The ordinary performer, especially one who performs outside the entertainment industry, is not adequately protected by those legal regimes. As these regimes provide the major forms of protection, it follows that other protection that has been suggested, such as criminal sanctions, actions under employment law and actions under the law of tort, will not provide adequate protection. If performers are to be given rights to control the exploitation of their performances then those rights should protect all performances by all performers. Those rights should emanate from a single legal source. They should be simple and uniform. The advantages of the other forms of protection are not lost if a system of performers' rights is established. That system supplements rather than supplants contract, copyright and unfair competition.

6

Performers and the Stucture of Ownership

I INTRODUCTION

THIS IS THE last of those chapters that address the questions posed in chapter 1. It is primarily concerned with a number of issues relating to the ownership of performers' rights. The person who owns those rights is the person who is able to exercise them and thereby to control the use that is made of a performer's performances. Ownership is therefore a critical factor in a system of performers' rights and it is important that the rights should be vested in the 'right' person.

The first issue is who should be the first owner of performers' rights? The proposition that a performer should be the first owner of the rights in his or her performances has not been challenged in the literature of performers' rights. A performer is the originator and first owner of a special kind of commodity, a performance.[1] The obvious question is whether all the individuals who have made all the performances that characterise modern society should be entitled to the protection of performers' rights. Although it is not an issue of ownership, the first section of this chapter identifies the individuals who should be regarded as performers. The next step is to investigate whether performers should be the first owners of performers' rights, for there are others who have a claim to ownership.

The second issue is should those rights be transferable? This issue is closely related to the first and is considered in the final section of the chapter. Whether the system of rights is oriented to the interests of performers or whether it has a more market-centred approach favouring producers determines the manner in which the provisions relating to ownership and the transfer of those rights are structured.

[1] Rose describes an author in the following words: 'The distinguishing characteristic of the modern author . . . is that he is a proprietor, the originator and first owner of a special kind of commodity, the "work".' See M Rose, 'The Author as Proprietor: Donaldson v Becket and the Genealogy of Modern Authorship' in B Sherman and A Strowel (eds), *Of Authors and Origins Essays on Copyright Law* (Clarendon Press, Oxford, 1994) 27.

II WHO IS A PERFORMER?

The exercise of identifying a performer is valuable for a number of reasons:

(i) It is crucial to identify the performers who should be protected. The criteria of eligibility in the international instruments are only complete when the relevant definitions are applied.[2]
(ii) The concept of a performer as the ultimate source of a performance is intimately associated with the concept of a performance. There is an inseparable link between a performer and his or her performance. The present discussion of a performer depends on the analysis of a performance made in chapter 2, and at the same time adds to the understanding of a performance.
(iii) Other issues, such as the duration of performers' rights, benefit from an understanding of the concept of a performer.

A Defining a Performer

There are various definitions of a performer. In the following section, three definitions are analysed: a dictionary definition; a legal definition; and a proposed definition that, it is submitted, best identifies the characteristics of a performer. It will become clear that the definition of a performer does not require the same depth of analysis that was applied to the definition of a performance.

1 Dictionary Definition

The *New Shorter Oxford English Dictionary* has two relevant entries:

> **performer** . . . A person who carries out or executes an undertaking, action, etc., esp. in a specified manner. . . . A person who performs a part in a play, a piece of music, etc., as a public exhibition of art or skill; a person who takes part in public entertainment.

Two useful points may be taken from this definition. First, a performer is a person; second, that person performs some activity, often as an entertainer. For the purposes of the law of performers' rights, however, a more precise definition is necessary.

[2] This is implicit in the Rome Convention and in TRIPS; however, it is explicitly stated in Art 3(2) of the WPPT.

2 *Legal Definition*

It has been noted already that Article 3(a) of the Rome Convention is the classic definition of performers.[3] It is not the place here to analyse the elements of Article 3(a): that analysis is done in chapter 8. It is sufficient to say that Article 3(a) lists four categories of performers and prescribes a range of activities that determine the status of those persons as performers.

At the national level, and again using the Australian legislation as a useful example, it is clear from the definition of a performance that two characteristics identify a performer: first, that a performer is a natural person; second, that a performer gives a performance as defined.[4] Section 248A(1) of the Copyright Act 1968 (Cth) provides that a performance is given by one or more 'qualified persons'. As originally drafted, a qualified person was defined as 'an Australian citizen, an Australian protected person or a person resident in Australia.'[5] That definition has since been widened to include a person who is a citizen, national or resident of a Rome Convention country;[6] and, a person who is a citizen, national or resident of a WTO country.[7]

3 *Principled Definition*

The status of a person as a performer is determined by the activity of making a performance. The definition of a performer therefore depends on the analysis of a performance, as the subject matter of protection under performers' rights, undertaken in chapter 2 and it draws upon that analysis. A performer should therefore be defined as follows:

> A performer is a natural person who has performed an activity that is defined as a performance.[8]

There are three important elements in this definition:

(i) A performer must be a natural person. This is important because performers' rights can be justified on the basis that a performer leaves an imprint of his or her personality on the performances that he or she makes.

[3] Art 3(a) states: '"performers" means actors, singers, musicians, dancers and other persons who act, sing, deliver, declaim, play in, or otherwise perform literary or artistic works.'

[4] A performer is not defined in the legislation of Australia or the United Kingdom. The term 'performance' is defined in the legislation of those states, see the discussion above in ch 2.

[5] S 248A(1) of the Copyright Act 1968 (Cth).

[6] Regulation 4A(2) and (3) of the Copyright (International Protection) Regulations 1969 (Cth).

[7] Regulation 4B(2)(d) of the Copyright (International Protection) Regulations 1969 (Cth).

[8] This is similar to Ricketson's description of an author: 'An "author" therefore is a person who has made a work, or an intellectual creation.' See S Ricketson, *The Berne Convention for the Protection of Literary and Artistic Works: 1886–1986* (Centre for Commercial Law Studies, Kluwer, London, 1987) [5.2].

(ii) The use of the past tense in the definition is deliberate. It is impossible to analyse the characteristics of a performer without referring to a performance. A person is not a performer until a performance has been made. Moreover, he or she reverts to being merely a person once the performance has been made, although retaining the status of performer in respect of any performance that he or she has made.

(iii) The identification of a performer depends on the identification of a performance. Once a performance has been identified, it follows that the person who made the performance, in the sense of providing the final intellectual element, is a performer. It also follows that any individual can be a performer provided he or she is capable of performing a performative activity that is specifically identifiable as a performance.

The proposed definition is very wide. It raises the question should it be restricted in some way?

B Is it Necessary to Restrict the Application of a Definition of a Performer?

A feature of modern life is that most individuals have a part to play in a performance nearly every day of the week as performers, spectators, authors or producers. These performances range from activities that would be accepted by the average person as performances, usually forms of drama and music, to a multiplicity of performances that include sports, ritual, play, education and many more that the average person might find hard to accept on first response as performances.

> American society is a riot of performances—rock concerts, discos, electioneering, wrestling, con games and stings, college and professional sports, vogueing, street theatre, parades, demonstrations and a panoply of religious rituals ranging from staid old church services to hot gospel sings [sic], to the rituals of Asian and African religions, to the practices of New Age shamanism.[9]

If all these activities qualify as performances, does that mean that the people who made those performances should all be considered to be performers for the purposes of performers' rights?[10] On first principles, the answer is yes. All

[9] R Schechner, 'A New Paradigm for Theatre in the Academy' (1992) 36 (4) *TDR The Drama Review* 7, 10. Schechner goes on to comment that hardly any of these performances get noticed in theatre departments. He could well have added that few of them are recognised by the law.

[10] There is a very practical problem with according rights to all performers. This has come to be known in the common law jurisdictions as the problem of the '10th spear carrier': H Laddie, P Prescott, M Vitoria, A Speck and L Lane, *The Modern Law of Copyright* 3rd edn (Butterworths, London, 2000) [12.70]; Australian Copyright Council, *Performers' Copyright* (Australian Copyright Council, Redfern, Sydney; 1996) [4.5.5]; O Morgan, 'Performers' Rights' in B Brown *et al Intellectual Property in New Zealand Copyright and Design* (Butterworths, Wellington, Issue No 3–March, 1997) G139. The problem arises when a performer with a small

performers should be protected against the unauthorised use of their performances.

That answer is conditional on recognising that, no matter how widely or how narrowly a performer is defined in the common understanding of the term, there are two factors that restrict the range of the individuals protected under a system of performers' rights. The first factor is expressly referred to in the definition proposed above: it is the notion of a performance. The law is only concerned with the rights of performers in performances that are recognised as performances for the purposes of the law. If a performance does not meet the criteria set out in the law then a performer will not have any rights in that performance under a regime of performers' rights. He or she is simply not a performer.[11]

Nationality is the second factor that will always arise in determining whether a performer is entitled to performers' rights. It would be unprecedented if a state did not protect its own nationals while protecting the nationals of other states. The issue of the nationality of a performer will arise, therefore, only in regards to the level of the protection that a state grants to the nationals of other states. A state must decide whether it will protect the nationals of other states and, if so, on what terms. It is not required to grant protection unless it is a party to a treaty that obliges it to do so.[12]

Like the great copyright conventions, the international instruments concerned with performers' rights have adopted the principle of national treatment. Where State A and State B are members of an international convention that has adopted the principle of national treatment, a national of State A is entitled to the same protection in State B that State B affords to its own nationals. National treatment is usually allied to a minimum level of protection: if a state does not provide its own nationals with the minimum rights prescribed under an international treaty, it must still provide the nationals of other contracting states with that minimum level of protection. There are a number of other features that distinguish one performer from another. They should not, however, affect the definition of a performer at an international level:

part in a cinematographic film, for example, refuses to consent to the further exploitation of the film. Provided that his or her part is sufficiently important that it could not be simply excised, it could prevent the exploitation of the entire project to the detriment of other performers as well as the producer.

[11] The most notable examples of performances that are not recognised as such are performances of expressions of folklore, performances by variety artists and performances by sportspersons. Performers in these three areas are not recognised as performers under the Rome Convention or TRIPS; performers of expressions of folklore are recognised as performers under the WPPT.

[12] In *Sony Music Australia Ltd and Michael Jackson v Tansing (t/a as Apple House Music)* (1993) 27 IPR 649, 655, Michael Jackson, the well-known performer, was unable to pursue a claim in Australia under the performers' rights provisions because at that time Australia was not obliged to extend protection to citizens of the United States and did not do so.

(i) Individuals who are professionally qualified or who perform for financial gain are more likely to suffer the unauthorised use of their performances than are amateurs. Nevertheless, all performers leave an imprint of their personality on their performances and, if that justifies the award of performers' rights, they should all be entitled to control the uses to which their performances are put.[13] Two examples make this clear: First, the unauthorised exploitation of a performance made by an amateur performer could cause greater emotional distress to that performer than a similar exploitation would cause to a professional performer. Second, a bootlegger may gain as much of an undeserved reward from a performance that was not intended to be commercially exploited as from a performance that was so intended.

(ii) It has been suggested that some performers are no more than conduits for an author's work. The counter-argument is that performers are essential to the dissemination of works and actually add something to those works.[14] The majority members of the Australian Copyright Law Review Committee that reported on performers' protection in 1987 drew attention to the practical problem of drawing a line between those performers whose artistic or creative contribution warranted protection and those performers whose contribution did not meet that standard.[15] The majority wisely did not suggest how the problem could be resolved.

(iii) Performers perform to a variety of standards. Some are good, some are bad and some are indifferent. The standard that a performer achieves is another possible criterion for according the performer rights in his or her performance. The application of a standard of merit would be fraught with practical and philosophical difficulties. Matters of merit and taste should not affect the question of who is a performer.

III FIRST OWNERSHIP OF THE RIGHTS

The owner of intellectual property rights has control over the subject matter of the rights. The significance of being the owner of exclusive intellectual property

[13] Some commentators suggest that performers should be restricted to principal performers such as soloists who perform a major part of a work: V Blanco Labra, 'The Three Subjects Protected by the Rome Convention' (1978) *Copyright* 25, 27 citing the theories of Henry Jessen. See the discussion of the definition of 'performers' in 'Draft Report' AP/CE/2/9 Prov, (Committee of Experts on a Protocol Concerning Audiovisual Performances, Geneva, 8 to 12 June 1998) [49]–[55] where the proposal to exclude extras from the definition of performers was supported by a number of delegates including an observer from FIA.

[14] A Mille, 'Performers' rights: A New Independent Institution of Intellectual Property Law' (1984) *Copyright* 289, 290; *Waring v WDAS Broadcasting Station, Inc.* 327 Pa. 433, 440 per Stern J, a case decided by the Supreme Court of Pennsylvania.

[15] Copyright Law Review Committee, Commonwealth of Australia, *Report on Performers' Protection* (Australian Government Publishing Service, Canberra, May 1987) [116].

rights is two-fold.[16] First, the owner of the rights is the person entitled to authorise or prohibit use or reproduction or the like. Second, the owner of the rights can dispose of those rights or otherwise deal with them in ways that may fetter his or her ability to exercise those rights, such as waiving his or her moral rights. Where the right is merely a right of equitable remuneration, ownership of that right is still important. The owner of the right is entitled to receive the remuneration due to him or her. Alternatively, the owner of a right of remuneration may waive the right to receive remuneration.

A system of performers' rights that is fashioned by an optimist will be sympathetic to performers and will empower performers with broad rights to ensure that they have the ability to control the use that is made of their performances. In terms of ownership of those rights, performers will invariably be the first owners under the optimist's system. In terms of the transfer of those rights, while some economic rights may be freely transferable, it is unlikely that a right to remuneration that assures a performer of a continuing economic benefit will be transferable. Moral rights will be unwaivable and inalienable. A system that is sympathetic to performers is more likely to acknowledge that a performer's personality is embodied in a performance.

Under a system fashioned by pessimists that is sympathetic to the needs of producers, economic rights will not necessarily be vested in performers. They may be allocated to producers on the basis that they are the people who made the arrangements and risked the investment that led to the making of the performance. Such a system will make it easier for producers to acquire ownership of performers' rights and hence to exploit performances in the marketplace. It is more likely to acknowledge that incentives should be made available to producers as the people who are in a position to decide whether performances will be made.

A decision as to which of these two approaches is to be preferred in an international system of performers' rights would be difficult enough if it were restricted to performances made with the knowledge and intention that they will be commercially exploited within the entertainment industry. But the variety of performances and the variety of ways in which they are made complicate the decision further. Ownership of rights in a performance is not an issue that can be restricted to the entertainment industry, no matter how widely that industry is defined. Performances that are made for other purposes are vulnerable to exploitation; they also have their own problems of ownership.[17]

[16] Ownership of performers' rights is usefully discussed in B Sherman and L Bently, *Performers' Rights: Options for Reform* (Department of Communications, Information Technology and the Arts, Canberra, 1995) Part 13 [13.1]–[13.7].

[17] The issue of ownership of a performance of an expression of folklore was discussed above in ch 3. See n 48 and accompanying text.

A Performers as First Owners

The proposition that a performer should be the first owner of rights that return a measure of control over his or her performances can be justified in a number of ways:

(i) The purpose of a system of performers' rights is to protect the interests of performers, to provide them with the ability to control the uses to which performances are put. It makes sense, therefore, that performers should be the first owners of those rights.

(ii) Performers should be first owners because of the importance of their contribution to the making of a performance. It is true that a performance can be seen as the culmination of the efforts of a number of people including an author, a producer, a director and a performer; individuals such as conductors, choreographers and lighting and sound engineers may all contribute to the production of a performance. However, a performance is nothing without a performer.

(iii) Performers are natural persons. Producers are often corporations or other legal persons. Performers can therefore be compared to authors as natural persons who are, subject to national legislation to the contrary, the first owners in their works.

(iv) Performances bear the imprint of the personality of the performers who made them and, to that extent, are inseparable from those performers. It is inappropriate that anybody else should be able to exercise the rights in a performance unless they have obtained them through the performer.

(v) First ownership should not be a complicated issue. Performers' rights arise on the making of a performance without the need for registration or other formalities.[18] Vesting first ownership in performers alone is a solution that combines the advantages of being certain and simple.

B Other Claimants to the First Ownership of Performers' rights

Other people, besides performers, have credible claims to be recognised as the first owners of rights in performances. Their claims are tested below.

1 *Producers as Employers*

Apart from a performer, a producer can lay the strongest claim to be the first owner of the rights in a performance. That claim can be expressed in terms of the performer-producer relationship that is at the heart of the production and

[18] This is explicitly stated in Art 20 of the WPPT which provides that: 'The enjoyment and exercise of the rights provided for in this Treaty shall not be subject to any formality.'

exploitation of a performance. A producer's claim is best illustrated by reference to the entertainment industry, which is the major source of performances that are commercially exploited. (It must be remembered that performers are also employed in areas as diverse as education and religious service.) Producers engage the vast majority of the performers in the entertainment industry either as employees or as independent contractors under contracts to make performances.[19] There are some performers who are exceptions and who combine the role of performer with that of producer but they are comparatively few.

The basis of the claim is that the producer, as an employer, is the person who has made arrangements for the performance, has taken the financial risk and has provided employment to the performer; is therefore entitled to the rights that afford control over the exploitation of that performance. A producer who commissions the making of a performance, has an identical claim to that of the producer-employer to the rights in a performance on the basis that the producer is the person that has made the arrangements, taken the risk and has commissioned the performer to perform. The producer can also argue that the state should recognise that performances that have been commercially exploited are commodities and that the state should provide rules that regulate the efficient dissemination of performances as commodities to the public. Rights in commodified performances that are made in the course of employment should, on this view, be accorded to the producer as the person best able to produce and exploit performances.

If the production and efficient dissemination of performances were the only considerations then, by analogy with copyright and other intellectual property, producers would have a strong claim to be recognised as the first owners of rights in a performance made by their employees or independent contractors in their employ.[20] There are, however, other considerations unique to the production of performances.

As noted above, the majority of performers in the entertainment industry are engaged under contracts of employment. The consequence of granting first ownership to employers would be that the majority of performers in that industry, and in other employment, would seldom if ever be entitled to be the owners

[19] For a United States perspective, see LS Gray and RL Seeber, 'Looking Ahead' in LS Gray and RL Seeber (eds), *Under the Stars Essays on Labor Relations in Arts and Entertainment* (ILR Press, Ithaca, 1996) 187. For a useful discussion of first ownership of works of copyright in the context of employers and authors see 'The Report of the Committee of Governmental Experts on Model Provisions for National Laws on Employed Authors (Geneva, January 27 to 31, 1986)' (1986) *Copyright* 72.

[20] It is commonplace for copyright legislation to include provisions vesting ownership in copyright in employers or persons who commission the making of works: see s 11 of the Copyright, Designs and Patents Act 1988 (UK); s 35 of the Copyright Act 1968 (Cth). The work for hire provision has great significance for the cinematographic film industry in the United States where performers are typically employed on a work for hire basis: §201(b) of the Copyright Act 1976 (US). For a discussion of the legal position of performers in the cinematographic film industry, see N Reber, *Film Copyright, Contracts and Profit Participation* (Wiley-VCH, Weinheim, 2000).

of performers' rights. Such a dramatic consequence would call the integrity of the system of performers' rights into question. Performers' rights, at least in part, protect performers' interests by providing them with a bargaining tool to combat the economic power of the producer. If performers' rights vest in the producer as the original owner, a performer will be unable to use those rights to negotiate with a producer before performing, and will be unable to exercise control over the exploitation of a performance by the producer and others. The purpose of the system of performers' rights as a means of returning control to performers is thereby undermined and the value of the rights as a bargaining tool is lost.

A decision to recognise the producer as the first owner of rights in a performance comes down to a preference for the claim of the person who made the arrangements for the performance and who has the capacity to exploit it over the claim of the person who performed the performance and endowed it with aspects of his or her personality. Clearly, both parties have conflicting interests to protect. Some sort of compromise is necessary. At an international level, this may be achieved by recognising performers as the first owners of economic rights (excluding the right to equitable remuneration), while also acknowledging that those rights are transferable. It would then be a matter for national law as to whether or in what form the method of transferring those rights was implemented.

2 *Joint Ownership*

The second claimant to be the first owner of rights in a performance is another performer as a joint owner. It is arguable that where the performances of a number of individuals are indistinguishable from one another the performers should hold the rights in those performances as joint owners.[21] While many performances are physically separable from one another, there are circumstances in which an individual can be identified by appearance but not by contribution. For example, spectators can see individual performers in a massed choir, but the voices of those performers blend so that it is impossible to distinguish the separate contribution made by those individuals. This is essentially a problem of coherence. Is the performative activity of an individual complete in itself or are there circumstances in which it is merely a part of a larger performance presented by a number of individuals? It was concluded in the earlier discussion of this issue that each individual makes a separate performance and that individual performers should have first ownership in their performances as individuals.[22] This conclusion was based on a matter of principle, namely, that

[21] In its bulletin on performers' rights, the Australian Copyright Council advocates joint ownership and collective administration of performers' rights: Australian Copyright Council above n 10 [5.7.1].

[22] See above ch 2, n 19 and accompanying discussion.

performers' rights are best justified as a means of protecting the expression of an individual's personality. It is suggested that an international treaty is not the place to construct a test of joint ownership—that task is best left to national law.

3 *Recording Rights*

The final situation in which a person other than a performer could claim to be the first owner of rights in a performance is when those rights flow from a performer's activity but are rights that exist in parallel to performers' rights. Although such rights have not been recognised under the international instruments that establish performers' rights, they have been formalised in legislation in the United Kingdom and New Zealand under the name of 'recording rights.'[23] Recording rights subsist in parallel to performers' rights; they are rights that can be characterised as neighbours to performers' rights in the way that performers' rights are neighbours to copyright.

An extensive system of recording rights arises under the United Kingdom legislation if a performer has granted the benefit of an exclusive recording contract to another person. 'A person having recording rights' can take action for infringement of those rights independently of the performer.[24] The first owner of recording rights is the person with whom the performer made the exclusive recording contract. The key component of recording rights is that of an exclusive recording contract. Section 185(1) of the Copyright, Designs and Patents Act 1988 (UK) states:

> An 'exclusive recording contract' means a contract between a performer and another person under which that person is entitled to the exclusion of all other persons (including the performer) to make recordings of one or more of his performances with a view to their commercial exploitation.[25]

A 'recording' is defined widely enough in the legislation to cover the most important ways in which a performance can be embodied in a fixation.[26] There is no equivalent provision in the Australian legislation which was used as an example earlier in this chapter; however various commentators, both Australian and from other jurisdictions, have suggested that consideration should be given to granting people other than performers the right to take action against

[23] The Copyright Act 1994 (NZ) is closely based on the Copyright, Designs and Patents Act 1988 (UK).

[24] Ss 185–188 of the Copyright, Designs and Patents Act 1988 (UK).

[25] The definition in the New Zealand legislation is identical: see s 169 of the Copyright Act 1994 (NZ).

[26] In s 180(2) of the Copyright, Designs and Patents Act 1988 (UK), 'recording' is defined as 'a film or sound recording' made directly from a performance or from a broadcast, cable programme or another recording. Under the New Zealand legislation a recording is a sound recording or film made directly from a performance or made from a broadcast or a cable programme: see s 169 of the Copyright Act 1994 (NZ).

bootleggers.[27] Recording rights in New Zealand sit somewhere between these suggestions and the rights granted under United Kingdom legislation. They have been reduced to the right to take action on behalf of the performer but are not limited to cases of bootlegging.[28]

The call for rights in performances to be vested in people other than performers suggests that when legal action needs to be taken, it is more likely to be taken by the producer than by the performer. The phonogram industry in Australia made this claim in a submission to the Music Industry Advisory Council ('MIAC') that reported in 1994.

> It is the record company who is responsible and bears the financial cost for protecting its artists against bootlegs locally and internationally. Artists expect and require record companies to take such actions on their behalf. A bootleg of a John Farnham concert released for sale in Germany is, and always ends up being, the responsibility of John Farnham's record company's licensee in Germany.[29]

If this claim can be substantiated, and performers did not contest it at the time it was made, then it does suggest that the majority of the CLRC were correct to conclude that performers were seeking a bargaining tool rather than a system of exclusive rights.[30] Recording rights can therefore be seen either as a further protection for performers, through the efforts of producers, or as a development of the law that questions the need for a system of performers' rights.

C Issues Common to First Ownership and to the Transfer of Ownership

There are certain issues that are fundamentally the same whether one is considering the first ownership of performers' rights by a person other than a performer or the transfer of those rights by a performer to that other person. Although the transfer of rights has not yet been analysed, it is convenient to raise the common issues at this point.

[27] The Australian Copyright Council suggested that record companies should be able to institute legal proceedings in respect of unauthorised recordings, Australian Copyright Council, above n 10, [5.7.3]. Sherman and Bently suggest that both recording and broadcasting organisations should have that ability, Sherman and Bently, above n 16, [13.1]. Thompson suggested that it would be to performers' advantage if phonogram producers and broadcasters, who were also given rights under the Rome Convention, also had rights against third parties, E Thompson, 'Performers and technological change 25 years after the Rome Convention' (1986) 125 *International Labour Review* 575, 576.

[28] Ss 196(2) and 197(1)(b) of the Copyright Act 1994 (NZ).

[29] Music Industry Advisory Council, *Performers' Copyright* (MIAC Secretariat, Canberra, 1994) 19.

[30] Copyright Law Review Committee, above n 15, [118].

1 *Economic Rights and Moral Rights*

All the arguments advanced above in favour of a performer being the first owner of the rights in his or her performance apply in respect of moral rights as they do for economic rights. Further, the scope of protection provided by moral rights suggests that the first owner of those rights should only be the performer. The right of attribution and the right of integrity are integral to the natural right theory and to the claim that performances are imbued with the personality of the performers. Nothing is more personal than a person's honour and reputation and the best judge of whether a use of a performance is prejudicial to a performer's honour is the performer.

The answer to the question of whether performers' rights should be transferable, may differ depending on whether the rights in question are solely economic rights or whether they include moral rights. Even advocates of strong performers' rights concede that some, at least, of the economic rights should be transferable.[31] It is difficult, however, to justify the exercise of moral rights in a performance by someone other than a performer. Even the transfer of moral rights to members of the performer's family or to a community organisation set up to exercise those rights is questionable. The need for compromise is a further argument in favour of performers retaining their moral rights. If moral rights are inalienable, performers retain some control over the use of a performance.

2 *Duration*

It was noted in the previous chapter that there are various options as to the duration of performers' rights. The first option was that the term of protection should be linked to the life of the performer. This suggests that the first owner should be the performer and that the rights should not be transferable. The second option was that performers' rights should be perpetual; this was rejected as oppressive. The third option was to link the rights to the economic life of the performance. The possibility that the first owner of those rights might be a person other than the performer or that they might be transferred to another person illustrates an argument for that option: if performers' rights can be owned by a person whose sole interest is in maximising economic returns from a performance, then surely this third option is the best one. This reasoning applies, of course, only to economic rights and only to performances that have commercial worth. Tying the duration of economic rights to the economic life of a performance would be likely to result in economic rights and moral rights having a different term of protection, a result which is consistent with the differing juridical bases for these rights.

[31] See 'FIA Comments on the WIPO Basic Proposal prepared for the Diplomatic Conference, December 2000' <http://www.fia-actors.com/new/wipo_2000_comments_eng.htm>; Australian Copyright Council, above n 10, [5.7.3].

IV TRANSFER OF THE RIGHTS

As well as issues as to first ownership of performers' rights, there are also issues within a system of rights as to the transferability of those rights.[32] (This section assumes that performers are the first owners of performers' rights.) As rights become more extensive, ownership and the transfer of ownership will become more of an issue and the pressure exerted on performers to transfer their rights will increase.[33] By agreeing to a transfer of the rights vested in him or her as the first owner, the performer relinquishes control, to the extent of the transfer, over his or her performance. Those rights can then be exercised for the benefit of the transferee. The transferability of performers' rights raises two important questions. The first is should performers' rights be transferable? The second is to whom should performers' rights be able to be transferred?

A Transfer to Whom?

Although it is logical to take up the question of who should be the transferee of rights only after it has been decided that the transfer is possible, answering that question first does shed some light on the overarching issue of transferability itself.

There are two categories of transferees. The first category comprises those people who, in their own interests, wish to control the exploitation of a performance. They can be characterised as producers, although there may be other people.[34] The interests of the producer and the performer coincide so far as they have a joint interest in preventing the unauthorised use of a performance and in maximising the economic returns on a performance. Their interests do not necessarily coincide in respect of the manner of the exploitation of a performance or in the proportions that each receive from the distribution of remuneration.

The second category of transferees comprises those people who either act on the performer's behalf or who have interests that are based on the interests of the performer. There are a number of groups included in the second category: (i) That group of people to whom a performer might willingly agree to assign the rights in a performance, namely agents, collecting societies and unions. A

[32] A number of those issues are canvassed by Sherman and Bently, above n 16 [8.6]. They include the possibility of transfer of exclusive rights; a presumption of transfer; non-assignable remuneration rights.

[33] The Diplomatic Conference on the Protection of Audiovisual Performances held in Geneva 7 to 20 December 2000 closed without adopting a new instrument because agreement could not be reached on a provision in the instrument relating to the transfer of economic rights. The failure of this Diplomatic Conference is discussed below in ch 13.

[34] In ch 4, n 20 and accompanying text, producers were defined as people who make the arrangements for the production and exploitation of performances. The term is wide enough to encompass a wide range of individuals. Other individuals who might be interested in obtaining the rights to a performance include users such as broadcasters.

performer would expect that class of people to exercise those rights on his or her behalf; (ii) Those individuals to whom the rights are transferred when the performer dies or is incapacitated. They would usually be beneficiaries under a will or members of a community group nominated by the state to exercise the moral rights of the performer;[35] (iii) Certain people could legitimately argue that they have a stronger claim than the performer to the performance and the rights in the performance. Protection of the integrity of expressions of folklore is considered to be a matter for the elders or other important individuals in indigenous groups around the world.[36]

The simple but important conclusion is that there are people to whom a performer would willingly agree to transfer his or her rights. There are other people to whom a performer would be less willing to transfer those rights.

B Should Performers' Rights Be Transferable?

As with the question of first ownership of performers' rights, there is a choice when considering whether performers' rights should be transferable. On the one hand, a system of rights that is sympathetic to the position of performers will ensure that performers maintain control over the continuing use of their performances partly by prohibiting the transfer of all or some of their rights.[37] On the other hand, a system of rights that is sympathetic to the position of producers will permit the free transfer of performers' rights.

There are good reasons for allowing performers to transfer the rights in their performances. (i) In principle, performers as owners of rights in the nature of property should be free to dispose of those rights as they see fit. If they dispose of them to their advantage, so much the better; but it should be their decision; (ii) Those rights also provide performers with leverage to obtain a better terms and conditions from producers; (iii) Pessimists would argue that it is equally important that performers' rights be freely transferable to provide producers with freedom of action to exploit the performances; (iv) Finally, it should always be possible to transfer the rights in a performance to individuals who have a better claim to the rights, such as tribal elders.

[35] Art 5(2) of the WPPT provides: 'The rights granted to a performer in accordance with paragraph (1) shall, after his death, be maintained, at least until the expiry of the economic rights, and shall be exercisable by the persons or institutions authorised by the legislation of the Contracting Party where protection is claimed.'

[36] For a perspective of the New Zealand Maori, see M McLean, *Maori Music* (Auckland University Press, Auckland, 1996).

[37] Under the United Kingdom legislation, performers' property rights are transmissible by assignment, testamentary disposition or operation of law: see s 191B of the Copyright, Designs and Patents Act 1988 (UK). Performers' rights are not assignable under the Australian legislation: see s 248N of the Copyright Act 1968 (Cth).

The arguments against allowing the transfer of performers' rights have already been referred to. If performers' rights are transferable, then there will be heavy pressure on performers to transfer their rights to their disadvantage:

> Multimedia convergence brings with it a powerful industrial model from the English-speaking world. It brings increased demands for the transfer of rights—known as the copyright model—which protects the producer, not the artist. This constitutes a major threat to the existence of the performer and production in small countries.[38]

Allowing performers to transfer their rights runs contrary to the justification for those rights. If performers' rights are justified on the natural right theory that a performance is an expression of a performer's personality, then it is at least arguable that those rights should be inalienable; they should be perpetually linked to the performer who made the performance. This argument is particularly strong in respect of moral rights. 'It is inconceivable that a third party should replace performers where their moral right is involved.'[39]

It was suggested above that compromise is necessary in respect of the ownership of performers' rights. Compromise is also required in respect of the transfer of those rights. The ability of performers to maintain a measure of control over the exploitation of their performances must be preserved while the operation of an efficient market in the products of the entertainment industry must be encouraged. The wishes of indigenous groups to maintain control of their own culture must also be respected. On balance, however, the arguments in favour of the transfer of rights to producers and others outweigh the contrary arguments.

1 *Transfer of Performers' Rights to Producers*

Gaines encapsulated the arguments for and against the transfer of rights to a producer, in reference to 'star contracts':[40]

> And it is the transferability of rights that is the basis of the mass marketing of the human image and the human voice in the communications industries. The basic film and television contract is markedly different from the employment contract in other industries (in which one agrees to be separated from one's labor power for the duration of the employment) because of what it is that the actor leaves with the employer. It is not exactly as though the actor leaves inventions or ideas with the employer. In contrast with the ordinary worker, who leaves the proceeds of his work with his

[38] M Waldorff, 'Audiovisual Performers: Rights, Collective Bargaining and Multimedia Convergence' in ILO, *Final Report: Symposium on Multimedia Convergence Geneva, 27–29 January 1997* (1997) 124, 125.

[39] D Gaudel, 'The Eternally Excommunicated—The Situation of Performers in France' (1980) 103 *Revue Internationale du Droit D'Auteur* 92, 130.

[40] In that context, the term 'star contracts' refers to contracts between producers and performers who have the status of stars in the entertainment world.

> employer, the screen actor may be permanently separated from tangible aspects of personhood—his or her voice and photographic likeness.[41]

In the first sentence of this quotation, Gaines identifies the major argument for the transfer of performers' rights to a producer in the entertainment industry. Quite simply, as the person who makes the arrangements for the production of a performance, the producer needs to be able to gather all the intellectual property rights relating to that performance under one umbrella. Without ownership of performers' rights, the producer's ability to exploit that performance will be reduced by the need to obtain the performers' consent to the use of each individual performance for each form of exploitation. If the performer's consent does not provide sufficient assurance to the producer, or to the financiers that the producer represents, that there will be no problems, the production of a performance may be put in jeopardy. In such circumstances, performers' rights are a disincentive to the production of performances.

The remainder of the quotation puts the performer's position. A performer leaves a permanent record of his or her voice or likeness in a performance. Even if the performance is not permanently fixed but is merely broadcast or communicated to the public, his or her voice or likeness is projected to a larger audience. (Of course, a performer who uses a musical instrument leaves a less tangible mark.) It is a logical extension of the natural right theory that a performer should not have to surrender any rights in a performance, embodying as it does aspects of his or her personality.

Clearly, if one is a pessimist, it is preferable that a producer should have clear title in order to be able to exploit a performance. The alternative for a producer who decides that a performance is worth exploiting, is to find other, less certain ways to deal with the problem of ownership. Licensing of the rights in performances may achieve the same result as the transfer of ownership. A licence to use a performance is less certain than outright ownership of the rights; a licence can be revoked or it may not cover the form of the intended use. A system of performers' rights should aim for simplicity and certainty, and this aim provides another argument for allowing the transfer of rights.

2 *Transfer of Performers' Rights to People Sympathetic to Performers*

In principle, the argument against the transfer of rights is that the nature of a performance and the rights that flow from it militate against the transfer of those rights from the performer to any other person. The use that is made of the performance once it is transferred is a secondary consideration. However, optimists who support an extensive system of rights supporting the protection of performers, and who might oppose the transfer of those rights to producers,

[41] JM Gaines, *Contested Culture—The Image, the Voice and the Law* (University of North Carolina Press, Chapel Hill, 1991) 155, endnote omitted.

should not oppose the transfer of performers' rights to a person who has the interests of a performer at heart, or who holds similar interests. For example, the collective administration of the economic rights by a collecting society facilitates the performer's control of the use that is made of a performance. It also makes it easier for users, such as broadcasters, and others to locate the person who owns the rights in a performance.

3 Methods of Transfer

The manner in which performers' rights are transferred, if transfer is permitted, will help determine whether the system of rights is oriented to the interests of performers or the interests of producers. There are various options:

(i) The most likely form of transfer of performers' rights is an assignment of the economic rights. As the bundle of rights expands to rival the bundle that comprises copyright, there will be an incentive to split those rights and to assign them separately, thereby maximising the benefit to the performer. Whether the assignment comprises only certain rights rather than an assignment of the whole bundle will depend on the relative bargaining power of the parties. It will also depend on the purpose of the assignment. An assignment to a collecting society might comprise only those rights that enable the society to complete its task on behalf of the performer. An assignment may also be subject to a statutory limitation, such as a requirement that the performer retain a non-assignable and unwaivable right to equitable remuneration.[42]

(ii) The international community is currently under pressure to recognise the principle of a rebuttable presumption of transfer.[43] Under this method, the question of assignment is not left to the parties. On the making of an agreement with a producer, a performer would be deemed to have transferred some or all of his or her rights in a performance. The presumption would be rebuttable, in that it would be subject to clear words to the contrary in the agreement or in a complementary agreement. National legislation would determine the rights that should be transferred to the producer. One option is that a right to equitable remuneration would not

[42] Council Directive 92/100/EC of 19 November 1992 on rental right and lending right and on certain rights related to copyright in the field of intellectual property provides that the performer retains an unwaivable right to equitable remuneration where he or she has transferred the rental right: Arts 4(1) and 4(2).

[43] The United States of America insisted on the inclusion of such a provision in the proposed instrument for the protection of audiovisual performances that was the subject of a Diplomatic Conference held in Geneva in December, 2000. The provisions of that instrument and the reasons for the failure of the Conference are discussed below in ch 13. A limited rebuttable presumption of transfer is provided for in an EC Directive: see Art 2(5) of Council Directive 92/100/EEC of 19 November 1992 on rental right and lending right and on certain rights related to copyright in the field of intellectual property. See also the discussion in Sherman and Bently, above n 16, [8.6.2].

be subject to the presumption of transfer. Another option is that moral rights would not be subject to the presumption.

(iii) On the death of a performer who is the owner of performers' rights, the options are for the performer to bequeath the rights by testamentary disposition or for some community group to be authorised to exercise the rights after the performer's death.[44]

C The Performer's Consent to the Use of a Performance

In the absence of a transfer of the relevant rights, a producer needs the security of knowing that all the performers involved in the making for example, of a phonogram, have consented to the making of the phonogram and to its exploitation.[45] It will be a less satisfactory outcome for a producer if it has to rely on a performer's consent to the use of a performance rather than depend on a transfer of the rights. There will always be the element of uncertainty as to whether the manner in which the performance is exploited is covered by the terms of the consent. This will usually be a matter of interpreting the terms of a contract. The position is more secure for producers if the consent takes the form of an exclusive licence and if national law gives the special status to exclusive licences in performers' rights that it has given in some jurisdictions to exclusive licences in copyright. In the United Kingdom and Australia, an exclusive licensee of copyright is in the same position as an assignee against everyone except the copyright owner.[46] However, only the United Kingdom has provided licensees with that status in respect of performers' property rights.[47] This is consistent with the approach taken to the assignment of performers' rights in those jurisdictions.[48]

Conceptually, the grant of consent is more satisfying than the transfer of rights because it recognises the enduring connection between the performance, as an expression of the performer's personality, and the performer. There are other, potentially more tangible, benefits for the performer. If the consent is

[44] Art 5(2) of the WPPT provides for the exercise of a performer's moral rights by persons authorised by the state. The Australian legislation does not provide for the testamentary disposition of performers' rights nor does it prohibit them. In *Rickless v United Artists Corpn* [1988] QB 40, the Court of Appeal held that the plaintiffs, the personal representatives of Peter Sellars, had a right of action under the relevant legislation although there was no reference in that legislation to the transmission of rights. It may be that the Courts in Australia would take a similar view. Under the United Kingdom legislation, performers' property rights are transmissible by assignment, testamentary disposition and by operation of law respectively s 191B of the Copyright, Designs and Patents Act 1988 (UK). Under 192A, performers' non-property rights are transmissible to a limited extent.

[45] An example of a blanket consent provision is given above in ch 5, n 17.

[46] S 101 of the Copyright, Designs and Patents Act 1988 (UK); s 119 of the Copyright Act 1988 (Cth).

[47] S 191L of the Copyright, Designs and Patents Act 1988 (UK).

[48] The United Kingdom legislation permits the assignment of performers' property rights; assignment is not permitted under the Australian legislation: see above, n 37.

limited to exploitation in one medium, the producer will be forced to negotiate for the performer's consent to the exploitation of the performance in other media. A narrow consent also provides a performer with freedom to negotiate with other entities, besides the original producer, for the further exploitation of the performance. On the downside, the option of granting consent does leave the performer with the obligation of policing unauthorised uses of a performance, although the producer may take over this obligation from the performer in the interests of protecting its investment.

Part III

The Structure of Protection

Historical Interlude

BACKGROUND TO THE INTERNATIONAL INSTRUMENTS

AT THIS POINT in the book, the focus changes from the problems and issues that underlie an international system of performers' rights to an analysis of the relevant provisions in the Rome Convention, TRIPS and the WPPT.[1] It is therefore an appropriate place to describe some of the background to these instruments.[2]

A The Rome Convention

The road to international protection for performers has not been an easy one. Initially, they sought protection under the Berne Convention. The claims of performers that they should be regarded as authors and their performances as works attracted sympathy, but those claims were rejected in 1928 at the Rome Revision Conference of the Berne Convention and again at the Brussels Revision Conference in 1948. At both conferences, resolutions, or '*voeux*', were adopted. The *voeu* adopted at Rome expressed the wish that participating governments consider what measures could be taken to protect the rights of performers. The *voeu* adopted at Brussels stressed the artistic quality of performances and expressed the wish that studies be undertaken, particularly in respect of the protection of performers as a neighbouring right.[3]

> 'Neighbouring rights' is a term that in its narrow sense covers the rights of performers, producers of phonograms and broadcasting organisations, that is, the beneficiaries

[1] It is important to bear in mind that performers are not the only beneficiaries of protection under the international instruments. Under both the Rome Convention and TRIPS, those beneficiaries are performers, phonogram producers and broadcasting organisations. Under the WPPT, the beneficiaries of protection are performers and phonogram producers.

[2] The background to the proposed audiovisual instrument is described in ch 13.

[3] The wording of the *voeu* was: 'VI Considering that the interpretations of the performers have an artistic character, the Conference expresses the wish that studies should be actively pursued with reference to the neighbouring rights of copyright and particularly the protection of performers.' Quoted in GHC Bodenhausen, 'Protection of Neighbouring Rights' (1954) 19 *Law and Contemporary Problems* 156, 157.

> under the Rome Convention. In a wider sense, the term covers a range of rights in subject matter such as cinematographic films, photographs and typographical arrangements.[4]

As a term to designate the rights of performers, it was first used in a *voeu* at the 1948 Brussels Revision Conference; from that point on, it was determined that protection for performers would be achieved outside the Berne Convention.[5]

In the decade that followed the Brussels Revision Conference, a series of meetings produced a number of draft conventions for the international community to consider. The final preparatory step was taken in 1960, when a Committee of Experts prepared the Draft International Convention concerning the Protection of Performers, Makers of Phonograms and Broadcasters ('the Hague Draft'), which was to serve as the basis for discussions at Rome. Despite the years of negotiation and preparation, there was no guarantee that a convention would be concluded at the Diplomatic Conference.[6] Although there was an unpromising start, the Conference did succeed in completing its work.[7]

The conclusion of the Rome Convention in 1961 established a major benchmark in the development of neighbouring rights and, particularly, the development of performers' rights. Although it has been criticised by performers and commentators for the low level of protection that it affords performers, the Rome Convention established a minimum level of protection for foreign performers.[8] It is always open to states, whether or not they are not parties to

[4] Jehoram has described neighbouring rights as: 'Rights neighbouring to copyright by definition are rights which are not copyrights themselves. They provide a strengthened protection against certain acts of unfair competition which can very loosely be associated with copyright infringements. Therefore they are situated "in the vicinity of copyright".' HC Jehoram, 'The Relationship between Copyright and Neighbouring Rights' (1990) 144 *Revue Internationale du Droit d'Auteur* 81, 83.

[5] The wording of the *voeu* is quoted above n 3.

[6] According to Ulmer—who was the head of the German delegation, Vice-President of the Conference and chaired Working Party II—from the outset, the merits of the Diplomatic Conference itself were questioned and, although the principles of the Hague Draft had been generally accepted, there was well-organised opposition from authors and broadcasters to the idea of a convention incorporating protection for performers. The arguments of the authors, for example, were adopted by the French delegation to the Diplomatic Conference: E Ulmer, 'The Rome Convention for the Protection of Performers, Producers of Phonograms and Broadcasting Organizations. Part I' (1963) 10 *Bulletin Copyright Society of the U.S.A.* 90, 95.

[7] The French delegation questioned the need for the Diplomatic Conference and pointed to contractual arrangements as a means of achieving the aim of the Convention: 'Summary Records of the Proceedings', *Records of the Diplomatic Conference on the International Protection of Performers, Producers of Phonograms and Broadcasting Organisations* (ILO, UNESCO and BIRPI, Geneva, 1968) [50].

[8] Examples of papers critical of the Rome Convention include: P Masouye, 'The Rome Convention: Realities and Prospects' (1985) *Copyright* 296; E Thompson, 'Performers and Technological Change 25 Years After the Rome Convention' (1986) 25 *International Labour Review* 575; R Rembe, 'Time for a Performer's Convention' (1991) 25 *Copyright Bulletin* 25; C Rodrigues, 'The Nature and Scope of Rules for Updating the Protection of Performers' rights' (Paper presented at the International UNESCO Symposium on Copyright and Communication in the Information Society, Madrid, 11–14 March, 1996) 143.

the Convention, to provide protection at a higher level than the conventional minima.

B TRIPS

The most influential step forward in the development of an international response to performers' rights has been the negotiation of the TRIPS Agreement as an annex to the WTO Agreement. TRIPS, which is binding on all WTO Members, established an international system for the protection of intellectual property, including minimum rights for performers, as a means of reducing 'distortions and impediments to international trade'.[9]

The regime of performers' rights established by TRIPS is based on the Rome Convention, although it is more restricted in a number of areas. 'The logic of the TRIPS Agreement is to follow existing intellectual property conventions as closely as possible, adding the necessary elements where necessary to update the international legal framework.'[10] TRIPS added nothing substantive to the development of the law of performers' rights. Rather, the significance of the TRIPS Agreement for performers' rights is that it has a high level of international acceptance.[11] Performers' rights moved from being a largely European concern to one affecting nearly all the world's developed states.

C WPPT

In 1997, an Assistant Director General of WIPO stated WIPO's view of the development of copyright and neighbouring rights in the 1970s and 1980s.[12] According to Ficsor, there were two features: first, a number of important technological developments; second, a process of 'guided development' as opposed to the establishment of new international norms. This guidance, which took the form of the preparation of recommendations, principles and model provisions for governments and legislators, included issues relating to neighbouring rights.

[9] Art II(2) of the WTO Agreement provides: 'The agreements and associated legal instruments included in Annexes 1, 2 and 3 (hereinafter referred to as "Multilateral Trade Agreements") are integral parts of this Agreement, binding on all Members.' See also Art 1(1) of the TRIPS Agreement which begins, 'Members shall give effect to the provisions of this Agreement.' The first sentence of the Preamble to the TRIPS Agreement begins: 'Desiring to reduce distortions and impediments to international trade . . . .'

[10] D Gervais, *The TRIPS Agreement: Drafting History and Analysis* (Sweet & Maxwell, London, 1998) 48.

[11] As of 1 January 2002, there were 144 Members of the WTO: World Trade Organisation, 'The Organization: Members and Observers' <http://www.wto.org/english/thewto_e/whatis_e/ tif_e/org6_e.htm>.

[12] M Ficsor, 'The Spring 1997 Horace S Manges Lecture—Copyright for the Digital Era: The WIPO "Internet" Treaties' (1997) 21 *Columbia-VLA Journal of Law & the Arts* 197, 197–199.

In 1974, a Model Law was produced that was intended to provide a framework for implementing the Rome Convention.[13] At the end of the 1980s, it was recognised by the international community that guidance was not enough: it was essential to develop new binding international norms. The international response to the development of performers' rights continued under the auspices of WIPO in parallel to the negotiations for the General Agreement on Tariffs and Trade ('GATT') that resulted in the WTO Agreement.

In 1992, as part of a move to reappraise substantive copyright standards, the Assembly of the Berne Union decided to establish two Committees of Experts, one to prepare a possible protocol to the Berne Convention and the other to prepare a possible new instrument for the protection of performers' rights and the rights of the producers of phonograms.[14] The First Session of the committees did not take place until 28 June to 2 July 1993, but their work accelerated after the adoption of the TRIPS Agreement. In 1961, at the Rome Diplomatic Conference, the Rome Convention had been adopted by a relatively small number of states, some of which had no experience with performers' rights in their national laws. By contrast, a much larger group were involved in the negotiations that led to the conclusion of the TRIPS Agreement; and by the time of the Geneva Diplomatic Conference, at which the WPPT and the WIPO Copyright Treaty ('WCT') were adopted on 20 December 1996, more states had had experience with performers' rights over a period of some years.

Both of these Treaties are intended to establish international standards in copyright and neighbouring rights that meet the challenges of the so-called 'digital agenda.'[15] With the exception of performers' rights in performances fixed in audiovisual media, the WPPT covers the same ground as the Rome Convention and TRIPS. It includes a number of provisions that extend the obligations provided for under those instruments. It also includes provisions for rights that were not included under those instruments. However, the WPPT only entered into force on 20 May 2002.

[13] The Model Law was adopted by the Intergovernmental Committee of the International Convention for the Protection of Performers, Producers of Phonograms and Broadcasting Organisations done at Rome in 1961. The purpose was to assist in the ratification of the Rome Convention by providing the simplest possible legislative framework for the implementation of the Rome Convention: *Model Law Concerning the Protection of Performers, Producers of Phonograms and Broadcasting Organisations with a Commentary on it* (ILO, UNESCO, WIPO, Geneva and Paris, 1974).

[14] 'Report Adopted by the Assembly' International Union for the Protection of Literary and Artistic Works (Berne Union) B/A/XIII/2 (Assembly, Thirteenth Session (3rd Extraordinary), Geneva, 21 to 29 September 1992) [22].

[15] 'Digital agenda' is used, particularly by the International Bureau of WIPO, to describe the issues concerning the clarification of existing norms and the creation of new norms to meet the challenges raised by digital technology, in particular, by the Internet. Ficsor, above n 12, 202.

D Preliminary Treaty Issues

There is no direct linkage between the three instruments, although certain provisions of the Rome Convention are incorporated by reference into the other two. The independence of the WPPT is explicitly stated in Article 1(3) of that Treaty, and there are non-derogation clauses in respect of existing obligations under the Rome Convention in Article 2(2) of TRIPS and in Article 1(1) of the WPPT.[16]

Further, there is no direct linkage between the three instruments and the copyright conventions, although the primacy of copyright was a major issue at the Rome Diplomatic Conference and resulted in the adoption of Article 1 of the Rome Convention. Article 1 provides:

> Protection granted under this Convention shall leave intact and shall in no way affect the protection of copyright in literary and artistic works. Consequently, no provision of this Convention may be interpreted as prejudicing such protection.

The Report of the Rapporteur-General of the Rome Diplomatic Conference states that Article 1 makes it clear that the need to obtain the authorisation of an author for the reproduction or other use of a work embodied in a performance is not affected by the provisions of the Rome Convention. Conversely, the need to obtain the authorisation of the performer does not cease to exist because authorisation of the author is also required.[17] Article 1(2) of the WPPT duplicates Article 1 of the Rome Convention and the Agreed Statement of the Diplomatic Conference concerning Article 1(2) repeats the gist of the Rapporteur-General's interpretation.[18]

As a final word on the international instruments, it is worth repeating two points. First, besides performers, producers of phonograms and broadcasting organisations are also beneficiaries of protection under the Rome Convention and TRIPS, and producers of phonograms are also beneficiaries of protection under the WPPT. The analysis that follows of the provisions in the international instruments is restricted, however, to performers' rights. Secondly, the provisions of the international instruments acquire the force of law in contracting

[16] Art 2(2) of TRIPS provides: 'Nothing in Parts I to IV of this Agreement shall derogate from existing obligations that Members may have to each other under the Paris Convention, the Berne Convention, the Rome Convention and the Treaty on Intellectual Property in Respect of Integrated Circuits.' Art 1(1) of the WPPT provides: 'Nothing in this Treaty shall derogate from existing obligations that Contracting Parties have to each other under the International Convention for the Protection of Performers, Producers of Phonograms and Broadcasting Organisations done in Rome, 26 October 1961 (hereinafter the "Rome Convention").'

[17] 'Report of the Rapporteur-General', Records of the Diplomatic Conference on the International Protection of Performers, Producers of Phonograms and Broadcasting Organisations (ILO, UNESCO and BIRPI, Geneva, 1968) 38.

[18] In this context an 'Agreed Statement' is a statement made between the parties to the WPPT relating to the interpretation of the Treaty. The significance of an Agreed Statement is discussed further in ch 9.

states only when they are incorporated into national law. Also, one must bear in mind that the international instruments are intended to cover circumstances that are truly international in nature; and those instruments provide only the minimum level of rights.

Against this background, it is now appropriate to begin the analysis of the international instruments.

7

National Treatment and the Protection of Foreign Performers

I INTRODUCTION

THE TITLE OF this chapter serves two functions. First, it is a reminder that the technology of exploitation has presented performers with problems that must be addressed on an international basis. The fundamental purpose of an international system of performers' rights is to provide for the protection of performers in states other than their state of origin, and this protection is contained in the three international instruments.

Secondly, the title 'National Treatment and The Protection of Foreign Performers' identifies the provisions that are examined in this chapter. The delegates to the Rome Diplomatic Conference acknowledged that the protection of foreign performers involves two issues: (i) Who are the people protected and what are the international circumstances under which protection should be granted to them (bearing in mind that the international instruments protect performers only in international circumstances)? (ii) What is the nature and extent of this protection?[1] The answers to those questions are to be found in the provisions of the international instruments that identify the beneficiaries of protection (the performers who meet the criteria of eligibility) and in the application of the principle of national treatment. In this chapter, therefore, the background description of the international instruments is followed by a general discussion of the principle of national treatment and of the criteria of eligibility. That discussion is followed, in turn, by an analysis of the provisions relating to national treatment and the criteria of eligibility in the Rome Convention, TRIPS and the WPPT. It is those provisions that form the basis for the international protection of performers.

[1] 'Report of the Rapporteur-General', Records of the Diplomatic Conference on the International Protection of Performers, Producers of Phonograms and Broadcasting Organisations (ILO, UNESCO and BIRPI, Geneva, 1968) 38.

II NATIONAL TREATMENT AND THE CRITERIA OF ELIGIBILITY

The ideal situation for performers would be for performers' rights to be harmonised on a world-wide basis, with the result that a performer who is a national of State A would be treated in the same way in State B as in State A without argument and with certainty. The ideal is seldom achieved in any situation. The first obstacle to the international harmonisation of performers' rights is that some states may simply not provide protection for foreign performers. Next, there is the issue of the level of protection that is granted. Some states may provide greater rights than others; and some states may make greater use of limitations and exceptions and of reservations to the rights provided under the international instruments. The result is that the protection of performers and their performances may be quite uneven. National treatment is the means that has been chosen for accommodating differences in national laws and ensuring a basic level of protection. It is a fundamental principle of the international instruments that provide for performers' rights.

In the words of the Rapporteur-General to the Rome Diplomatic Conference, 'Simply stated, national treatment is the treatment that a State grants under its domestic law to domestic performances.'[2] National treatment is a simple concept to grasp, but it has always been a controversial issue. The strict application of the principle of national treatment presents a difficulty in that it does not allow for the situation where a state provides a low level of protection, but nationals of that state wish to take advantage of the high level of protection available in another state. Naturally, states that provide a high level of protection are reluctant to grant national treatment if a similarly high level of protection is not available to their nationals in other states.

The people protected and the circumstances under which they are protected are determined by reference to the criteria of eligibility. The latter are also known as the 'points of attachment'. They are the conditions that must be satisfied if a performer is to be granted national treatment. The provisions that embody those criteria are crucial to the protection of foreign performers. They should be read together with: (i) the provisions that provide for national treatment; and (ii) the definition of 'performers' in the relevant treaties. The issues of national treatment and criteria of eligibility are discussed together in the following sections of this chapter. The definition of 'performers' is discussed in the next chapter.

The difficulties of providing for the uniform protection of performers on an international scale are reflected in provisions in the international instruments that restrict the application of national treatment:

[2] 'Report of the Rapporteur-General', Records of the Diplomatic Conference on the International Protection of Performers, Producers of Phonograms and Broadcasting Organisations (ILO, UNESCO and BIRPI, Geneva, 1968) 39.

(i) National treatment is invariably granted only to those performers of other contracting states who meet the relevant criteria of eligibility. They must also meet the definition of 'performers'.
(ii) The obligation to provide national treatment to the nationals of other contracting states may be limited to the rights contained in a particular treaty. This means that if a state grants protection to its domestic performers in the form of rights that are not contained in that treaty, it is not obliged to offer that protection to the nationals of other contracting states.
(iii) If limitations and exceptions and reservations are permitted, the level of protection in one state may vary significantly from the level of protection that is available in another state.
(iv) The application of material reciprocity means that the protection that State A offers to the nationals of State B is at the level of protection that the nationals of State A enjoy in State B.[3]

The problem of the varying levels of protection is balanced to some extent by requiring that contracting states must accord minimum standards of protection to the nationals of other contracting states. Where the obligation to offer the same rights to foreigners as a state offers to its own nationals is adjusted in this way, it expands the scope of protection provided to foreign performers. It ensures that, as between contracting states, a national of State A has a guaranteed minimum level of protection in State B, whatever the level of protection for domestic performers that is provided in State B.

The importance of establishing the minimum standards of protection that must be accorded to the nationals of other contracting states stems from the proposition that the protection that a state affords to its own nationals is not a matter for the international instruments. The matter was canvassed at the Rome Diplomatic Conference and the Report of the Rapporteur-General is clear on this point:

> A question applicable to [Articles 4, 5, and 6] was whether the Convention should apply only to international situations, or also to national situations. Simply stated, the question was whether a Contracting State must apply the Convention only to foreign or also to domestic performances, phonograms and broadcasts. . . .
>
> It was generally agreed that the question was probably of little practical significance, since it was unlikely that a State would not grant at least the same advantages to domestic performances, etc., as to foreign ones. On the other hand, several delegations, and particularly that of the United States, emphasized that domestic situations

[3] Reciprocity is discussed in the context of the copyright conventions in SM Stewart, *International Copyright and Neighbouring Rights* 2nd edn (Butterworths, London, 1989) [3.20]; and in S Ricketson, *The Berne Convention for the Protection of Literary and Artistic Works: 1886–1986* (Centre for Commercial Law Studies, Kluwer, London, 1987) [1.27].

> should not be regulated by international treaty. . . . [T]he Convention covers only international situations.[4]

It would be unusual if performers who are nationals of a state that has become a party to one of the international instruments did not receive the minimum level of protection dictated by that instrument. However, those instruments do not guarantee the protection of performers in their state of origin: they are intended to apply only to international situations. What they do guarantee is that the protection of the nationals of other states is at least the conventional minima.

III ROME CONVENTION

National treatment, as it applies to performers, is defined in Article 2(1)(a) of the Rome Convention. It provides:

> For the purposes of this Convention, national treatment shall mean the treatment accorded by the domestic law of the Contracting State in which protection is claimed:
>
> (a) to performers who are its nationals, as regards performances taking place, broadcast, or first fixed, on its territory.

A Contracting State must therefore treat foreign performers in the same way as it treats its own nationals in respect of performances made by those performers within its territory. The various factual circumstances in Article 2(1)(a) mirror the criteria of eligibility in Article 4. Ulmer has commented that:

> 'The wording of article 2(1) of the Rome Convention makes it clear that national treatment shall mean the domestic protection granted by the contracting countries regardless of which of the above mentioned criteria they apply, singly or in conjunction with each other, to determine whether the case is domestic.'[5]

The meaning of national treatment is refined by Article 2(2). It provides:

> National treatment shall be subject to the protection specifically guaranteed, and the limitations specifically provided for, in this Convention.

This provision does two things. First, it provides that national treatment is subject to the minimum protection specified in the Convention: that is, Contracting States must provide the conventional minima to the performers of other Contracting States. Apart from the rights provided in Article 7, the provisions that complete the minimum protection of performers are those providing for a right to remuneration, for duration, for exceptions and reservations and for

[4] 'Report of the Rapporteur-General', above n 1, 41. Arts 4, 5 and 6 provide for the points of attachment for performers, producers of phonograms and broadcasting organisations.

[5] E Ulmer, 'The Rome Convention on Neighboring Rights. Part II' (1963) *10 Bulletin. Copyright Society of the USA*. 165, 169.

formalities.[6] Secondly, Article 2(2) provides that the protection guaranteed in the Convention is itself subject to the limitations provided in the Convention. This provision was intended to make it clear that the protection provided under the Convention may be less than that provided under national law. Article 2(2) therefore brings into play, for example, the important provisions as to reservations in Article 16 that qualify the right of remuneration in Article 12. Thus, State A, which has legislated for a remuneration right for its domestic performers, may still declare a reservation in accordance with Article 16. In those circumstances, State A has avoided the obligation to provide a right of remuneration for foreign performers.[7]

Turning now to the criteria of eligibility, Article 4 provides:

> Each Contracting State shall grant national treatment to performers if any of the following conditions is met:
>
> (a) the performance takes place in another Contracting State;
>
> (b) the performance is incorporated in a phonogram which is protected under Article 5 of this Convention;
>
> (c) the performance, not being fixed on a phonogram, is carried on a broadcast which is protected by Article 6 of this Convention.

The three criteria govern the international situations in which performers will be protected under the Rome Convention. These criteria either have a direct connection to the place where the performance is made, or an indirect connection through the criteria of eligibility for producers of phonograms and broadcasting organisations. The criteria are in the alternative; if any one of them is met the performer may claim the protection provided under the Convention. It is not explicitly stated as such in the Convention, but to be a beneficiary of protection an individual must also meet the definition of 'performers' in Article 3(a).

The nationality of the performer was considered as another criterion of eligibility; that is, if a performer is a national of State A, that criterion alone would qualify him or her for protection in State B, assuming both to be parties to the Rome Convention. The majority of the delegates to the Rome Diplomatic Conference rejected this option because they considered that the practical problems associated with nationality were too great, particularly as performances may be given by groups of performers all of different nationalities.[8] This objection was unwarranted. The criteria are alternatives; therefore, if there are problems with groups of performers meeting the criterion of nationality, then it would surely be possible to turn to one of the other criteria, such as the place in

6 Respectively, Arts 12, 14, 15, 16 and 11 of the Rome Convention.

7 'Report of the Rapporteur-General', above n 1, 39.

8 Ulmer Part II, above n 5, 172; C Masouye (W Wallace trans), *Guide to the Rome Convention and to the Phonograms Convention* (World Intellectual Property Organisation, Geneva, 1981) [4.7].

which the performance took place. If nationality had been included as a criterion, it would have disposed of a problem that was identified by the delegation of the Federal Republic of Germany. This arises if a state uses nationality of a performer in its national legislation as one of the criteria of eligibility:

> If, say, Switzerland were to grant protection, in its domestic legislation, to performers of Swiss nationality only, then, according to Article 4, a German artist performing in Germany, Italy, or France would be protected in Switzerland, always provided the Convention had been ratified by the countries concerned. In the event of a performance in Switzerland, however, he would enjoy legal protection neither on the strength of domestic legislation nor on the strength of the Convention.[9]

The German delegation proposed that a performer of a Contracting State who performs in another Contracting State should enjoy the same rights as a national of that other Contracting State. Other delegations were divided as to whether this was an international situation to which the Convention applied and the proposal was withdrawn. The better view is that the Germans were correct and that the situation described was an international situation. On this basis, the failure to address the issue properly constitutes a significant gap in protection. As noted above, both TRIPS and the WPPT incorporate the Rome Convention's criteria of eligibility, and therefore this gap has been carried forward into those instruments.

IV TRIPS

In line with the major intellectual property conventions, national treatment is a cornerstone of TRIPS.[10] The pertinent provisions are Articles 1(3) and 3(1) which follow the same pattern as the Rome Convention. The relevant sections of Article 1(3) provide:

> Members shall accord the treatment provided for in this Agreement to the nationals of other Members. In respect of the relevant intellectual property right, the nationals of other Members shall be understood as those natural or legal persons that would meet the criteria for eligibility for protection provided for in . . . the Rome Convention . . . were all Members of the WTO members of those conventions.[11]

[9] Ulmer Part II, above n 5, 172.

[10] Associated with the principle of national treatment is the principle of most-favoured-nation treatment. Art 4, which provides for the principle of most-favoured-nation in TRIPS, is a provision that does not have a counterpart in other intellectual property instruments. 'Its purpose is to ensure uniformity of the multilateral trade environment. Its principal relevance in this framework would be where an advantage, favour (e.g. as regards registration, deposit or fees) has been granted bilaterally and is not subject to the national treatment clause.' D Gervais, *The TRIPS Agreement: Drafting History and Analysis* (Sweet & Maxwell, London, 1998) [2.30]. Art 4 is subject to a similar exception as prevails in Art 3. Exemptions are made for rights not provided for in TRIPS and for advantages deriving from the international agreements which entered into force before TRIPS was concluded.

[11] The notes to Arts 1 and 3 of TRIPS have been omitted. They do not materially affect the present discussion.

The relevant sections of Article 3(1) provide:

> Each Member shall accord to the nationals of other Members treatment no less favourable than it accords to its own nationals with regard to the protection of intellectual property, subject to the exceptions already provided in . . . the Rome Convention . . .. In respect of performers, producers of phonograms and broadcasting organizations, this obligation only applies in respect of the rights provided under this Agreement.

Read together, these two Articles incorporate a general requirement that Members of the WTO must provide to the nationals of other Members the level of protection provided for in TRIPS. This provision differs from Article 4 of the Rome Convention in that it appears to establish nationality as the prime criterion of eligibility. Appearances can be deceptive: Article 1(3) goes on to restrict the meaning of nationals to those people who would meet the criteria of eligibility provided in the Rome Convention. Nationality is not part of those criteria. The above discussion of those criteria is therefore directly applicable, including the need to have regard to the definition of 'performers'.

The requirement in Article 3(1) that the protection be no less favourable than that provided for a Member's own nationals recognises that it is possible, however unlikely it would be in practice, that a Member would provide the nationals of other Members with treatment that is more favourable than the treatment it accords its own performers. However, Article 3(1) also recognises that an unrestricted rule of national treatment would have obliged Members to extend protection, particularly in the form of a right to equitable remuneration, to the nationals of other Members, and those states would be unlikely to reciprocate. The obligation to grant minimum protection to the nationals of other Members therefore extends only to the rights provided under the TRIPS Agreement. A state may be obliged to grant to the nationals of other states, who may or may not be WTO Members, a higher degree of protection than is established in TRIPS because, for example, it has become a party to the Rome Convention. However, if that state is also a Member of the WTO, it is not obliged by the rule of national treatment to grant to the other Members of the WTO the higher level of protection. The rights that a Member grants to the nationals of other Members are also subject to the exceptions in the Rome Convention. States that had implemented those exceptions in their national legislation before TRIPS was concluded are therefore not disadvantaged by having to amend their legislation.

V WPPT

In the draft treaty ('Basic Proposal') that was presented to the 1996 Geneva Diplomatic Conference at which the WPPT was adopted, national treatment and the international application of protection followed in part the model of the Rome Convention and in part the model of TRIPS.[12] However, significant changes were made to the Basic Proposal.

As to international protection, Article 3 provides:

> (1) Contracting Parties shall accord the protection provided under this Treaty to the performers and producers of phonograms who are nationals of other Contracting Parties.
>
> (2) The nationals of other Contracting Parties shall be understood to be those performers or producers of phonograms who would meet the criteria of eligibility for protection provided under the Rome Convention, were all the Contracting Parties to this Treaty Contracting States of that Convention. In respect of these criteria of eligibility, Contracting Parties shall apply the relevant definitions in Article 2 of this Treaty.[13]

So far as the international application of protection under the WPPT is concerned, Article 3 follows the TRIPS style of drafting. There is a general obligation to provide protection to performers who are the nationals of other Contracting Parties. This provision is followed by the incorporation by reference of the criteria of eligibility provided under the Rome Convention. (As with the discussion of Article 1(3) of TRIPS, the above analysis of those criteria is directly applicable.) Additionally, Article 3(2) directs Contracting Parties to have regard to the relevant definitions in Article 2, perhaps because they have been updated since the Convention was concluded.[14] (The relevant definitions are those of: 'performers', 'publication', 'fixation', 'producer of phonograms' and 'phonograms'.) Such a requirement is implicit in the corresponding provisions of the Rome Convention, but it is not appropriate to TRIPS as that Agreement does not include definitions.

As to national treatment in the WPPT, Article 4 provides:

> (1) Each Contracting Party shall accord to the nationals of other Contracting Parties, as defined in Article 3(2), the treatment it accords to its own nationals with regard to the exclusive rights specifically granted in this Treaty, and to the right to equitable remuneration provided for in Article 15 of this Treaty.

[12] This drafting was explained by Mr Liedes (the Chairman of the Committees of Experts) in United States Department of Commerce, Patent and Trademark Office 'Briefing on Request for Comments on the Chairman's Text of the Diplomatic Conference on Certain Copyright and Neighbouring Rights Questions, To be Held in Geneva from 2 to 20 December 1996', (Arlington, 12 November 1996) 36. The draft treaty and commentary were contained in a document that was known as the 'Basic Proposal': Chairman of the Committees of Experts on a Possible Protocol to the Berne Convention and on a Possible Instrument for the Protection of the Rights of Performers and Producers of Phonograms, 'Basic Proposal for the Substantive Provisions of the Treaty for the Protection of Performers and Producers of Phonograms to be Considered by the Diplomatic Conference' CRNR/DC/5 ('Basic Proposal') (Diplomatic Conference on Certain Copyright and Neighbouring Rights Questions, Geneva, 2 to 20 December 1996).

[13] Art 3(3) of the WPPT has not been reproduced. It relates to producers of phonograms.

[14] The definition of 'performers' in Art 2(a) of the WPPT was expanded to include performers who perform 'expressions of folklore'.

> (2) The obligation provided for in paragraph (1) does not apply to the extent that another Contracting Party makes use of the reservations permitted by Article 15(3) of this Treaty.

At the Geneva Diplomatic Conference, agreement was not easily reached over the provisions dealing with national treatment. It is not surprising that there was disagreement. The Basic Proposal provided for a right of remuneration, which is incorporated in Article 15 in the WPPT, for the use of performances fixed in phonograms for broadcasting or communication to the public.[15] There was therefore concern among the states of the European Community that national treatment would require states that provided for a right of remuneration to accord that right to the nationals of Contracting Parties that did not provide for that right.

> It was readily apparent that the intensity of the conflict over the terms of a national treatment requirement in the PPT [*sic*] would depend on the level of minimum rights agreed on for the Treaty.[16]

As originally drafted, Article 4(1) included a clause that confined national treatment to the protection generally provided in the Basic Proposal. This was replaced in the WPPT itself with the clause that refers specifically to the exclusive rights and the right to equitable remuneration provided in the Treaty. National treatment does not extend beyond those obligations. Another important change was made in Article 4(2). In the Basic Proposal, Article 4(2) was based on and bore a close resemblance to Article 2(2) of the Rome Convention. The substitution of the re-drafted Article 4(2), which reduces the obligation of national treatment according to the use that is made of the reservation provision in Article 15(3) reflects the level of dissension at the Geneva Diplomatic Conference. In practical terms, Article 4 in its final form means that states that have implemented, or intend to implement, remuneration schemes in respect of analog sound recordings will not have to allow the nationals of the United States to participate in those schemes.[17]

The decision not to include a provision making national treatment subject to the limitations and exceptions in the Treaty itself means that the WPPT differs from Article 2(2) of the Rome Convention and Article 3(1) of TRIPS. It is a matter of interpretation by individual states of their obligations under the WPPT as to whether they will limit national treatment in accordance with the limitations and exceptions that they have made to the exclusive rights in the WPPT. The obvious question, and one that cannot be answered here, is whether they

[15] Art 15 is reproduced in ch 9, where the right of remuneration is discussed.

[16] C Cresswell, 'Copyright Protection Enters the Digital Age: the New WIPO Treaties' (1997) 15 (1) *Copyright Reporter* 4, 17.

[17] The United States has a remuneration scheme that is limited to copying by digital media: Cresswell, above n 16, 18; R F Martin, 'The WIPO Performances and Phonograms Treaty: Will the US Whistle a New Tune?' (1997) *Journal of the Copyright Society of the USA* 157, 167.

will legislate for a right of remuneration for their own performers while declaring a reservation in accordance with Article 15, thereby avoiding the obligation to provide the right for foreign performers.

VI CONCLUSIONS

This chapter considered the issue that is fundamental to an international regime of performers' rights: the level of protection that is to be granted to foreign performers. Goldstein has suggested that the 'knee-jerk' answer to the question of copyright protection for the works of foreign authors is that they should not be protected, because this would raise the cost of those works above what they would be if they were unprotected.[18] It is possible to give the same answer to the protection of foreign performers and their performances. A more considered response would acknowledge that works and performances made by foreign authors and performers should be protected. The need to protect foreign performers is accepted in this text. The analysis of the principle of national treatment, which determines the nature and extent of the protection that is accorded to foreign performers, formed the major part of the above discussion. The way in which the international instruments dealt with the issue of identifying the performers who should be protected was also analysed. It was seen that performers must satisfy criteria of eligibility.

The analysis of the national treatment provisions disclosed that there is a conflict between two basic objectives. The first objective is to obtain protection for performers on a truly international scale by the accession of as many states as possible to the relevant instrument. The second is to provide protection that is harmonised at a particular level. The seemingly insurmountable hurdle to achieving these two objectives is that not all states are prepared to provide protection at the same level. Under the strict application of the principle of national treatment, the nationals of all contracting states would receive the same protection abroad as they receive at home. Such perfectly uniform national treatment may be unattainable.

In a situation in which some states are not prepared to provide a certain level of protection, there are two possible responses: (i) The relevant instrument can permit those states to provide a lower level of protection; (ii) Accession to the international instrument can be limited to those states that can agree on a higher level of protection. In the second option the international range of the instrument is reduced. The first option should be preferred. The question, therefore, is what sort of protection does Rome-style national treatment provide? The rights provided in the instrument are mandatory but there is no obligation

[18] P Goldstein, *Copyright's Highway—The Law and Lore of Copyright from Gutenberg to the Celestial Jukebox* (Hill and Wang, New York, 1994) 180. See also WR Cornish, 'The International Relations of Intellectual Property' (1993) *Cambridge Law Journal* 46, 48.

to grant other rights, not provided for in the instrument, to foreign performers. In addition, a contracting state may take advantage of the limitations and exceptions and of the reservations in the particular instrument. The trade-off for allowing these departures from strict national treatment is the expectation that more states will be able to accede to the instruments. There are further expectations: first, those contracting states that provide a low level of rights will be encouraged by the example of other states to extend those rights; second, that as new treaties are negotiated or old ones are updated, existing rights will be harmonised upwards.

Have the provisions in the three instruments achieved the correct balance between wide international protection and a lack of harmony of protection? There will never be a perfect answer; performers should take what they can get while it is on offer.

While the major emphasis in this chapter has been on national treatment, the criteria of eligibility should not be forgotten. The failure to include nationality as a criterion is a significant shortcoming that means that certain performers are unprotected.[19] Where a number of performers present a performance, nationality may be a problem if there is only a single performance, analogous to a number of authors collaborating to produce a single work. But what appears to have been overlooked by opponents of nationality as a criterion is that in a group performance, such as an opera, there is not one performance but a number of performances. The rights of the performers do not attach to the totality of their performances but remain separately attached to their individual performances. In the case of an opera, the rights are those that the performers have in their individual performances as, for example, singers, actors, musicians or other performers. Nationality is therefore not an issue because it is necessary to consider only the nationality of each individual performer. The problem lies in obtaining the consent of each individual to the exploitation of the performance, and that is a practical problem for the producer.

[19] Refer to the example above at n 9 and accompanying discussion.

8

The Right Holder and the Subject Matter of Protection

I INTRODUCTION

IN ANY SYSTEM of intellectual property rights, a key issue is, who is the person who is the right holder? Another key issue is: what is the subject matter to which the rights extend? In this chapter those two issues are examined together. A performer is the originator of a performance and the first right holder in respect of that performance. The subject matter of protection is the performance.

The view taken herein is that a performer is defined by reference to the activity that he or she performs. It is not a matter of defining the activity by reference to the performer. Outside of a performative activity, a performer reverts to merely being an individual and his or her activities are simply activities rather than performative activities. On this basis, the fundamental criterion of protection is a performance. However, that is not the view embodied in the international instruments. In the Rome Convention and the WPPT it is clear that a performance is regarded as being the activity of a performer behaving as a performer.[1] Whichever view is taken, the two concepts of a performer and a performance are inseparable.

In the next section of this chapter, a detailed analysis is undertaken of the definition of 'performers' as it appears in the international instruments. This is followed by a discussion of the provisions that relate to the transfer of ownership. An analysis of the term 'performance' follows.

II PERFORMERS

The significance of the definition of 'performers' is that, together with the criteria of eligibility analysed in the previous chapter, it determines who is protected under the international instruments. It is implicit in the Rome

[1] 'Performers' are defined in Art 3(a) of the Rome Convention and in Art 2(a) of the WPPT. There is no definition of 'performers' in TRIPS.

Convention and TRIPS, and explicit in the WPPT, that contracting states should have regard to that definition when interpreting the criteria of eligibility.[2]

The classic definition of performers, in Article 3(a) of the Rome Convention, was introduced in chapter 2 as part of the task of formulating a principled definition of a performance. In the present chapter, that definition and its derivative, Article 2(a) of the WPPT, is discussed in the different context of a provision in an international instrument. The classic definition is impliedly incorporated into the relevant provisions of TRIPS.[3]

A Rome Convention

Article 3(a) states:

> 'performers' means actors, singers, musicians, dancers and other persons who act, sing, deliver, declaim, play in, or otherwise perform literary or artistic works.

1 *The Agreed Interpretation*

There are two interpretations of Article 3(a). They are labelled here as the 'agreed interpretation' and the 'alternative interpretation'. The term 'agreed interpretation' refers to that interpretation agreed on by the delegates to the Rome Diplomatic Conference and by the learned commentators who have since analysed the provision—namely that the consistent factor amongst the categories of performers referred to in Article 3(a) is that performers must perform literary or artistic works. Thus, the Rapporteur-General reported that: 'As stated in connexion with Article 3, "performers" are defined as persons who perform literary or artistic works.'[4] Similarly, the Basic Proposal stated: 'The definition in the Rome Convention is . . . entirely built on the performances of literary and artistic works.'[5]

[2] The final sentence of Art 3(2) of the WPPT provides: 'In respect of these criteria of eligibility, Contracting Parties shall apply the relevant definitions of Art 2 of this Treaty.'

[3] See the discussion below of Art 14(1) of TRIPS and performers as right holders.

[4] 'Report of the Rapporteur-General', *Records of the Diplomatic Conference on the International Protection of Performers, Producers of Phonograms and Broadcasting Organisations* (ILO, UNESCO and BIRPI, Geneva, 1968) 46. This interpretation has been supported by such commentators as Masouye, Nordemann and Stewart: see C Masouye (W Wallace trans), Guide to the Rome Convention and to the Phonograms Convention (World Intellectual Property Organisation, Geneva, 1981) [3.1]; W Nordemann, K Vinck, PW Hertin, (English version by G Meyer based on the translation by R Livingston), International Copyright and Neighboring Rights Law: commentary with special emphasis on the European Community (VCH Publishers, New York, 1990) 355; SM Stewart, International Copyright and Neighbouring Rights 2nd edn (Butterworths, London, 1989) [7.16].

[5] Chairman of the Committees of Experts on a Possible Protocol to the Berne Convention and on a Possible Instrument for the Protection of the Rights of Performers and Producers of Phonograms, 'Basic Proposal for the Substantive Provisions of the Treaty for the Protection of Performers and Producers of Phonograms to be Considered by the Diplomatic Conference' CRNR/DC/5 ('Basic Proposal') (Diplomatic Conference on Certain Copyright and Neighbouring Rights Questions, Geneva, 2 to 20 December 1996) [2.03].

According to the agreed interpretation of Article 3(a), there are four categories of performers:

(i) Actors, singers, musicians and dancers who act, sing, deliver, declaim and play in literary or artistic works;
(ii) Actors, singers, musicians and dancers who otherwise perform literary or artistic works;
(iii) Other than actors, singers, musicians and dancers, those persons who act, sing, deliver, declaim and play in literary or artistic works;
(iv) Other than actors, singers, musicians and dancers, those persons who otherwise perform literary or artistic works.[6]

By implication, there is a fifth category of performers who are not protected under Article 3(a). That category is comprised of those persons who perform, but who do not perform literary or artistic works. By restricting 'performers' to those who perform literary or artistic works, delegates to the Rome Diplomatic Conference were left in a quandary: what to do about performers who do not perform works?

> The main policy question was whether the protection of the Convention should cover only performers who perform "works" in the copyright sense, or whether it should go wider so as to protect artistes like variety artistes and circus performers.[7]

The objections to extending protection to artists that do not perform works were two-fold. First, it was acknowledged that a number of events that were not protected were economically significant, but it was thought that a wider definition of performer would make it difficult for national legislatures to determine just how far protection should extend.[8] Second, the influence of users of performances was directed towards minimising the ambit of protection, particularly to protect the interests of broadcasters.[9] The main concern was that a wider definition could lead to uncertainty, because users could not be sure that a performance was protected. A demand for some certainty as to an aspect of performers' rights, while legitimate, bears no more weight than the concern for certainty that a broadcaster would have to ensure that an underlying work is no

[6] It was agreed by the delegates to the Rome Diplomatic Conference that conductors of musicians or singers were included in the definition of 'performers' on the basis that they impart their personality to the performance of a work: 'Report of the Rapporteur-General', above n 4, 40; Masouye, *Guide to the Rome Convention*, above n 4, [3.4].

[7] 'Working Documents', *Records of the Diplomatic Conference on the International Protection of Performers, Producers of Phonograms and Broadcasting Organisations* (ILO, UNESCO and BIRPI, Geneva, 1968) 260. The concern of some delegations for variety artistes and circus performers is not explained in the Records of the Rome Conference. Certainly, the argument was accepted that this group of performers were at risk from the new technology in the sense that people would not go to see their performances if they had been broadcast: Masouye, above n 4, [9.1].

[8] 'Report of the Rapporteur-General', above n 4, 46.

[9] Masouye, above n 4, [9.3].

longer protected by copyright; or the concern that a producer has to secure all the relevant rights to a performance that it wants to exploit.

Another argument against a wider definition of 'performers' was that states always have the ability in their national legislation to protect performers who do not perform literary or artistic works. Although some delegates to the Diplomatic Conference proposed that all performers should be protected, the view prevailed that the Convention should not protect performers who did not perform works.[10] This settled the matter so far as the Convention was concerned. However, Article 9 was still included in the Convention. It provides:

> Any Contracting State may, by its domestic laws and regulations, extend the protection provided for in this Convention to artists who do not perform literary or artistic works.

Although regarded by some delegations as unnecessary, because it is always open to a Contracting State to grant protection at a higher level than that specified in the Convention, Article 9 was considered by others to have merit as a reminder to Contracting States that they could, within their own laws, extend protection to the likes of variety artistes. The Convention, after all, provides only a minimum level of protection. Article 9, however, does emphasise the restrictive nature of Article 3(a).

2 *Literary or Artistic Works*

It was agreed at the Rome Diplomatic Conference that the expression 'literary or artistic works', which is at the heart of the definition of performers, had the same meaning that it has in the Berne and Universal Copyright Conventions. In particular, it was agreed that it included musical, dramatic and dramatico-musical works.[11] Article 2(1) of the Berne Convention defines literary and artistic works. It comprises a general definition and then 'a list of examples, intended to be illustrative of the kind of subject matter falling within the general definition.'[12] Besides musical and dramatic works, the list includes a number of other works that would naturally be of interest to performers, including 'choreographic works and entertainments in dumb show' and 'cinematographic works'. The connection, one might say subservient attachment, to the copyright treaties is emphasised by a number of provisions in the Rome Convention including Articles 23 and 24, which require that signatory states must be party to the Universal Copyright Convention or a member of the Berne Union.

Apart from performers who clearly do not perform literary or artistic works, there are two categories of performers who are potentially excluded from

[10] 'Report of the Rapporteur-General', above n 4, 46.
[11] *Ibid* 39–40.
[12] S Ricketson, *The Berne Convention for the Protection of Literary and Artistic Works: 1886–1986* (Centre for Commercial Law Studies, Kluwer, London, 1987) [6.1].

protection by the narrowness of the definition in Article 3(a). The first category comprises those performers who perform works that are no longer protected by copyright. In the second category are those performers whose performances are improvised.

The problem of the first of these categories can be disposed of swiftly. It is generally accepted that performers who perform works that are no longer protected by copyright are in fact protected.[13] If they were not, then, for example, performances of great composers like Beethoven and Bach would not be protected. This would be unacceptable for a number of reasons. Denying these performances protection would run contrary to the role performers' rights have in advancing the culture of the state. Denying them protection would also change the role of performers' rights from protecting the expression of a performer's personality in a performance to protecting the works themselves, a role already filled by copyright.

As to the question of improvised performances, where it is difficult to say that a work of copyright has been performed, the answer for performers is less satisfactory. The commentary to the Model Law on performers' rights suggests that the term 'literary or artistic works' is generally regarded as broad enough to include 'oral works, pantomimes and improvisations.'[14] (The Model Law was intended to provide a framework for implementing the Rome Convention.[15]) However, the answer is not nearly as clear-cut as this. It would stretch the definition of 'performers' in Article 3(a) to an unacceptable degree to include performers of improvisations in its ambit; consequently they, and their performances, are probably unprotected under the Rome Convention. Although it would be very unlikely to find any performance that was totally improvised—that is, composed on the spot without reference to any other material—it is a problem that is best addressed by national legislation.[16]

[13] Masouye, above n 4, [3.1]; see also Nordemann, above n 4, 355.

[14] The Intergovernmental Committee of the International Convention for the Protection of Performers, Producers of Phonograms and Broadcasting Organisations done at Rome in 1961 *Model Law Concerning the Protection of Performers, Producers of Phonograms and Broadcasting Organisations with a Commentary on it* (ILO, UNESCO, WIPO, Geneva and Paris, 1974) 7.

[15] The Model Law was adopted by the Intergovernmental Committee of the International Convention for the Protection of Performers, Producers of Phonograms and Broadcasting Organisations done at Rome in 1961. The purpose was to assist in the ratification of the Rome Convention by providing the simplest possible legislative framework for the implementation of the Rome Convention.

[16] The definition of 'performance' in the Australian legislation, s 248A(1) of the Copyright Act 1968 (Cth), includes an improvisation in a number of the categories. The definition in the United Kingdom legislation, s 180(2) of the Copyright, Designs and Patents Act 1994 (UK), does not have a similar provision. The *WIPO Glossary of Terms of the Law of Copyright and Neigboring Rights* defines 'improvisation' in the following terms: 'Creating a work simultaneously with its performance. Public improvisation means that expression and disclosure of the work happen simultaneously.'

3 An Alternative Interpretation

As an alternative to the agreed interpretation of Article 3(a), there are two categories of performers:

(i) Actors, singers, musicians and dancers;
(ii) Those persons, other than actors, singers, musicians and dancers, who act, sing, deliver, declaim and play in literary or artistic works.

By implication, there is a third category of performers: those persons other than actors, singers, musicians and dancers who perform, but who do not perform literary or artistic works.

While a case can be made for this interpretation, it is less plausible than the agreed interpretation, for several reasons. First, the significance of works as being the source of protected performances is reduced under this interpretation.[17] Performers in the category of actors, singers, musicians and dancers are included in the class of performers even if they do not perform works; therefore, most variety artists would be protected and there would be little reason for Article 9 in the Rome Convention, which provides for the extension of protection to performers who do not perform literary or artistic works. Secondly, if the alternative interpretation were correct, the majority of performers of expressions of folklore would be protected, in which case the agitation to include those performers in the protection of the WPPT was unnecessary.[18] The third and most telling objection to the alternative interpretation is that Article 32 of the Vienna Convention on the Law of Treaties provides: 'Recourse may be had to supplementary means of interpretation, including the preparatory work of the treaty and the circumstances of its conclusion.' In the case of Article 3(a), the supplementary means of interpretation are in favour of the agreed interpretation: as quoted above, the Report of the Rapporteur-General stated that performers are 'persons who perform literary or artistic works'.

[17] The definition of 'performance' in the United Kingdom legislation places little reliance on the performance of a literary or artistic work: s 180(2) of the Copyright, Designs and Patents Act 1988 (UK). The definition of 'performance' in the Australian legislation, which was discussed above in ch 2, refers to the performance of works with two exceptions, a performance of a dance and a performance of a circus act or variety act: s 248A(1) of the Copyright Act 1968 (Cth).

[18] The International Bureau of WIPO issued a Memorandum before the first session of the Committee of Experts that addressed the definition of 'performers' and that repeated comments first made at the Rome Conference. It questioned the value of Art 9 of the Rome Convention and noted that a provision of wide extent would 'create legal uncertainty' for users such as broadcasting organisations. The Memorandum then went on to state that an extension of the definition of performers to cover variety and circus performers and folklore was justified: Memorandum Prepared by the International Bureau of WIPO, 'Questions Concerning a Possible Instrument for the Protection of the Rights of Performers and Producers of Phonograms' INR/CE/I/2 (Committee of Experts on the Possible Protection of the Rights of Performers and Producers of Phonograms, First Session, Geneva, 28 June to 2 July 1993) [13]–[17]

B TRIPS

Article 14(1) of TRIPS contains provisions that clearly identify performers as right holders. The first sentence of Article 14(1) provides (in part):

> In respect of a fixation of their performance on a phonogram, performers shall have the possibility of preventing the following acts when undertaken without their authorisation . . . .

An accurate interpretation of Article 14(1) is complicated by the fact that neither performers nor performance are defined. However, there is a clear indication in Article 14(6) that the classic definition of performers is applicable. Article 14(6) permits Members of the WTO to 'provide for conditions, limitations, exceptions and reservations' to the rights granted to performers to the extent provided for in the Rome Convention. Another strong indication is to be found in Article 1(3) of TRIPS, which incorporates by reference the eligibility criteria for nationals (which in this context are performers), that are found in the Rome Convention. It would be difficult to construe those articles of TRIPS without adopting the meaning given to 'performers' in the Rome Convention. On this basis, the above discussion of Article 3(a) is entirely relevant to an understanding of the TRIPS provisions.

A Member may therefore reasonably restrict protection to people who perform literary or artistic works, the category protected under the Rome Convention. Alternatively, although there is no counterpart in TRIPS to Article 9 of the Convention, a Member may extend protection to variety artists, performers of expressions of folklore or sportspersons, all of whom are denied protection under the Rome Convention, and still comply with its obligations under Article 14(1). It has also been suggested that since the rights granted in fixations of performances under Article 14(1) are limited to performances fixed in phonograms, this limits the term 'performers' to 'musical performers'. This suggestion ignores the other performances of works that can be fixed on a phonogram.[19]

C WPPT

The WPPT is consistent with the Rome Convention in that it defines 'performers', who are right holders under the Treaty. The definition in Article 2(a) of the WPPT is modelled on Article 3(a) of the Rome Convention and, in fact, makes only two substantive changes to the earlier wording. It adds 'interpret' to the

[19] D Gervais, *The TRIPS Agreement: Drafting History and Analysis* (Sweet & Maxwell, London, 1998) [2.78]. The works of Shakespeare and other playwrights form just one example of non-musical performances that are fixed on phonograms. Another example is talking books for the blind.

enumeration of the activities of performers, and it includes 'expressions of folklore' as material that may be performed by performers. Article 2(a) states:

> 'performers' are actors, singers, musicians, dancers, and other persons who act, sing, deliver, declaim, play in, interpret, or otherwise perform literary or artistic works or expressions of folklore.

The similarity to the classic definition of 'performers' in the Rome Convention is marked and the conclusions reached above in relation to the classic definition can be applied to the definition in the WPPT.

Does the inclusion of 'interpret' as a separate activity add anything to the definition of 'performers'? It is commonplace to hear the colloquial or non-legal use of a phrase such as, 'the musician interpreted the work in his or her own way'. When the term is included in a provision of an international instrument, however, there is a presumption that it has a specific meaning, although that meaning is not included in the WPPT. Nevertheless, since the definitions in the WPPT were intended to 'modernise and complete' the definitions in the Rome Convention, a performer who interprets a work must do something that is not covered, or is not clearly covered, by the list of activities in the earlier, Rome Convention definition.[20]

There is some assistance to be found in dictionary definitions. The most relevant meaning given to 'interpret' in the *New Shorter Oxford English Dictionary* is:

> **Interpret** . . . Bring out or represent stylistically the meaning of (a creative work, a dramatic role, etc.) according to one's understanding of the creator's ideas.

It is submitted that this meaning covers a situation in which a performance is only loosely based on a literary or artistic work. This would help to broaden the application of the definition, although it seems likely that interpretative performances were always covered in the classic definition, probably by the words 'or otherwise perform.'[21]

While the value of including 'interpret' in the list of performative activities is doubtful, there is no doubt at all that the inclusion of 'expressions of folklore' as a form of performance does extend the definition of a performer. Justification for the inclusion of this term was given in the Memorandum prepared by the International Bureau of WIPO for the first meeting of the Committee of Experts whose deliberations led eventually to the conclusion of the WPPT:

[20] Liedes, Chairman of Main Committee I, is reported as saying that the definitions in the Basic Proposal 'had been modernised and completed with new elements': Summary Minutes, Main Committee I of the Diplomatic Conference on Certain Copyright and Neighboring Rights Questions CRNR/DC/102 ('Summary Minutes') (Diplomatic Conference on Certain Copyright and Neighboring Rights Questions, Geneva, 2 to 20 December 1996) [360].

[21] These points were also made by at least one of the delegates to the Geneva Conference: 'Summary Minutes', above n 20, [389], comments of Ms Daley the delegate of Jamaica.

> The absence [from Article 3(a) of the Rome Convention] of a reference to performances of expressions of folklore seems to be a great deficiency in the definition of 'performers.' . . . [I]t was clarified that expressions of folklore do not correspond to the concept of literary and artistic works (and, thus, should be granted *sui generis* protection). At the same time, it is hardly questionable that the performances of expressions of folklore (such as folk songs, instrumental folk music, folk dances, folk plays, folk poetry and folk tales) deserve the same protection as the performances of literary and artistic works. It is justified to extend the scope of the definition of performers to cover [this category].[22]

In respect of rights granted under the WPPT, performers of expressions of folklore are to be protected to the same extent as performers of literary or artistic works. It was understood that performers of expressions of folklore that qualify as literary or artistic works under the Berne Convention, such as a folk song that had been written down, would be protected under the existing classic definition. The purpose of the new definition is to ensure that performers of expressions of folklore enjoy protection irrespective of the material on which their performances are based.[23] The inclusion of those performers in Article 2(a) is a step towards recognising that a wider range of performers and performances should be protected than are currently protected by the international instruments.

Somewhat surprisingly, the definition of 'performers' in the WPPT does not include variety artistes or circus performers. The International Bureau of WIPO recommended to the earliest meetings of the Committees of Experts that these performers should be included in the new instrument; this recommendation was made at the same time as the recommendation was made to include performers of expressions of folklore.[24] While there appeared to be no opposition in those preliminary meetings to the inclusion of variety artistes and circus performers, they were, in fact, omitted from the definition in the Basic Proposal. Their inclusion was suggested by at least one delegate to the Geneva Diplomatic Conference, but this suggestion was not taken any further.[25]

The failure to add variety artistes and circus performers to the list of recognised performers is a serious blow for those performers; on a grander scale it is symptomatic of the reluctance of the international community to recognise the rights of performers who do not perform literary or artistic works. While the WPPT, like TRIPS, does not contain a counterpart to Article 9 of the Rome Convention; it is open to Contracting Parties to provide protection in their own legislation for performers who do not perform literary or artistic works.

[22] Memorandum Prepared by the International Bureau of WIPO, above n 18, [17].
[23] Basic Proposal, above n 5, [2.04].
[24] Memorandum Prepared by the International Bureau of WIPO, above n 18, [17]. Memoranda prepared by the International Bureau for subsequent meetings of the Committee of Experts repeated the recommendation.
[25] The delegate for Senegal, Mme Youm Diabe Siby, suggested the inclusion of variety artistes and circus performers. 'Summary Minutes', above n 20, [367].

However, the inclusion of performers of expressions of folklore does demonstrate that the categories of performers are not permanently closed, however grudgingly they may be opened. It is easy to point to the inclusion of performers of expressions of folklore in the WPPT as a major step forward in the evolution of the protection of performers and performances at the international level. The reality is that this extension of the category of performers paralleled continuing pressure to gain intellectual property protection for expressions of folklore generally.[26] There has been no such international pressure on behalf of performers such as variety artistes or sportspersons.

III TRANSFER OF OWNERSHIP OF THE RIGHTS

Ownership of performers' rights and the transferability of those rights are serious issues that underpin the grant of those rights. The fundamental principle in each of the international instruments that provide for performers' rights is that performers who satisfy the criteria of eligibility and the definitions of 'performers' are the first right holders. None of the international instruments, however, has an explicit provision as to the transfer of ownership of performers' rights.[27]

Although the transferability of performers' rights was a subject of discussion at the Rome Diplomatic Conference and in meetings of the Committees of Experts that preceded the Geneva Diplomatic Conference, there was not enough support to warrant the inclusion of provisions relating to the transfer of the rights in either the Rome Convention or the WPPT. TRIPS is silent, not just on the transferability of performers' rights, but on the transferability of intellectual property rights generally. Nonetheless, there are certain oblique references to transferability of performers' rights in the Rome Convention and in the WPPT, and a general provision was included in the 23 July 1990 draft of TRIPS, but not in the final instrument.

As there are no provisions in the Rome Convention, TRIPS or the WPPT that explicitly provide for the transfer of rights, the transferability of performers' rights has to be considered in the light of other provisions in the three instruments.

[26] For an overview, see International Bureau of WIPO, '1967, 1982, 1984: Attempts to Provide Intellectual Property Protection for Folklore by Intellectual Property Rights' UNESCO-WIPO/FOLK/PKT/97/19 (Paper presented at the UNESCO-WIPO World Forum on the Protection of Folklore in Phuket, Thailand, 8 to 10 April 1997)

[27] The Diplomatic Conference that met in Geneva in December, 2000 to consider a new instrument for the protection of audiovisual performances could not agree on a provision relating to the transfer of economic rights and, consequently, the instrument was not concluded. The matter is discussed in ch 13.

A Rome Convention

At the Rome Diplomatic Conference, the issue of the transferability of rights was raised in the discussion of Article 7, which is the article that determines the rights performers shall enjoy. In the discussion over the inclusion of an exclusive right to authorise or prohibit in Article 7, some delegates expressed concern that performers would assign an exclusive right to a professional association of performers. It was suggested that if this were to happen it would provide the association with a weapon that it could use to advance the interests of performers against the interests of producers. It was pointed out, however, that professional associations of performers would hardly be likely to exercise their rights in a way that was obstructive on an international scale.[28] Also in the discussion of Article 7, the delegation of Austria proposed a provision permitting a performer to exercise the rights after he or she had transferred those rights to another party. The proposal was rejected, some delegates stated that it was contrary to the principle of freedom of contract.[29]

There is only one provision of the Rome Convention that refers to the transfer of rights. The provision is Article 11, which provides for formalities as a condition of protection for phonograms. The relevant part of Article 11 provides:

> If the copies or their containers do not identify the principal performers, the notice shall also include the name of the person who . . . owns the rights of such performers.

It can be argued that this provision implies that a performer is not the only person who can own the rights, and therefore that performers' rights may be transferred.

B TRIPS

The possible transfer of rights was considered prior to the conclusion of TRIPS. In the Draft of 23 July 1990 (W/76) of TRIPS, Clause 1A proposed that:

> Protected rights shall be freely and separately exploitable and transferable. [Assignees and exclusive licensees shall enjoy all rights of their assignors and licensors acquired through voluntary agreements, and shall be entitled to enjoy, exercise and enforce their acquired exclusive rights [in their own names.]][30]

This provision did not proceed.

[28] 'Summary Records of the Proceedings', *Records of the Diplomatic Conference on the International Protection of Performers, Producers of Phonograms and Broadcasting Organisations* (ILO, UNESCO and BIRPI, Geneva, 1968) [1065.1].

[29] 'Report of the Rapporteur-General', above n 4, 45.

[30] Unfortunately, Gervais does not explain why the provision did not proceed. The square brackets in this quotation have been retained because this is the way in which he records the material: Gervais, above n 19, [2.83].

C WPPT

The question of the transfer of the economic rights was discussed at the meetings of the Committees of Experts that preceded the Geneva Diplomatic Conference. However, there was not enough support for provisions relating to the transfer of rights to be included in the provisions of the draft treaty.[31] The issue is not reported as having arisen at the Conference itself. Nonetheless, some commentators have referred to the opening clause of Article 5(1), which is modelled on Article 6*bis*(1) of the Berne Convention, as suggesting that performers' economic rights are transferable.[32] The opening words of Article 5(1) are:

> Independently of a performer's economic rights, and even after the transfer of those rights . . ..[33]

In the absence of an explicit provision as to the transfer of rights, it seems that it is open to a Contracting Party to proscribe or to allow the transfer of economic rights.

So far as the transfer of moral rights themselves are concerned, Article 5 does not directly address the issue. Article 5(2), which is also modelled on the corresponding provision of the Berne Convention, does permit those rights to be exercised by persons or institutions authorised by the state. The first sentence of Article 5(2) provides:

> The rights granted to a performer in accordance with paragraph (1) shall, after his death, be maintained, at least until the expiry of the economic rights, and shall be exercisable by the persons or institutions authorised by the legislation of the Contracting Party where protection is claimed.

This provision does not explicitly recognise the transfer of the rights; rather it acknowledges that as the rights subsist after the death of the performer there must be a person or institution that is permitted to exercise them. If those rights were not exercisable by another person then it would be pointless to provide that they should be maintained after the performer's death.

[31] Memorandum Prepared by the International Bureau of WIPO, 'Questions Concerning a Possible Instrument for the Protection of the Rights of Performers and Producers of Phonograms' INR/CE/III/2 (Committee of Experts on the Possible Protection of the Rights of Performers and Producers of Phonograms, Third Session, Geneva, 12 to 16 December 1994) [87].

[32] C Cresswell, 'Copyright Protection Enters the Digital Age: the New WIPO Treaties on Copyright and on Performances and Sound Recordings' (1997) 15 Copyright Reporter 4, 12; M Ficsor, 'The Spring 1997 Horace S Manges Lecture—Copyright for the Digital Era: The WIPO "Internet" Treaties' (1997) 21 *Columbia-VLA Journal of Law and the Arts* 197, 221.

[33] The opening clause of Art 6*bis*(1) of the Berne Convention provides: 'Independently of the author's economic rights, and even after the transfer of the said rights . . . .'

IV PERFORMANCE

In each of the three international instruments that provide for performers' rights, the subject matter of protection is a performance by a performer. None of the international instruments defines 'performance', although that term is used in the substantive provisions. It is left to contracting states to determine in their own legislation the essential elements of a performance. For an understanding of what constitutes a performance in those instruments, it is necessary to draw on the analysis of the definitions of 'performers' in Article 3(a) of the Rome Convention and Article 2(a) of the WPPT.

A Rome Convention

It is made clear in Article 7 that the subject matter of protection in the Rome Convention is a performance made by a performer. As an example, Article 7(1)(a) provides that, with some exceptions, performers shall have the possibility of preventing the broadcasting or communication to the public of their performances. The delegates to the Rome Diplomatic Conference regarded it as superfluous to define a performance, and that approach has been followed in TRIPS and the WPPT:

> The Hague Draft contained a definition of 'performance' but not of 'performers'. In view of the addition of a definition of 'performers', the Conference found it superfluous to define 'performance' separately; obviously, performance means the activities of a performer *qua* performer. It was, however, agreed that whenever the Convention uses the expression 'performance'. . . it must be understood as a generic term which also includes recitation . . . and presentation.[34]

Returning to the earlier analysis of Article 3(a), it can be concluded that a performance is protectable if it is a performative activity of an actor, singer, musician or dancer; or if it is a performative activity of other persons who act, sing, deliver, declaim, play in or otherwise perform. The key element is, of course, that the activity must be a performative activity: in the context of Article 3(a), a performative activity is a performance of a literary or artistic work. In this way, the Rome Convention established a distinction between performances of literary or artistic works and performances other than of works. It is only performances of the former that are protected.

[34] 'Report of the Rapporteur-General', above n 4, 40. Art 7 of the Hague Draft states: 'For the purposes of this Convention, "performance" means the recitation, presentation or performance of a literary or artistic work. It shall be a matter for national laws and regulations to extend the protection to artistes who do not perform literary or artistic works.'

The limitation to literary and artistic works reflected a number of the factors that were influential at the Rome Diplomatic Conference. First, a very important factor was the influence of the broadcaster's lobby.[35] Broadcasters were determined to limit the scope of protection granted to performers.

> The great difficulty about extending protection to those who do not perform works is to decide how far to go without making too many difficulties for the broadcasting organizations, i.e. to keep protection within defined limits.[36]

A second factor was the influence of the copyright tradition. Although a formal connection was not established between the Rome Convention and the copyright conventions, the influence of the Berne Convention can be seen in the content and structure of the Rome Convention.[37] Third, the provisions of the Rome Convention represent the demands made by performers in the European tradition; although, as has been pointed out elsewhere, 'performance is an inclusive term.'[38]

B TRIPS

As noted above in the discussion of performers, neither 'performers' nor 'performance' is defined in TRIPS. Just as clearly as Article 14(1) identifies performers as right holders, it identifies a performance as the subject matter of protection. It was suggested earlier that the meaning of 'performers' in Article 3(a) of the Rome Convention should be adopted to interpret the relevant provisions of TRIPS. It is now suggested that the description of a performance derived from Article 3(a) of the Rome Convention can be applied in its entirety to TRIPS.

[35] The European Broadcasting Union had a significant advantage over the other non-governmental organisations at the Rome Diplomatic Conference in that its principal legal adviser, Dr Straschnov, was also a member of the delegation of Monaco and took a very active part in the Conference. Ulmer notes that he 'carried weight with other delegations whose members were close to broadcasting organizations': E Ulmer, 'The Rome Convention for the Protection of Performers, Producers of Phonograms and Broadcasting Organizations. Part I' (1963) 10 *Bulletin. Copyright Society of the U.S.A.* 90, 96

[36] Masouye, above n 4, [9.3].

[37] The influence can be seen, for example, in the provisions for national treatment and the points of attachment and in the provisions relating to limitations and exceptions. As discussed above, the Rome Convention requires that Contracting States must be a party to either the Berne Convention or the Universal Copyright Convention.

[38] See the comments of Schechner, ch 2, n 15.

C WPPT

The approach to the subject matter of protection in the WPPT is consistent with the approach first adopted at the Rome Convention. The essence of performing is still measured, in large part, by whether or not it is a performance of a literary or artistic work, a peculiarly European concept. Exceptions to this standard are only grudgingly conceded. However, the WPPT does broaden the understanding of a performance beyond the constraints imposed by the Rome Convention by the inclusion of 'expressions of folklore' as an activity of a performer. The use of the term 'otherwise perform . . . expressions of folklore' in Article 2(a) permits Contracting Parties to recognise virtually any form of behaviour as a performance provided that it is associated with an expression of folklore.

The other change that is included in Article 2(a)—namely the recognition of 'interpretation' as a form of activity characteristic of performers—is unlikely to have any significant effect. As indicated above, 'interpret' is probably covered by the phrase 'or otherwise perform'.

V CONCLUSIONS

There appears to be a general consensus at an international level as to the matters discussed in this chapter, and from this discussion a number of important conclusions can be drawn:

(i) The definition of 'performers' is based on the performance of literary or artistic works. The consequence of concentrating on performances of works is that performers in three major classes of performances (variety, folklore and sports) are excluded from protection. The point of principle, that performers must perform literary or artistic works, has always been shaky. The inclusion of Article 9 in the Rome Convention as a reminder to Contracting States that they could extend protection to a wider group of performers than those who perform literary or artistic works was an acknowledgment that there was uncertainty as to the definition of 'performers'. The decision to include performers of expressions of folklore as part of the definition of 'performers' in the WPPT is recognition that different cultures have different views on what constitutes a performance; without this recognition, international agreements that have been established to protect foreign performers will not provide complete protection for those performers.

(ii) It is unsatisfactory to have to search for clues about the transferability of rights in provisions that do not have transferability as a primary concern. The argument in response is that the transfer of performers' rights is not really within the scope of the international instruments; it is a matter that owes more to conditions within states rather than the international situation that is the proper province of international instruments.[39] Nevertheless, ownership of the rights is so important that provisions relating to ownership should be spelt out.

(iii) An important feature of all three instruments is that once the threshold requirement is reached, be it a performance of a work or a performance of an expression of folklore, no distinction is made as to the context in which the performance is made, the content of the performance, nor the merits of the performance or the talent of the performer.

Other aspects of the system of performers' rights have been criticised by commentators for a number of reasons, but the definition of 'performers' and the understanding of 'performance' have not provoked any real concern. Nor have these matters greatly concerned the delegates to the diplomatic conferences that have concluded the performers' rights instruments. Likewise, while the question of the transfer of performers' rights has been considered from time to time, it is only recently that there has been real interest in providing for the transfer of performers' rights. This lack of concern about such important provisions is disappointing; it suggests that the level of priority given to these matters is low. The same criticism cannot be levelled at the provisions that determine the scope of the rights accorded to performers. There has been considerable debate about the provisions which are analysed in the following two chapters.

[39] The increasingly common practice of making audiovisual productions in several countries has led the United States to argue in respect of performers' rights in audiovisual performances that such rights must be balanced 'with the need for a simple rule that will achieve a requisite level of certainty as audiovisual production and distribution increasingly continues to cross national boundaries.' See the statement on the transfer of rights in: Agenda Item 4: Protection of Audiovisual Performances, 'Submission of the United States', SCCR/3/7 (Standing Committee on Copyright and Related Rights, Third Session, Geneva, 16 to 20 November 1999).

9

The Primary Economic Rights

I INTRODUCTION

THIS CHAPTER ANALYSES the scope of protection afforded to performers by the primary economic rights under the Rome Convention, TRIPS and the WPPT. The term 'primary economic rights' is used because the rights analysed in this chapter are the rights that were first granted to performers. The expression also distinguishes them from the rights analysed in the next chapter, the 'extended rights'; in that context 'extended' is used to denote rights that take the protection of performers beyond the primary rights.

It was suggested in chapter 4 that there are two basic economic rights: the right of making available, and the right of reproduction. In the international instruments, however, performers' rights are divided into a number of separate rights. For the sake of consistency, the division of the basic rights that is adopted in those instruments is followed throughout. The four economic rights that are recognised in the Rome Convention are: the right of broadcasting and communication to the public; the right of fixation; the right of reproduction; and the right to equitable remuneration.[1] Although fixation is a form of reproduction, and the remuneration right is an aspect of the right of broadcasting and communication to the public, they are all treated separately in the international instruments and will also be treated separately here.

II RIGHT OF BROADCASTING AND COMMUNICATION TO THE PUBLIC

The consequences for performers of the development of broadcasting and public communication have been described in an earlier chapter.[2] They were key factors leading to performers' demands for rights to enable them to control the use of their performances.

[1] The possibility of other protection is recognised in the Rome Convention. Art 21 provides: 'The protection provided for in this Convention shall not prejudice any protection otherwise secured to performers, producers of phonograms and broadcasting organizations.'

[2] Ch 4, n 8 and n 9 and accompanying text.

A Rome Convention

1 *The Protection Provided by Article 7*

Article 7 sets out the protection that the Rome Convention guarantees to performers. The obligation to provide a minimum level of protection to performers is couched in the form of a general goal or purpose, rather than an exclusive right. Performers are to have 'the possibility of preventing' certain acts when those acts are undertaken without the performers' consent. Those acts are then outlined. The legal means that would enable the performer to prevent these acts are not spelt out; they are a matter of complete freedom of choice under national legislation, a drafting device that enabled the United Kingdom to retain criminal sanctions as the means of protecting performers and still comply with the Convention.[3] The obligation to provide 'the possibility of preventing' certain acts can be couched in the language of exclusive rights. A prime example is Section 2 of the Model Law Concerning the Protection of Performers, Producers of Phonograms and Broadcasting Organisations ('Model Law').[4] It is not a question of how protection is achieved, but rather one of ensuring that the minimum protection provided for under the Convention is implemented.

> [P]erformers are only guaranteed a certain legal position which is to be safeguarded by appropriate sanctions, the details of which are left to the discretion of the contracting countries. References to performers' 'rights' in the Convention . . . are merely made for the sake of simple terminology; strictly speaking, we should refer, not to performers' rights, but rather to the legal position of performers.[5]

National legislation may provide the conventional minima or it may provide for greater rights than those prescribed in the Convention. Of course, it would not be surprising for a state to regard the Convention as a prescription of the maximum rather than of the minimum. What a Contracting State must not do is to enact legislation that provides a lower standard than the Convention.

[3] 'Report of the Rapporteur-General', *Records of the Diplomatic Conference on the International Protection of Performers, Producers of Phonograms and Broadcasting Organisations* (ILO, UNESCO and BIRPI, Geneva, 1968) 43. Masouye suggests that other options include employment law, unfair competition, unjust enrichment and the provision of an exclusive right: C Masouye (W Wallace trans), *Guide to the Rome Convention and to the Phonograms Convention* (World Intellectual Property Organisation, Geneva, 1981) [7.4].

[4] The opening sentence of s 2 of the Model Law is: 'Without the authorisation of the performers, *no person shall do any of the following acts*.'(Emphasis added). The Intergovernmental Committee of the International Convention for the Protection of Performers, Producers of Phonograms and Broadcasting Organisations done at Rome in 1961 *Model Law Concerning the Protection of Performers, Producers of Phonograms and Broadcasting Organisations with a Commentary on it* (ILO, UNESCO, WIPO; Geneva and Paris, 1974).

[5] E Ulmer, 'The Rome Convention for the Protection of Performers, Producers of Phonograms and Broadcasting Organizations. Part III' (1963) 10 *Bulletin. Copyright Society of the U.S.A.* 219, 220.

2 *Article 7(1)(a)*

The first sub-paragraph of Article 7(1) provides performers with some protection against the broadcasting or communication to the public of their performances when this is done without their consent. Before analysing that provision, it is worthwhile considering the meaning of the terms 'broadcasting' and 'communication to the public' as they are used in the Rome Convention. Broadcasting is defined in Article 3(f) as: 'the transmission by wireless means for public reception of sounds or of images and sounds.' Communication to the public is not defined. The distinction between communication to the public and broadcasting lies in the means of transmission, which is by wireless means for broadcasting and by wired means for communication to the public. As these two means of transmission to the public are specified together, as a right of broadcasting and communication to the public, and that right covers the same content, all aspects of those forms of exploitation are covered. In other words, the right granted under Article 7(1)(a) covers the transmission of both audio and audiovisual performances whether by wireless or by wired means.

It has been suggested that communication to the public does not apply to a situation in which the public is present at the place where the performance takes place.[6] On that view, the use of amplification equipment within an auditorium does not constitute communication to the members of the public present in that auditorium. If, however, the performance is transmitted by the same equipment to persons outside the auditorium, there would be a communication to the public. (The same approach was taken in the drafting of the WPPT.[7]) This approach is to be doubted for at least two reasons. First, such a narrow position ignores the realities of the exploitation of performances by modern technology, particularly within large stadiums. The concept of 'communication to the public' should cover transmission to spectators physically present at the performance. Second, there is no definition of the activity in the Rome Convention and the definition of 'communication to the public' in Article 2(g) of the WPPT speaks of 'the transmission to the public by any medium, *otherwise than by broadcasting*' (emphasis added). There is no basis for reading down this provision. The more relevant objection is that the examples just referred to are examples of situations in which the communication to the public does not involve an international situation, and therefore it is unnecessary to provide for them in an international instrument. This was recognised by the delegates to the Rome

[6] Masouye, above n 3, [7.12].

[7] Chairman of the Committees of Experts on a Possible Protocol to the Berne Convention and on a Possible Instrument for the Protection of the Rights of Performers and Producers of Phonograms, 'Basic Proposal for the Substantive Provisions of the Treaty for the Protection of Performers and Producers of Phonograms to be Considered by the Diplomatic Conference' CRNR/DC/5 ('Basic Proposal') (Diplomatic Conference on Certain Copyright and Neighbouring Rights Questions, Geneva, 2 to 20 December 1996) [2.24].

Diplomatic Conference, who decided that international situations might be rare but were still possible.[8]

The issue of who constitutes the public to whom the communication is made is left by the Convention to national legislation and national courts. As the right of broadcasting and communication is a right to control transmission of a performance to the public, the emphasis should be on the authority of the person making the transmission and not on the circumstances of the reception of that transmission.

In respect of broadcasting and communication to the public, Article 7(1)(a) provides:

> The protection provided for performers by this Convention shall include the possibility of preventing:
>
> (a) the broadcasting and communication to the public, without their consent, of their performance, except where the performance used in the broadcasting or the public communication is itself already a broadcast performance or is made from a fixation.

When Article 7(1)(a) is analysed, it proves to be quite narrow:

(i) A performer's consent is required for a broadcast or a communication to the public of an unfixed performance. The performer's consent is not required if the performance has already been broadcast. This is the issue of rebroadcasting, which is discussed below.

(ii) A performer's consent is not required if the performance is embodied in a fixation. This is a serious restriction, given that the majority of performances that are broadcast and communicated to the public are embodied in fixations. It also leaves a gap in the protection of performances that have been fixed without consent. For example, a performer has no right to prevent the broadcast or communication to the public of a bootleg phonogram. The fact that the making of the phonogram is subject to prohibition under Article 7(1)(b) as a fixation made without consent is irrelevant to sub-paragraph (a). The sanction in Article 7(1)(a) is on the act of broadcasting or communication to the public, not on the fixation of an unfixed performance; a broadcast of a bootleg phonogram is still a broadcast of a performance that is embodied in a fixation.

It can be seen that the level of protection guaranteed to performers in relation to broadcasting is low, and it is reduced by Article 7(2)(1) which permits Contracting States to determine the level of protection available to performers in respect of uses of their performances in broadcasting in cases in which the

[8] 'Report of the Rapporteur-General', above n 3, 44.

performers had consented to the broadcasting.[9] The strength of the broadcasters' lobby at the Rome Conference was responsible for these provisions rather than the application of principle to the problem.[10]

Article 7(2)(1) provides:

> If broadcasting was consented to by the performers, it shall be a matter for the domestic law of the Contracting State where protection is claimed to regulate the protection against rebroadcasting, fixation for broadcasting purposes and the reproduction of such fixation for broadcasting purposes.

Article 7(2)(2) provides:

> The terms and conditions governing the use by broadcasting organisations of fixations made for broadcasting purposes shall be determined in accordance with the domestic law of the State where protection is claimed.

The first use of a performance that Article 7(2)(1) reserves to the regulation of national law is rebroadcasting, which is defined in Article 3(g) as: 'the simultaneous broadcasting by one broadcasting organisation of the broadcast of another broadcasting organisation.' Article 7(2)(1) reflects the technology issues of the time: commercial satellite transmissions had not begun in 1961 and sound and television communications were relayed across Europe.[11] While rebroadcasting was a major concern of the delegates to the Rome Diplomatic Conference, the advance of technology has reduced the importance of rebroadcasting today.[12] The other activities that are left to the regulation of national law, by virtue of Article 7(2)(1) and Article 7(2)(2), are the making of fixations for broadcasting purposes, the reproduction of those fixations and the use of those fixations. Those activities are still issues of some concern.

Finally, there is an important proviso in Article 7(2)(3), which provides that if Contracting States do regulate the matters considered in sub-paragraphs (1) and (2), performers should still be free 'to control, by contract, their relations with broadcasting organisations'. The Report of the Rapporteur-General notes that during the discussion of this provision it was agreed that, in this context, 'contract' includes 'collective contracts.'[13] Delegates to the Diplomatic Conference appear to have recognised that there was likely to be an imbalance of bargaining

[9] Although it is not clear that Art 7(2) refers to situations in which the performer has consented to the broadcast of his or her performance, this was made clear during the discussion of the provision. 'Summary Records of the Proceedings', *Records of the Diplomatic Conference on the International Protection of Performers, Producers of Phonograms and Broadcasting Organisations* (ILO, UNESCO and BIRPI, Geneva, 1968) [1100].

[10] The broadcasters had the advantage of Straschnov's unique position as the principal legal officer of the European Broadcasting Union and as a member of the delegation of Monaco: E Ulmer, 'The Rome Convention for the Protection of Performers, Producers of Phonograms and Broadcasting Organizations. Part I' (1963) 10 *Bulletin Copyright Society of the U.S.A.* 90, 96.

[11] There is a description of the practice of rebroadcasting in Masouye, above n 3, [7.24].

[12] 'Summary Records of the Proceedings', above n 9, [1074.2].

[13] 'Report of the Rapporteur-General', above n 3, 45. Performers can therefore look to their professional bodies for assistance in reaching agreements with broadcasters.

power between performers and broadcasters that might be met by performers seeking the support of a guild or union.

B TRIPS

The right of broadcasting and communication to the public forms part of Article 14 of TRIPS, which, so far as performers are concerned, is the most important provision in that Agreement. In respect of all the rights provided, Article 14 includes the phrase 'the possibility of preventing', which is taken from the Rome Convention and is to be interpreted in the same way.

The relevant part of Article 14(1), the second sentence, provides:

> Performers shall also have the possibility of preventing the following acts when undertaken without their authorisation: the broadcasting by wireless means and the communication to the public of their live performance.

The words used are similar to the Rome Convention, but not exactly the same. Broadcasting under Article 14(1) is explicitly a transmission by wireless means but, like the Rome Convention, communication to the public is not defined. As broadcasting in the context of TRIPS is a wireless means, it is logical to assume that the 'wired/wireless' distinction applies and that communication to the public involves transmission by wire. Article 14(1) introduces the unfortunate term 'live performance' which is not defined in Article 14, nor anywhere else in TRIPS. The difficulties associated with that term have already been considered.[14] The Rome Convention is of no assistance. The term was deliberately not used in the Convention because it was regarded as ambiguous, having different connotations in different languages.[15]

The term 'live performance' can be explained on the basis that it is a performance that takes place in the presence of an audience when there is no intervening form of exploitation between the performance and the audience. There is a distinction to be made between a live performance and an unfixed performance. The latter includes a performance that is broadcast or communicated to the public, provided that the content of the programme has not been previously fixed. Thus, a live performance is an unfixed performance, but an unfixed performance may also be one in which the technology of broadcasting or communication to the public intervenes between the performance and the public. On this interpretation, the effect of the broadcasting and communication to the public provision is the same as in the Rome Convention. A performance that is broadcast by one organisation and then rebroadcast by another organisation is

[14] The question of a live performance was discussed in ch 4, n 58 and accompanying text.

[15] 'Report of the Rapporteur-General', above n 3, 43–44.

no longer a live performance and is therefore not protected, either by TRIPS or by Article 7 of the Rome Convention.[16]

The other notable point about the right of broadcasting and communication to the public is that it encompasses both 'live' audio and 'live' audiovisual performances. This is notable because the other rights granted under Article 14 are restricted to performances fixed on phonograms.[17]

C WPPT

1 *Exclusive Rights*

Apart from the remuneration right, the economic rights in the WPPT are couched in the language of exclusive rights and therefore set new standards not present in either the Rome Convention or TRIPS. The most important effect of the new standards adopted in the WPPT is that states will not be able to provide purely criminal sanctions as they were able to under the Rome Convention and TRIPS. There is no reason, however, why criminal sanctions cannot be provided in addition to civil remedies.

2 *Article 6(i)*

Article 6 of the WPPT is divided into two paragraphs. The first paragraph is concerned with broadcasting and communication to the public. The interpretation of this provision is assisted by the definitions in Article 2, which include an updated definition of 'broadcasting' and a definition of 'communication to the public'. It will be recalled that the latter definition was lacking in the other two instruments.

The definition of broadcasting in Article 2(f) is in three parts. It states:

> 'broadcasting' means the transmission by wireless means for public reception of sounds or of images and sounds or of the representations thereof; such transmission by satellite is also 'broadcasting'; transmission of encrypted signals is 'broadcasting' where the means for decrypting are provided to the public by the broadcasting organisation or with its consent.

The first part repeats the Rome Convention definition that covers the transmission by wireless means for public reception of sounds or of images and sounds

[16] The International Bureau of WIPO concur that the effect is the same as Art 7(1)(a) but they have a different interpretation. In their view, the provision in TRIPS does not include any reference to rebroadcasting, and therefore it can be assumed that it is not covered in Art 14(1): International Bureau of WIPO, *Implications of the TRIPS Agreement on Treaties Administered by WIPO* (WIPO, Geneva, 1997) [59].

[17] A phonogram is not defined in TRIPS. Logically, however, it is a sound recording: see the discussion below, n 24 and accompanying text.

or of their representations.[18] The second part is new: it explicitly states that transmission by satellite is included in broadcasting. Whether satellite transmissions should be equated to broadcasting has been a matter of some discussion but it is now settled affirmatively for the purposes of the WPPT.[19] The third part of the definition introduces a new concept: it includes in broadcasting, 'the transmission of encrypted signals . . . where the means for decrypting are provided to the public by the broadcasting organization or with its consent'. It was stated in the Basic Proposal that the third part dealt with encrypted satellite transmissions.[20] There are, however, other circumstances that fit the words of the provision. For example, pay-TV operators transmit encrypted signals and provide decryption devices but their broadcasts may be land-based.

The definition of 'communication to the public' in Article 2(g) is entirely new as the term is not defined in either the Rome Convention or TRIPS. Article 2(g) states:

> 'communication to the public' of a performance or a phonogram means the transmission to the public by any medium, otherwise than by broadcasting, of sounds of a performance or the sounds or the representations of sounds fixed in a phonogram. For the purposes of Article 15, 'communication to the public' includes making the sounds or representations of sounds fixed in a phonogram audible to the public.

In the context of the WPPT, it can be seen that 'communication to the public' is simultaneously broad and narrow in scope. It is broad in that it encompasses 'transmission to the public by any medium, otherwise than broadcasting', which should signal to legislators that the right of communication to the public includes transmissions of unfixed performances over the Internet and any medium that succeeds it. The definition is narrow in the content that is transmitted. Broadcasting encompasses images and sounds and representations thereof; communication to the public is restricted to sounds or the representations thereof. This distinction is emphasised by explicitly excluding broadcasting from the definition of communication to the public.

With those definitions in mind, it is now possible to comment on the substantive provision. Article 6(i) provides:

[18] The use of the term 'representations' in the definitions of 'phonogram', 'broadcasting' and 'communication to the public' was explained in the Basic Proposal in the following way: 'The definition of a phonogram is modernised by extending its coverage to phonograms that are not fixations of sounds. Phonograms may be produced for instance utilising digital technology that fixes data which can be used to generate sounds even though no 'real' sounds have yet been produced. The data, of course, can be made audible by means of appropriate electronic equipment.' See Basic Proposal, above n 7, [2.07].

[19] There is a useful discussion in: International Labour Organisation, *Satellite and Cable Television—The Rights of Performers and Producers of Phonograms* (International Labour Office, Geneva, 1989) 3–10.

[20] Basic Proposal, above n 7, [2.22].

> Performers shall enjoy the exclusive right of authorizing, as regards their performances:
>
> (i) the broadcasting and communication to the public of their unfixed performances except where the performance is already a broadcast performance.

Even a cursory glance will show that, although performers will now enjoy an exclusive right, that right is subject to the same restrictions that are present in the other instruments and that were discussed above: it applies only to unfixed performances that have not yet been broadcast. The value of Article 6(i) lies not so much in the exclusive right that it grants but in clarification of the terms that it uses.

III RIGHT OF FIRST FIXATION

Bootlegging was one of the first problem areas that technology created for performers. This problem is addressed in the right of first fixation. The law of performers' rights treats the first fixation of a performance separately from any rights that a performer may have in the reproduction of fixations of a performance.[21] By analogy with Article 9 of the Berne Convention, the right of first fixation could have been treated as a component of a right of reproduction.[22]

A Rome Convention

Article 7(1)(b) requires the consent of a performer to the fixation of his or her unfixed performance, that is, to the first fixation of a performance. Fixation is not defined either in the Rome Convention or in TRIPS. It is appropriate to refer to the definition of the 'first fixation of sounds' in the *WIPO Glossary of Terms of the Law of Copyright and Neighboring Rights*. It states:

> The original embodiment of sounds of a live performance, or of any other sounds not taken from another existing fixation, in some enduring material form such as tapes, records or other appropriate device permitting them to be perceived, reproduced or otherwise repeatedly communicated.

Although this definition refers explicitly to sounds, it can be adapted, *mutatis mutandis*, to include images as well as sounds. The essence of fixation is in the requirement of stability of form which enables the performance to be perceived, reproduced or otherwise communicated.

[21] Art 3(e) of the Rome Convention states: '"reproduction" means the making of a copy or copies of a fixation.' There is no definition of 'reproduction' in TRIPS or the WPPT.

[22] Art 9(1) of the Berne Convention provides authors with an exclusive right to authorise the reproduction of their works 'in any manner or form'. This provision is supplemented by Art 9(3) which provides: 'Any sound or visual recording shall be considered as a reproduction for the purposes of this Convention.'

Article 7(1)(b) is simply and clearly drafted. It provides:

> The protection provided for performers by this Convention shall include the possibility of preventing: . . .
>
> (b) the fixation, without their consent, of their unfixed performance.

Although there were no cheap and efficient means of embodying performances in audiovisual media available to bootleggers in 1961, 'clandestine filming, either live or off-the-air' was considered to be a possibility and bootleg audiovisual fixations are covered by the provision.[23] However, the practical problems of making an audiovisual fixation of a performance to the standard required of a cinematographic film, without the consent of the performers, mean that it is unlikely that the unauthorised use of audiovisual technology to capture performances will be extensive.

The requirements of the broadcasting industry, and its influence at the Rome Diplomatic Conference, meant that the right of first fixation is subject to a specific exception in Article 15(1)(c) of the Rome Convention. This exception permits Contracting States to provide for an exception to the protection guaranteed by the Convention for 'ephemeral fixation by a broadcasting organisation by means of its own facilities and for its own broadcasts'. This can be justified on the basis that it is a technical requirement for delayed broadcasts; and on this basis the exception should be made subject to the destruction of the fixation within a specific and short period.

B TRIPS

The right of first fixation is dealt with in the first sentence of Article 14(1) of TRIPS. It provides:

> In respect of a fixation of their performance on a phonogram, performers shall have the possibility of preventing the following acts when undertaken without their authorisation: the fixation of their unfixed performance and the reproduction of such fixation.

This provision is narrower than Article 7(1)(b) of the Rome Convention, in that the fixation must be made on a phonogram whereas the Rome Convention contemplates fixation in any medium. However, in other respects, Article 14(1) of TRIPS corresponds to Article 7(1)(b) of the Rome Convention and therefore the comments made about Article 7(1)(b) are applicable here.

[23] Clandestine filming was raised in discussions over the Hague Draft. Report of Mr W Wallace, Rapporteur General, 'Comité d'experts sur la protection des artistes interprètes ou exécutants, des producteurs de phonogrammes et des organismes de radiodiffusion' (Réunion de la Haye, 9–20 mai 1960) (1960) *Le Droit D'Auteur* 167 at [59].

Although 'phonogram' is not defined in TRIPS, the heading to Article 14 reads 'Protection of Performers, Producers of Phonograms (Sound Recordings) and Broadcasting Organisations'. For the purposes of Article 14, a phonogram is therefore a sound recording and the protection granted by TRIPS in fixations of performances relates only to sound recordings.[24] The suggestion that protection under Article 14(1) is restricted to musical performers has been criticised in the previous chapter.[25]

In the absence of a definition in TRIPS, the definition of 'first fixation of sounds' in the *WIPO Glossary of Terms of the Law of Copyright and Neighbouring Rights*, which was cited above, is relevant. By virtue of Article 14(6), the exception under Article 15(1)(c) of the Rome Convention would also apply to the interpretation of the right of first fixation in TRIPS.[26]

C WPPT

The WPPT contains a definition of 'fixation'. Article 2(c) states:

> 'fixation' means the embodiment of sounds, or of the representations thereof, from which they can be perceived, reproduced or communicated through a device.

This definition has an important part to play in determining the level of protection that the WPPT, in Article 6(ii), provides to performers against the unauthorised first fixation of their performances. There is uncertainty because there are two conflicting interpretations of Article 6(ii). That Article provides:

> Performers shall enjoy the exclusive right of authorizing, as regards their performances: . . .
>
> (ii) the fixation of their unfixed performances.

A broad interpretation of this provision was advanced in the Basic Proposal, namely, that a performer has the right to control the fixation of an unfixed performance in any medium.[27] However, the definition of 'fixation' in Article 2(c) supports a narrow interpretation, as it would seem to restrict Article 6(ii) to the

[24] The International Bureau of WIPO arrived at the same conclusion as to the meaning of phonogram, but by a more convoluted method. As TRIPS includes, by reference, some provisions of the Rome Convention that use the term phonogram, in their view, this indicates that the definition in the Rome Convention applies. Art 3(b) of the Rome Convention defines phonogram as meaning 'any exclusively aural fixation of the sounds of a performance'. International Bureau of WIPO, above n 16, [56].

[25] As noted above, ch 8, n 19, Gervais has suggested that protection under Art 14(1) is restricted to performers of music. D Gervais, *The TRIPS Agreement: Drafting History and Analysis* (Sweet & Maxwell, London, 1998) [2.78].

[26] The first sentence of Art 14(6) of TRIPS provides: 'Any Member may, in relation to the rights conferred under paragraphs 1, 2 and 3 provide for conditions, limitations, exceptions and reservations to the extent permitted by the Rome Convention.' This provision is discussed below in ch 11.

[27] Basic Proposal, above n 7, [6.02].

right to control the fixation of an unfixed performance of sounds. This is in line with the general tenor of protection within the WPPT, which is restricted to audio fixations as opposed to audiovisual fixations.

In favour of the first, broader interpretation, the definition of 'fixation' is at least wider than a phonogram (the definition of 'phonogram' excludes fixations incorporated in audiovisual works).[28] It could therefore encompass an audiovisual fixation. It is possible—after all—to fix the sounds of a performance, for example, on a video cassette in a handheld video camera. The relevant performer's rights would then relate only to the embodiment of the sounds of the performance leaving the purely visual aspects unprotected under the WPPT. But this is a tortuous and unsatisfactory resolution of the issue and the narrow interpretation is more convincing. It is likely, however, that the matter will be determined in national legislation by the form of existing legislation. If a state has already granted performers a right of fixation in unfixed performances in audio and audiovisual media as part of its obligations under the Rome Convention or under TRIPS, it can be expected to continue this approach.

IV RIGHT OF REPRODUCTION

As soon as a performance is fixed, it is available to be exploited in a number of ways, the most important of which is through copies being made of that performance. It is clearly in the interests of performers to be able to control the reproduction of their performances. In the current international instruments, the right of reproduction is restricted to the copying of performances that are fixed; more specifically, the right is restricted (with the exception of certain unauthorised works) to the copying of performances fixed in phonograms. As discussed above, the right of first fixation covers the making of a copy of an unfixed performance by embodying it in a fixation.

It should be understood that in the law of performers' rights copying involves making or using exact, accurate copies of performances by means of some form of technology. This avoids the difficult question of whether the law should concern itself with reproduction in the sense of one performer copying the performance of another; that is left to national legislation.

A Rome Convention

Article 7(1)(c) of the Rome Convention provides that a performer's consent is required for the reproduction of a fixation of a performance in three narrow situations. It is useful to consider first the meaning of 'reproduction'. It is defined in Article 3(e) of the Convention as follows:

[28] Art 2(b) of the WPPT.

'reproduction' means the making of a copy or copies of a fixation.

A general right of reproduction that would have required the consent of the performer to all reproductions was rejected at the Rome Diplomatic Conference on the grounds that obtaining the further consents of the performer, in addition to that of the producer of the phonogram, would cause problems for broadcasting organisations.[29]

The circumstances in which a performer may prevent the reproduction of a fixation made without his or her consent are set out in Article 7(1)(c) which provides:

> The protection provided for performers by this Convention shall include the possibility of preventing: . . .
>
> (c) the reproduction, without their consent, of a fixation of their performance:
>
> (i) if the original fixation itself was made without their consent;
> (ii) if the reproduction is made for purposes different from those for which the performers gave their consent;
> (iii) if the original fixation was made in accordance with the provisions of Article 15, and the reproduction is made for purposes different from those referred to in those provisions.

The requirements in clauses (i) and (iii) are complementary, for the requirement of consent is always subject to the permitted exceptions in Article 15.[30] Interesting issues are raised by the situation covered by clause (ii), in which the reproduction is made for a purpose different from those for which a performer may have originally given consent. This situation involves questions of interpretation of the agreement between the performer and the producer, which is a matter for national courts to decide on a case by case basis.[31]

Apart from the three situations covered in clauses (i), (ii) and (iii), there was another situation considered at the Rome Diplomatic Conference which became

[29] 'Summary Records of the Proceedings' above, n 9, [1423.1]–[1434]

[30] Art 15 is discussed in ch 11. It provides for specific exceptions in para (1): private use; reporting of current events; ephemeral fixation by broadcasters; and, use for teaching or research. Art 15(1)(c) was mentioned above in connection with an exception to the right of first fixation. Art 15(2) sets out a general test in respect of other exceptions that Contracting States may include in national legislation.

[31] A number of reported performers' rights cases in the United Kingdom concern situations in which the performer claims that the consent which he or she gave did not extend to the purpose to which the defendant is putting a fixation of a performance. An example is *Ekland v Scripglow Limited* [1982] FSR 431. In that case, the well-known actress, Britt Ekland, had agreed to appear in an introductory role in a so-called video magazine that was to be released in the form of a video cassette. Subsequently, and without obtaining Ekland's consent, the first defendant made and distributed a cinematographic film that included her performance. Ekland successfully sought an injunction to prevent the distribution of the film. The defendants argued that Ekland gave consent to the making of the cinematographic film by consenting to the making of the video magazine. Peter Gibson J rejected this submission. He found that the contract related only to the video magazine. The issue of consent is discussed above, ch 5, n 16, and accompanying text.

known as the 'fourth case'. The situation envisaged was where a person, other than the one to whom the performer had originally given consent to make a fixation of a performance, makes a reproduction of the fixation without the performer's consent. Under Article 7(1)(c), a performer appears to be unable to prevent this exploitation if the reproduction was made for the purposes for which the original consent was made. A performer is therefore not protected against phonogram piracy as pirated phonograms are reproductions of fixations that were originally made with the performer's consent. The delegates to the Conference rejected the fourth case because the majority felt that it was sufficient to give the producer of the phonogram the right of reproduction in these cases.[32]

1 *Article 19*

The level of protection for performances fixed in audiovisual fixations was an issue at the Rome Diplomatic Conference and it has remained contentious to the present day.[33] The performers' right to object to reproductions made for different purposes was reduced in respect of audiovisual fixations by Article 19, which is one of the provisions that, together, exclude the cinematographic film industry from the ambit of the Convention.[34] Apart from Article 19, the exclusion of the interests of the film industry is achieved by the definition of 'phonogram', which is restricted to the fixation of sounds and the narrow protection offered by Article 7 itself. The attitude of the majority of the delegates to the Conference is summed up in the request made by the French delegation that the 'section which dealt with Article 19 should be preceded by a short paragraph stating that the Conference had, as a matter of principle, sought to exclude everything relating to the film industry.'[35] The request was, however, not agreed to.

Article 19 provides:

> Notwithstanding anything in this Convention, once a performer has consented to the incorporation of his performance in a visual or audiovisual fixation, Article 7 shall have no further application.

Obviously, Article 19 has a significant effect. However, it comes into play only after a performer has given his or her consent to the first fixation of a performance in visual or audiovisual media. The protection that performers are guaranteed under Article 7(1)(b) against fixations made without their

[32] 'Report of the Rapporteur-General', above n 3, 44.
[33] The failure to conclude a new instrument protecting audiovisual performances is discussed in ch 13.
[34] It was understood by delegates to the Rome Diplomatic Conference that Art 19 was intended to assist the film industry by permitting the broadcast of films on television without the need to obtain further consents. 'Summary Records of the Proceedings' above n 9, [584.3].
[35] *Ibid* [707].

consent—the right of first fixation—is unaffected by Article 19. The most likely situation in which Article 19 will override the wishes of a performer is in that contemplated under clause (ii) of Article 7(1)(c): the reproduction of a fixation of a performance where the copy was made for a purpose different from those purposes to which consent was originally given.

Essentially, Article 19 sets up a purpose test. If a performer consents to the fixation of a performance for the purposes of inclusion in an audiovisual fixation then he or she loses the right, given under the Convention, to object to the use of that performance for other purposes for which consent has not been given. Examples of this situation include the exploitation of the soundtrack of a film by releasing it on a recording, or the incorporation of a performance from a film in another film or in an advertisement.[36] The inclusion of an already successful phonogram on the soundtrack of a cinematographic film raises an interesting problem. Does the incorporation of the phonogram bring Article 19 into play so that the producer of the cinematographic film can issue a separate version? There is no clear answer. It is suggested that the owner of the rights in the performance embodied in the phonogram should provide for this situation in the contract with the producer of the cinematographic film. It was understood by the delegates to the Rome Diplomatic Conference that Article 19 does not affect a performer's freedom of contract.[37]

B TRIPS

In TRIPS, the performers' right of reproduction is tacked onto the right of first fixation in the first sentence of Article 14(1). That article provides:

> In respect of a fixation of their performance on a phonogram, performers shall have the possibility of preventing the following acts when undertaken without their authorisation: the fixation of their unfixed performance and the reproduction of such fixation.

Performers are to have the possibility of preventing the reproduction of a fixation of a performance that is made without their authorisation. As with the right of first fixation, the reproduction right is restricted to fixations of performances embodied in a phonogram. It is also narrower than the corresponding provision in the Rome Convention for another reason. It relates solely to the reproduction of fixations made without authorisation, whereas, as has been seen above, Article 7(1)(c) of the Rome Convention at least provides for other possibilities.

[36] These examples are suggested by various commentators: Masouye, above n 3, [19.2]; W Nordemann, K Vinck, PW Hertin, (English version by G Meyer based on the translation by R Livingston), *International Copyright and Neighboring Rights Law: commentary with special emphasis on the European Community* (VCH Publishers, New York, 1990) 417.

[37] 'Report of the Rapporteur-General', above n 3, 53.

C WPPT

Article 7 of the WPPT is drafted in a way that combines Article 10 of the Rome Convention, which provides an exclusive right of reproduction for producers of phonograms, with language taken from Article 9(1) of the Berne Convention, which provides for an author's exclusive right of reproduction.[38] A definition of 'reproduction' in the WPPT was considered unnecessary, as the meaning of the term was said to be clear from the wording of Article 7 and Article 11.[39] Article 7 provides:

> Performers shall enjoy the exclusive right of authorizing the direct or indirect reproduction of their performances fixed in phonograms, in any manner or form.

Article 7 is an exclusive right, but it provides an unqualified right of reproduction only in respect of performances that are fixed in phonograms. It is therefore a partial right against reproduction and narrower than some aspects of the reproduction right in the Rome Convention. (As discussed above, Article 7(1)(c) of the Rome Convention covers reproduction in audiovisual media, although Article 19 reduces the protection it provides.) In other ways, however, Article 7 is a significant advance over the level of protection in the Rome Convention and TRIPS:

(i) It is an exclusive right. It therefore covers the reproduction of both authorised and unauthorised fixations of a performance. This alone represents a significant increase in the ability of performers to control the exploitation of their performances; at the least, it strengthens the bargaining position of performers in relation to producers.

(ii) Reproduction by direct or indirect means, which is taken from Article 10 of the Rome Convention, is included. Indirect reproduction covers any form of remote copying, the most common being the reproduction of a fixation of a performance from a broadcast. This is now an explicit part of the right of reproduction.

(iii) The words 'in any manner or form' taken from Article 9(1) of the Berne Convention indicate that all methods of reproduction are included in the right. Practices common to digital technology are covered, such as the transfer of a performance fixed in an analog medium to one fixed in a digital medium.[40] The words are also broad enough to cover the next generation of technology.

[38] Basic Proposal, above n 7, [7.05]–[7.07]. Art 9(1) of the Berne Convention provides: 'Authors of literary and artistic works protected by this Convention shall have the exclusive right of authorising the reproduction of these works, in any manner or form.'

[39] *Ibid* [2.10]. Art 11 provides for the right of reproduction enjoyed by producers of phonograms.

[40] Basic Proposal above, n 7, [7.04]–[7.07].

1 *The Issue of Temporary Copies*

At the Geneva Diplomatic Conference, the WPPT was not the only treaty concluded and it was probably not the most important. Also concluded at the Conference was the WIPO Copyright Treaty ('WCT'). The form and scope of the WPPT was strongly influenced by the discussions around the WCT. This was particularly true of the right of reproduction. The most contentious issue that arose at the Conference was whether, in copyright, the right of reproduction included temporary copies of works in the digital environment. The issue in the WCT centred on two questions: are temporary copies that are made as a function of activities such as 'browsing' and 'caching' on the Internet reproductions; and do they require the authorisation of the right holder?[41] The issue is the same in respect of performances embodied in phonograms that can be accessed by digital technology: is the temporary copying of a performance, where it is required by technology, reproduction for the purposes of the reproduction right; and if it is a copy, can it be exempted?[42]

The issue of temporary copies became critical to the successful conclusion of the Diplomatic Conference. Both the draft copyright treaty and the draft performers' rights treaty contained provisions that made it clear that temporary reproduction was subject to the reproduction right.[43] The Basic Proposal makes the point that a uniform interpretation of the ambit of the right of reproduction is needed that is acceptable on a worldwide basis.[44] It then goes on to claim that: 'The only way to harmonise effectively the interpretation of the scope of the right of reproduction is to confirm that temporary reproduction falls within the scope of the right.'[45] In the event, the delegates to the Conference did not see it this way.[46]

[41] 'Browser' is defined as: 'A program which allows a person to read hypertext. The browser gives some means of viewing the contents of nodes (or 'pages') and of navigating from one node to another: *Free On-Line Dictionary of Computing* <http://www.nightflight.com/foldoc> 'Cache' is defined as: 'A small fast memory holding recently accessed data, designed to speed up subsequent access to the same data': *Free On-Line Dictionary of Computing* <http://www.nightflight.com/foldoc/>.

[42] The question has arisen before for performers and performances in the form of 'rebroadcasting' and 'ephemeral fixation' at the Rome Diplomatic Conference. In both those cases, the Rome Convention permits Contracting States to legislate in favour of the broadcaster, Art 7(2)(1) and Art 15(1)(c).

[43] Art 7(2) of the draft performers' treaty stated: 'Subject to the provisions of Art 13(2), it shall be a matter for legislation in Contracting Parties to limit the right of reproduction in cases where a temporary reproduction has the sole purpose of making the fixed performance perceptible or where the reproduction is of a transient or incidental nature, provided that such reproduction takes place in the course of use of the fixed performance that is authorised by the performer or permitted by law.'

[44] Basic Proposal, above n 7, [7.18].

[45] *Ibid* [7.19].

[46] Hawkins reports that, 'There was intense and divisive debate about whether the proposed provision on the reproduction right was an *extension* of the existing reproduction right in Berne or whether it was only a *clarification* of the scope of the existing reproduction right.' C Hawkins, 'Overview of the New WIPO Standards' in D Saunders and B Sherman (eds), *From Berne to*

The discussions at the Diplomatic Conference were largely confined to reproduction in the context of copyright and Article 9(1) of the Berne Convention. Those discussions were critical for Article 7 of the WPPT because of the similarity between that provision, as it appeared in the Basic Proposal, and Article 9(1) of the Berne Convention. Although the language of Article 9(1) is in broad terms, a number of countries at the Geneva Diplomatic Conference indicated that they did not regard it as applying to temporary electronic copies.[47] The end result was that Article 7 of the WPPT was agreed to in its abbreviated form, that is, without the draft Article 7(2), together with an Agreed Statement that is identical, *mutatis mutandis*, to the Statement agreed in respect of Article 1(4) of the WCT. (The relevance of Article 1(4) of the WCT in the present context is that it obliges Contracting Parties to comply with Articles 1 to 21 of the Berne Convention—that is, including Article 9(1) of that Convention.)

The status of Agreed Statements is provided for in Article 31 of the Vienna Convention on the Law of Treaties. Article 31(1) provides that a treaty shall be interpreted in good faith and in accordance with the ordinary meaning given to the terms of the treaty in their context and in view of the treaty's object and purpose. In relation to context, Article 31(2)(a) provides:

> The context for the purpose of the interpretation of a treaty shall comprise, in addition to the text, including its preamble and annexes:
>
> (a) any agreement relating to the treaty which was made between all the parties in connection with the conclusion of the treaty.

Sinclair interprets this provision as meaning that the agreement should be related to the treaty; that it must be concerned with a matter of substance; that it must clarify certain concepts in the treaty or limit its application; and that it must be drawn up when the treaty is concluded. An agreement that meets these requirements—and the Agreed Statements to the WPPT do meet the requirements—forms part of the context and is treated 'as an element in the general rule of interpretation.'[48] Various commentators have pointed out that because the Agreed Statements concerning Article 1(4) of the WCT and Article 7 of the WPPT were the only Statements not adopted by consensus, there is some doubt as to their value as aids to interpreting the provisions in those Treaties.[49]

Geneva: Recent Developments in International Copyright and Neighbouring Rights (Australian Key Centre for Cultural and Media Policy, Nathan, Qld, 1997) 10.

[47] See the report of the discussion in Summary Minutes, Main Committee I of the Diplomatic Conference on Certain Copyright and Neighboring Rights Questions CRNR/DC/102 ('Summary Minutes') (Diplomatic Conference on Certain Copyright and Neighboring Rights Questions, Geneva, 2 to 20 December 1996) [247]–[298]; C Cresswell, 'Copyright Protection Enters the Digital Age: the New WIPO Treaties on Copyright and on Performances & Sound Recordings' (1997) 15 *Copyright Reporter* 4, 8.

[48] I Sinclair, *The Vienna Convention on the Law of Treaties* 2nd edn (Manchester University Press, Manchester, 1984) 129.

[49] The status of agreed statements was discussed at the Geneva Diplomatic Conference. In particular, see the comments of Mr Abbasi of the delegation of Pakistan doubting the status of a

The text of the Agreed Statement concerning Article 7 of the WPPT reads:

> Agreed statement concerning Articles 7, 11 and 16: The reproduction right, as set out in Articles 7 and 11, and the exceptions permitted thereunder through Article 16, fully apply in the digital environment, in particular to the use of performances and phonograms in digital form. It is understood that the storage of a protected performance or phonogram in a digital form in an electronic medium constitutes a reproduction within the meaning of these Articles.

The first sentence of the Agreed Statement is a generally accepted understanding, namely, that the reproduction right applies in the digital environment and that it is open to limitation (although any limitation would have to meet the three-step test in Article 16(2) of the WPPT, which is discussed in chapter 11). However, the reference in the second sentence to the 'storage' of performances in a digital form in an electronic medium constituting reproduction is problematic. Because there is uncertainty as to the meaning of storage, this sentence leaves it open to Contracting Parties to interpret the application of Article 7 in the digital environment widely or narrowly. In view of the lack of consensus that marked the conclusion of this provision, it will be interesting in the future to review, for example, the way in which national legislation determines the liability of parties that deal with performances on the Internet.

2 *Right of Modification*

The Basic Proposal included a provision that would have given performers an exclusive right of modification of fixed performances. This right was included 'to cover any possible situation in which digital or other technological manipulation might be used to circumvent traditional notions of reproduction.'[50] There was little support for the inclusion of this provision in the WPPT, and it was eventually deleted on the basis that the need for protection was sufficiently covered by the right of reproduction.[51] If the international community does accept this interpretation of the ambit of the reproduction right, it represents an extremely important development. There should now be no doubt that practices such as sampling infringe a performer's exclusive right of reproduction.[52]

statement agreed by consensus: 'Summary Minutes', above n 47, [1101]. See also the comments of A Kérever, 'The New WIPO Treaties: the WIPO Copyright Treaty and the WIPO Performances and Phonograms Treaty' (1998) 32 *Copyright Bulletin* 3, 5; D Nimmer, 'A Tale of Two Treaties Dateline: Geneva—December 1996' in M Nimmer and D Nimmer, *Nimmer on Copyright: A Treatise on the Law of Literary, Musical and Artistic Property and the Protection of Ideas* (Mathew Bender, New York, 1978–Release 42–6/97) 17.

[50] Basic Proposal, above n 7, [8.04].

[51] 'Summary Minutes', above n 47, [221]–[245] and [921].

[52] Another recent phenomenon, 'morphing', will also constitute an infringement of the reproduction right if that right is extended to include performances fixed in audiovisual media.

V RIGHT OF REMUNERATION

Together with a right to control bootlegging, one of the earliest demands of performers was for a right to equitable remuneration for uses that were made of their performances. Before the Rome Convention was concluded, this right was among the rights accorded to performers that were most widely recognised in national law.[53]

A right to equitable remuneration for the secondary use of performances fixed on phonograms is merely a right to receive remuneration for the use. A right holder does not have the right to authorise or prohibit the use of performances for broadcasting or communication to the public. The remuneration right is still a form of protection for performers, as it establishes that they are entitled to share in the returns from the on-going exploitation of their performances. It therefore provides performers with some leverage in their negotiations with producers.

It is worth noting that it is the act of broadcasting or communicating to the public that is crucial. It does not matter that members of the public do not receive the broadcast or the communication to the public. It is also worth noting that it is a right that is shared with the producers of phonograms.

A ROME CONVENTION

There is a right of remuneration in the Rome Convention, but it was adopted only after a lengthy debate. The resistance to the inclusion of Article 12 in the Convention was so strong that it resulted in a number of votes; and the issue reached crisis proportions when several delegations threatened that they would not be able to sign the Convention if the provision was included.[54] The prospect of a Convention without Article 12 was described as 'a splendid portal leading to a deserted courtyard.'[55] Despite the opposition, the final vote achieved the required two-thirds majority for the inclusion of the provision in the form proposed in the Hague Draft and the provision was adopted.[56] Article 12 has been described as the most important provision in the Convention.[57] It provides:

> If a phonogram published for commercial purposes, or a reproduction of such phonogram is used directly for broadcasting or for any communication to the public,

[53] International Labour Organisation, 'Rights of Performers in Broadcasting, Television and the Mechanical Reproduction of Sound' in *Report III of the ILO Advisory Committee on Salaried Employees and Professional Workers Second Session* (ILO, Geneva, 1951) 72.

[54] 'Summary Records of the Proceedings', above n 9, [478].

[55] The speaker was Mr Tiscornia, the Head of the Delegation of Argentina, *ibid* [557.2].

[56] Most of the provisions were adopted unanimously; however, the final vote on Art 12 was 20 votes to 8 with 9 abstentions, a bare two-thirds majority, *ibid* [562]–[564].

[57] Masouye, above n 3, [12.1].

a single equitable remuneration shall be paid by the user to the performers, or to the producers of the phonogram or to both. Domestic law may, in the absence of agreement between the parties, lay down the conditions as to the sharing of this remuneration.

The obligation that Article 12 imposes on Contracting States to provide for equitable remuneration is reduced by the stipulations in the wording of the Article itself:

(i) The right is limited to the use of phonograms. Phonogram is defined in Article 3(b) as 'any exclusively aural fixation of sounds of a performance or of other sounds'. It therefore excludes audiovisual fixations.
(ii) The phonogram, or a reproduction of it, must be 'published for commercial purposes'. Publication is defined in Article 3(d) as 'the offering of copies of a phonogram to the public in reasonable quantity'. The usual example of phonograms not published for commercial purposes are the fixations of performances made by broadcasters for technical purposes.[58]
(iii) The use for broadcasting or communication to the public that attracts obligations under Article 12 is the direct use of a phonogram. The obligation to pay remuneration would therefore fall mainly on broadcasters. Performers and phonogram producers are unable to claim remuneration for indirect use such as rebroadcasting or the communication to the public of a broadcast by means of a radio in a restaurant.
(iv) The remuneration must be equitable, but it is payable only as a single grant. The difficult question of how the remuneration is to be calculated is left open.
(v) There is an obligation to make a payment, but that payment need not be paid to performers. In the absence of agreement, it is for national law to prescribe the way in which the remuneration is to be shared. The options are to prescribe that the payment be made: (a) to the performers alone; (b) to the producers alone; (c) to the performers and the producers; (d) to the performers with an obligation to pay the producers; (e) to the producers with an obligation to pay the performers.

1 *Article 16(1)(a)*

Article 16(1)(a) allows Contracting States to make a series of reservations in respect of Article 12.[59] This flexibility was intended to encourage countries that

[58] *Ibid* [12.6].
[59] 'Reservation' is defined in the Vienna Convention on the Law of Treaties. Art 2(1)(d) states: '"reservation" means a unilateral statement, however phrased or named, made by a State, when signing, ratifying, accepting, approving or acceding to a treaty, whereby it purports to exclude or to modify the legal effect of certain provisions of the treaty in their application to that State.' Reservations are discussed at length in ch 11.

might not otherwise have done so to accede to the Convention.[60] Unfortunately for performers, a possible effect of Article 16(1)(a) is that there might not be any remuneration to collect. Article 16(1)(a) provides:

> Any State, upon becoming party to this convention, shall be bound by all the obligations and shall enjoy all the benefits thereof. However, a State may at any time, in a notification deposited with the Secretary-General of the United Nations, declare that:
>
> (a) as regards Article 12:
>
> (i) it will not apply the provisions of that Article;
> (ii) it will not apply the provisions of that Article in respect of certain uses;
> (iii) as regards phonograms the producer of which is not a national of another Contracting State, it will not apply that Article;
> (iv) as regards phonograms the producer of which is a national of another Contracting State, it will limit the protection provided for by that Article to the extent to which, and to the term for which, the latter State grants protection to phonograms first fixed by a national of the State making the declaration; however, the fact that the Contracting State of which the producer is a national does not grant the protection to the same beneficiary or beneficiaries as the State making the declaration shall not be considered as a difference in the extent of the protection.

Of the four possible reservations, the first two permit a state to refuse to apply the provisions of Article 12 in national legislation or to restrict its application. A reservation under clause (i) is a total reservation that excludes the operation of Article 12. Australia is one of the few states that have made such a reservation.[61] The consequences for performers of a total reservation are obvious. Under clause (ii), a Contracting State can restrict the application of Article 12 'in respect of certain uses'.

> This was understood by the Conference to mean that a country may decide not to grant payments in the case of uses in broadcasting, or in the case of public communication, or in the case of certain kinds of broadcasting or public communication.[62]

It has been suggested that broadcasts that might be exempt include cultural or religious broadcasts, and that an example of an exemption in respect of

[60] Masouye, above n 3, [16.1].

[61] 'Notifications Concerning Treaties Administered by WIPO in the field of Copyright, Rome Convention, Accession, Australia' (1992) *Copyright* 301. The United Kingdom has also declared a reservation in respect of Art 16(1). It will not apply Art 12 in respect of uses of phonograms in public at premises where persons reside or sleep or at a place where the activities are basically not for profit. In certain other circumstances the United Kingdom will not apply Art 12 unless a phonogram has been published in a Contracting State that has not made a reservation. 'Rome Convention for the International Protection of Performers, Producers of Phonograms and Broadcasting Organisations, Ratification by the United Kingdom of Great Britain and Northern Ireland' (1963) *Copyright* 244.

[62] 'Report of the Rapporteur-General', above n 3, 52.

communication to the public would be when no entrance fee was charged to the event at which a phonogram is used.[63]

The remaining two reservations are intended to prevent the unfairness of a one-way flow of royalties. The wording of clauses (iii) and (iv) of Article 16(1)(a) also ties the rights of the performer firmly to the status of the producer. Clause (iii) relates back to the points of attachment for phonograms in Article 5; it permits a Contracting State to restrict the application of Article 12 to phonograms produced by a producer who is a national of a Contracting State.

> The most obvious example is the wish to exclude from payment phonograms from the United States, because the United States is not a member of the Convention and does not grant payment for secondary uses in its own law.[64]

Clause (iv) has two limbs. The first limb provides for the application of the principle of material reciprocity:

> A State may limit the protection given to secondary use rights under its domestic law, even if the phonogram was fixed by a producer who is a national of another Contracting State, to the extent that similar protection is granted in the latter state.[65]

In short, a state may restrict or cut back protection to the extent of the protection it receives. Without material reciprocity, there would be scope for considerable disadvantage given the different levels of reservations.[66] That same limb provides that 'the possibility of comparison and cutting back' includes the term of protection; that is, it includes the rule of comparison as to duration.[67] Material reciprocity is restricted, however, by the second limb of clause (iv): a state may not compare and cut back in respect of beneficiaries. This prevents the reservation from being used to direct payment to performers at the expense of producers, or vice versa.[68]

The analysis of Article 16 suggests some interesting options, but it does raise the question how valuable is Article 12 to the individual? A performer who is disadvantaged under the national law of a state is not in a position to enforce compliance by the offending state with the provisions of the Rome Convention. In Europe, organisations representing performers and producers of phonograms reached an agreement as early as 1954 to share remuneration. Agreements, such as the 1954 agreement between the International Federation of the Phonographic Industry and the International Federation of Musicians as to

[63] See SM Stewart, *International Copyright and Neighbouring Rights* 2nd edn (Butterworths, London, 1989) [8.30]; Nordemann, above n 36, 413.

[64] Stewart, above n 63, [8.30]. Nordemann also gives the United States situation as an example of unfairness that could arise, Nordemann, above n 36, 413.

[65] 'Report of the Rapporteur-General', above n 3, 52.

[66] Masouye describes some lengthy examples. Masouye, above n 3, [16.9].

[67] 'Report of the Rapporteur-General', above n 3, 52.

[68] *Ibid* See also Nordemann, above n 36, [414].

the sharing of revenue, are a practical solution to the problem of securing remuneration for performers for the secondary uses of their performances.[69]

B TRIPS

There is no right of equitable remuneration in TRIPS.

C WPPT

The right to equitable remuneration is the only primary right that was not elevated to the level of an exclusive right in the WPPT. That reluctance can be attributed to the difficult nature of the provision:

> The remuneration right proposed in this Article is an attempt to reconcile two extremes: on the one hand, there is the position that performers and producers of phonograms are not entitled to any right to remuneration in respect of the fruits of their labour; on the other hand, there is the position that the right to remuneration should be broad or even that the right should be exclusive.[70]

In general, Article 15 of the WPPT corresponds to Article 12 of the Rome Convention, although the position of performers is improved in two ways. First, the right to remuneration includes indirect as well as direct uses of phonograms; and second, the right is explicitly granted to performers and producers of phonograms, and the provision cannot be interpreted as permitting payment to either party alone. However, performers have not been given a guarantee under the WPPT that they will receive equitable remuneration. The Summary Minutes of Main Committee I of the Geneva Diplomatic Conference show that there was strong support for the inclusion of the reservation provision.[71]

Article 15(1) provides:

> Performers and producers of phonograms shall enjoy the right to a single equitable remuneration for the direct or indirect use of phonograms published for commercial purposes for broadcasting or for any communication to the public.

Three limiting factors in Article 15(1) have been carried over from the Rome Convention and the comments made above about those factors in the context of the Convention need not be repeated. First, the right is a right to 'a single equitable remuneration'; secondly, the right relates to the use of phonograms and excludes audiovisual fixations; and thirdly, those phonograms must be

69 The 1954 IFPI/FIM Agreement originally required producers to pay performers 25% of public performance revenues—this was increased in 1976 to 33%. JS Wolsey, "Performers" rights—The New Regime and Opportunities in Europe' (1994) 45 *Copyright World* 26, 27.

70 Basic Proposal, above n 7, [12.09].

71 For example, by Australia, see 'Summary Minutes', above n 47, [370].

'published for commercial purposes'. The definition of 'publication of a fixed performance or a phonogram' in Article 2(e) of the WPPT is essentially the same as in the Rome Convention, although it does require that the publication be made with the consent of the performer.

However, the right of remuneration in the WPPT differs significantly from that in the Rome Convention in that the right now includes indirect use by way of broadcasting or communication to the public. The extension of the right is emphasised by the inclusion in the definition of 'communication to the public' of a specific reference to Article 15. The second sentence of Article 2(g) states:

> For the purposes of Article 15, 'communication to the public' includes making the sounds or representations of sounds fixed in a phonogram audible to the public.

The right of remuneration therefore applies to the direct use of a phonogram, such as a disc jockey playing phonograms in a discotheque, and to the indirect use, such as making the sounds fixed in a phonogram audible in a public place by means of a radio.[72] It has also been suggested that the obligation applies to cable retransmission as well as to cable-originated transmission.[73]

Under Article 15(2), the national legislation of Contracting States bears the responsibility for establishing the way in which the equitable remuneration is to be paid to the performers and producers of phonograms and the way in which it is to be shared. The Basic Proposal noted that: 'These are logistical concerns that are beyond the scope of international agreements.'[74] Article 15(2) does envisage that performers and producers of phonograms will come to an agreement on how to share the single equitable remuneration, but recognises that the parties should be able to turn to national law in the absence of agreement.

Article 15(3) attempts to reconcile the two extremes, no right of remuneration versus an exclusive right, by following the structure of the Rome Convention and permitting reservations to the remuneration right. Article 15(3) provides:

> Any Contracting Party may, in a notification deposited with the Director General of WIPO, declare that it will apply the provisions of paragraph (1) only in respect of certain uses, or that it will limit their application in some other way, or that it will not apply these provisions at all.

These are the only reservations permitted by the WPPT.[75] The provision is based on Article 16 of the Rome Convention and provides for three options: (i) Contracting Parties may declare that they will not apply the provisions of paragraph (1) for 'certain uses'. That term will probably be interpreted as it has been in the

[72] For these and other examples, see Basic Proposal, above n 7, [2.27].
[73] Cresswell, above n 47, 7.
[74] Basic Proposal, above n 7, [12.06].
[75] Art 21 of the WPPT. As of October 15, 2001, no reservations had been recorded to Art 15: World Intellectual Property Office, 'Actions in Respect of Treaties Administered by WIPO not yet in Force' <http://www. wipo.org/treaties/ip/index.html>.

Rome Convention. (ii) They may declare that they will limit the application of those provisions 'in some other way'. This will enable Contracting Parties to apply limitations, such as material reciprocity. (iii) Contracting Parties may declare that they will not apply the provisions of paragraph (1) at all.

Article 15(4) states that phonograms that have been 'made available', as that term is used in respect of the right of making available in Articles 10 and 14, shall be considered to have been published for commercial purposes, a requirement under Article 15(1).[76] Paragraph (4) brings the right to equitable remuneration, in a minor way, into line with digital technology; for example, performances that are fixed in phonograms and that are downloaded from the Internet and later used for broadcasting or communication to the public are protected.

There are also two Agreed Statements concerning Article 15. The first was adopted as a concession to the United States after it was clear that the Diplomatic Conference would not accept a proposal by that state to include a limited exclusive right in Article 15:

> It is understood that Article 15 does not represent a complete resolution of the level of rights of broadcasting and communication to the public that should be enjoyed by performers and phonogram producers in the digital age. Delegations were unable to achieve consensus on differing proposals for aspects of exclusivity to be provided in certain circumstances or for rights to be provided without the possibility of reservations, and have therefore left the issue to future resolution.

The International Bureau of WIPO has interpreted this statement as meaning: 'This statement is a reference to the position that, in the cases of certain near on-demand services, exclusive rights are justified.'[77] It is suggested that neither the Agreed Statement nor WIPO's interpretation of that Statement throw much light on Article 15. The Article should be taken at face value.

The second Agreed Statement concerning Article 15 records an understanding in relation to the publication of phonograms that embody performances of expressions of folklore. As noted above, Article 15(1) provides for the payment of equitable remuneration for the secondary uses of phonograms published for commercial purposes. The understanding recorded in the Agreed Statement is that Article 15 does not prevent the grant of a right of remuneration to performers of expressions of folklore, even if the phonograms embodying their performances are not published for commercial gain. The right of remuneration in the WPPT represents the conventional minimum, and this Statement acknowledges that Contracting Parties are free to grant rights that are more extensive than those required under the Treaty.

[76] The right of making available is discussed in ch 10.

[77] International Bureau of WIPO, 'New Trends in the Protection of Copyright and Neighbouring Rights: The WIPO Performances and Phonograms Treaty (1996)' WIPO/CR/GE/97/4b (Introductory Seminar on Copyright and Neighbouring Rights, Geneva, 8 to 10 October 1997) 10.

VI CONCLUSIONS

In this chapter, the scope of protection for performers under the primary economic rights was analysed. The analysis shows that, with some variation, the protection provided by the three international instruments is very similar. The two high points are to be found in the Rome Convention and the WPPT: the Rome Convention provides the highest level of protection for performances embodied in audiovisual fixations, while the WPPT's right to remuneration is stronger than that in the Convention. Of course, these rights represent the conventional minima and a state can introduce a higher level of rights in national law. The protection afforded by TRIPS, which is taken largely from the Rome Convention, can be regarded as representing the lowest common denominator.

In the opening chapter, the nature of the problem that faces performers was identified as a lack of control over the uses that are made of their performances. In assessing the scope of protection, therefore, the fundamental question is: do the primary economic rights provide performers with the means to control the exploitation of their performances? The analysis undertaken in this chapter shows that there are significant gaps in the protection available to performers under the primary economic rights:

(i) If the justification of a regime of performers' rights is to be found in the natural right theory, the failure to provide for moral rights is a serious gap.

(ii) Both the Rome Convention and TRIPS couch the award of rights in terms of 'the possibility of preventing', as opposed to the grant of an exclusive right. It is true that the form in which a civil right of action is drafted in an international agreement will probably, if not inevitably, mean that a performer has exclusive rights in national law and one could say, therefore, that the form of words used makes no difference. However, the form of words used in the Rome Convention and TRIPS does make one important difference, and that is that it permits a contracting state to comply with the obligations of either instrument by way of criminal sanctions rather than a civil action.

(iii) The international instruments have taken an approach to the audiovisual issue that has responded to pressure from the cinematographic film industry. This has resulted in a very low level of protection for performances embodied in audiovisual media. It was suggested in the discussion of technology and the development of performers' rights that the fact that a performance is exploited by means of audiovisual as opposed to audio media should not affect the protection that is available to a performer.

(iv) TRIPS is the instrument that has had the greatest influence in securing recognition of performers' rights on a truly international scale. The fact that TRIPS does not provide a right of equitable remuneration is a serious shortcoming.

(v) Associated with the last point is the uneven standard of protection afforded by the three instruments. In particular, one would have thought that the most recently drafted of the three, the WPPT, would provide uniform protection at the highest level. But it does not. The Rome Convention remains the current benchmark for the international protection of performances embodied in audiovisual fixations. There is neither a moral obligation nor an economic incentive to belong to either the Rome Convention or to the WPPT. The instrument that has the widest claim to international influence is TRIPS.

The other forms of protection that are available to performers (which were identified in an earlier chapter as primarily contract, copyright and unfair competition) fill a number of the gaps in the primary economic rights. Reliance on other legal regimes is only a stop-gap solution that emphasises the inadequacies of the system of performers' rights. The primary economic rights are only part of the protection available to performers. The extended rights need to be analysed to determine whether they plug the gaps that have been identified and whether, together with the primary economic rights, they approximate an appropriate system of protection. That analysis is undertaken in the next chapter.

10

The Extended Rights

I INTRODUCTION

THIS CHAPTER CONTINUES the analysis of the protection afforded to performers under the international instruments. The term 'extended rights' is used to refer to those rights that take the protection of performers beyond the primary rights discussed in the previous chapter. The extended rights take the form of both economic rights and moral rights, and they respond to both old issues and new issues relating to the use of performances. The economic rights discussed in this chapter are the right of distribution, the right of rental and the right of making available. The moral rights discussed are the right of attribution and the right of integrity.

The discussion is mainly concerned with provisions of the WPPT, an agreement that responded to three imperatives in the field of performers' rights: first, it addressed existing rights (those provisions were discussed in the previous chapter); second, it introduced new rights that do not owe their existence to new technology; third, it introduced new rights that do owe their existence to new technology.

II RIGHT OF DISTRIBUTION

The right of distribution enables the right holder to set conditions concerning the distribution of copies of a performance. It is closely related to the right of reproduction: 'In practice, it flows from the right of reproduction.'[1] The connection between distribution and reproduction is obvious, for in the commercial world there is little or no value in having the right to make copies of a performance without also having the right to distribute those copies. There is no definition of distribution in the international instruments. In the *WIPO Glossary of Terms of the Law of Copyright and Neighbouring Rights*, the 'distribution of a work' is defined as:

> Generally understood as offering copies of a work to the general public or any section thereof, mainly through appropriate commercial channels.

[1] C Masouye (W Wallace trans,) *Guide to the Berne Convention for the Protection of Literary and Artistic Works (Paris Act, 1971)* (World Intellectual Property Organisation, Geneva, 1978) [9.4].

An act of distribution is an act that involves the transfer of ownership or possession of a copy of a performance, bearing in mind that ownership or possession may change hands either separately or together.

The right of distribution makes performers' rights directly applicable to decisions about the marketing of a performance. A performer who exercises his or her right to authorise the distribution of copies of a performance may require that only limited numbers of copies be distributed in particular markets or that the distribution of the copies be prohibited in certain markets. The assessment that a performer makes of the best avenues for distribution may not match the assessment made by the producer or the investors in the performance. The grant of a right of distribution can therefore be viewed in two ways: either it expresses an assumption that a performer is in a position, by virtue of expertise and information available to him or her, to make decisions as to the best avenues for the distribution of a performance; or the assumption is that the right is to be used to secure better contractual terms from a producer. It can be expected that a producer will seek to obtain the transfer to itself of the distribution right. It is reasonable to conclude, therefore, that the right of distribution can and should be subject to contractual arrangements between performer and producer.

A discussion of the distribution right that does not address the doctrine of exhaustion is incomplete. The right of distribution is exhausted and it ceases to exist, either partially or completely, once the right holder puts a copy of a performance on a market. If national exhaustion or regional exhaustion is legislated for, the right holder is able to exercise the right of distribution in markets other than the one in which an initial authorised distribution took place. If a state chooses to recognise the international exhaustion of the right of distribution, the right is exhausted if an authorised copy of a performance is distributed anywhere in the world with the right holder's consent. It is important to note that it is only the right of distribution that is exhausted in this way; the other rights granted to a performer are not exhausted, and in particular the right of reproduction is unaffected. A further spin on the issue of exhaustion is that national legislation may provide that the right of distribution is maintained in a restricted form as a right of rental or a public lending right, but that it is not maintained in respect of other forms of distribution. Exhaustion of rights is such a divisive issue that none of the international instruments obliges contracting states to choose between national, regional or international exhaustion.

A Rome Convention

There is no right of distribution in the Rome Convention. The Records of the Rome Diplomatic Conference do not record any discussion of the right or of the issue of exhaustion of rights.

B TRIPS

There is no right of distribution in TRIPS, although there was an unsuccessful attempt to introduce a right of distribution into an earlier draft.[2] There is, however, a specific reference to exhaustion of rights in relation to dispute resolution. Article 6 provides:

> For the purposes of dispute settlement under this Agreement, subject to the provisions of Articles 3 and 4 nothing in this Agreement shall be used to address the issue of the exhaustion of intellectual property rights.[3]

This article is a compromise reached after debate between the states that favoured national exhaustion and those that favoured international exhaustion. The compromise is that exhaustion is excluded from dispute settlement, and therefore international exhaustion cannot be invoked as a direct violation of TRIPS.[4] All rights that are conferred under TRIPS 'in respect of the use, sale, importation or other distribution of goods' are subject to Article 6.[5]

C WPPT

The WPPT includes a right of distribution. Article 8(1) provides:

> Performers shall enjoy the exclusive right of authorizing the making available to the public of the original and copies of their performances fixed in phonograms through sale or other transfer of ownership.

There are a number of important points that can be made about this provision:

(i) The distribution right is an exclusive right.

(ii) The term 'making available' is used in Articles 8, 10 and 15 of the WPPT, which are, respectively, the right of distribution, the right of making available and the right to remuneration. This term is not defined. In the context of those rights, to make a performance available to the public is to grant access to that performance so that members of the public may listen to the performance or view it. To make a performance available includes granting access to members of the public present at a performance in person. It also includes granting access to the public by means of

[2] The draft of 23 July 1990 (W/76) included a provision that stated: 'The protection for performers shall include the possibility of preventing: . . . the offering to the public, selling or otherwise distributing copies of the fixation containing the performance.' See D Gervais, *The TRIPS Agreement: Drafting History and Analysis* (Sweet & Maxwell, London, 1998) [2.75].

[3] Arts 3 and 4 of TRIPS are provisions dealing with national treatment and most-favoured-nation-treatment.

[4] Gervais, above n 2, [2.40].

[5] This restriction is explicit in the note to Art 28 of TRIPS.

a broadcast or communication of an unfixed performance or of a fixation of a performance. A copy of a performance may also be made available either embodied in a tangible object (such as a phonogram) or in an intangible form (such as an electronic copy accessed by means of an interactive system). The demarcation between copy-related rights and non-copy-related rights that was made in chapter 4 is not relevant here.[6] The term 'making available' is used in respect of both categories of rights.

(iii) It has been suggested that there may be some problems for national legislation or the courts in determining who or how many people constitute the 'public.'[7] The better approach is to focus on the activity that involves the exploitation of a performance. The relevant act is that of making the performance available to the public; it is not a matter of making the performance available in public. Whether a member of the public avails himself or herself of the opportunity to access that performance is irrelevant to the act of making available. If a member of the public does take advantage of access to the performance, it is also irrelevant to the act of making available whether he or she obtains access in a private or domestic situation or from a public forum, or whether he or she does so as an individual or as a member of a group.

(iv) The reference to 'the original and copies of their performances fixed in phonograms' is a clumsy piece of drafting that illustrates the dangers of lifting provisions from instruments dealing with copyright and applying them to neighbouring rights.[8] How can an original performance be fixed in a phonogram? Once it is fixed it is a copy of the original performance. Presumably, therefore, the intention is to distinguish between the original (first) copy of a performance and the copies of that copy.

(v) Apart from the issue of drafting, the reference to 'the original and copies of their performances fixed in phonograms' is limited in two ways: (a) There is an Agreed Statement concerning Articles 2(e), 8, 9, 12 and 13. It states that, in the context of the right of distribution and the right of rental, '"copies" and "original and copies" . . . refer exclusively to fixed copies that can be put into circulation as tangible objects'. The right granted under Article 8 is therefore to be distinguished from the right of making available under Article 10, which governs the making available of

[6] Ch 4, n 51, and accompanying discussion.

[7] A Mason, 'Developments in the Law of Copyright and Public Access to Information' [1997] 11 *European Intellectual Property Review* 636, 640; S Fox, 'Learning to Live with 1s and 0s: Response to the New WIPO Treaties' in D Saunders and B Sherman (eds), *From Berne to Geneva: Recent Developments in International Copyright and Neighbouring Rights* (Australian Key Centre for Cultural and Media Policy, Nathan, Qld, 1997) 22–23.

[8] Art 6(1) of the WCT provides: 'Authors of literary and artistic works shall enjoy the exclusive right of authorising the making available to the public of *the original and copies of their works* through sale or other transfer of ownership' (emphasis added). This terminology is also used in Art 9 of the WPPT (the right of rental). Similar language is used in Art 11 of TRIPS: 'originals or copies of their copyright works'.

intangible copies on an interactive on-demand system. (b) The right of distribution is a right to authorise or prohibit the distribution of copies of performances fixed in phonograms. It is therefore consistent with the restriction of protection in the Treaty to the fixation of the sounds of a performance.[9]

(vi) The final words of Article 8(1) make it clear that the right of distribution applies only to transactions involving a transfer of ownership. The distribution of performances involving the temporary transfer of possession, such as rental or public lending, is outside the ambit of this provision. The Basic Proposal included a right of importation as part of the right of distribution.[10] There was little support for this provision, tied as it is to the issue of exhaustion of rights, and it was abandoned.

The exhaustion of rights was one of the issues that was hotly debated at the Geneva Diplomatic Conference.[11] The exhaustion of the distribution right in the WPPT is dealt with in paragraph (2) of Article 8 which provides:

> Nothing in this Treaty shall affect the freedom of Contracting Parties to determine the conditions, if any, under which the exhaustion of the right in paragraph (1) applies after the first sale or other transfer of ownership of the original or a copy of the fixed performance with the authorisation of the performer.

Although there was a far-reaching discussion on the matter, consensus as to the conditions under which the distribution right is exhausted could not be achieved. The WPPT therefore leaves it to Contracting Parties to determine those conditions for themselves. A number of countries recorded their understandings as to the effect of Article 8(2).[12]

[9] Art 2(b) of the WPPT states: '"phonogram" means the fixation of the sounds of a performance or of other sounds, or of a representation of sounds, other than in the form of a fixation incorporated in a cinematographic or other audiovisual work.' Note also the definition of 'fixation' in Art 2(c) of the WPPT.

[10] Art 9(1)(ii) in Alternative E of the draft of the WPPT presented to the delegates to the Geneva Diplomatic Conference provided performers with an exclusive right to authorise the importation of the original and copies of their performances as one of the alternatives: Chairman of the Committees of Experts on a Possible Protocol to the Berne Convention and on a Possible Instrument for the Protection of the Rights of Performers and Producers of Phonograms, 'Basic Proposal for the Substantive Provisions of the Treaty for the Protection of Performers and Producers of Phonograms to be Considered by the Diplomatic Conference' CRNR/DC/5 ('Basic Proposal') (Diplomatic Conference on Certain Copyright and Neighbouring Rights Questions, Geneva, 2 to 20 December 1996).

[11] C Cresswell, 'Copyright Protection Enters the Digital Age: The New WIPO Treaties on Copyright and on Performances and Sound Recordings' (1997) *Copyright Reporter* 4, 11; see also J Reinbothe, M Martin-Prat and S von Lewinski, 'The New WIPO Treaties: A First Resume' (1997) 4 *European Intellectual Property Review* 171, 172.

[12] The term 'understanding' refers to a statement that sets forth a state's interpretation of a treaty provision. It is part of the context of a treaty for interpretation purposes as required by Art 31 of the Vienna Convention on the Law of Treaties. The Australian delegation made the following statement: 'Australia agrees to paragraph (2) in Art 8 in the WIPO Copyright Treaty, and in Arts 9 and

III RIGHT OF RENTAL

The right of rental can either be treated as part of the general right of distribution or it can be implemented as a separate right. TRIPS and the WPPT take the second approach. Rental entails a transfer of possession, but not of ownership, for a limited time and for profit-making purposes. It is sometimes associated with public lending, in which possession is also transferred for a limited time. However, rental is distinguished from public lending in that the transfer of possession is for profit-making purposes which is not the case in public lending. A right to authorise or prohibit the distribution of their performances by rental puts performers in a strong position to negotiate royalties for this use.

A Rome Convention

There is no right of rental in the Rome Convention.

B TRIPS

The possibility that performers could be the beneficiaries of the grant of an exclusive right of rental in phonograms is raised in Article 14 of TRIPS. If it applies, it is by way of a complicated interpretation of two provisions. The first sentence of Article 14(4) provides:

> The provisions of Article 11 in respect of computer programs shall apply *mutatis mutandis* to producers of phonograms and any other right holders in phonograms, as determined in a Member's law.

Article 11 of TRIPS requires Members to provide authors and their successors in title with an exclusive right of rental. It provides:

> In respect of at least computer programs and cinematographic works, a Member shall provide authors and their successors in title the right to authorise or prohibit the commercial rental to the public of originals or copies of their copyright works. . . . In respect of computer programs, this obligation does not apply to rentals where the program itself is not the essential object of the rental.

16 in the WIPO Performances and Phonograms Treaty, on the understanding that the paragraph will not affect existing, as well as future, national legislation providing for the importation of copies of works and phonograms that have been made by or with the consent of the rightholders.' The New Zealand and the Singapore delegations associated themselves with this statement: Summary Minutes, Main Committee I of the Diplomatic Conference on Certain Copyright and Neighboring Rights Questions CRNR/DC/102 ('Summary Minutes') (Diplomatic Conference on Certain Copyright and Neighboring Rights Questions, Geneva, 2 to 20 December 1996) [1029], [1035] and [1036].

If performers are to take advantage of Article 11 and Article 14(4), the first point to be determined is whether performers are right holders in phonograms. On one interpretation, they are such right holders, because Article 14(1) obliges Members to grant performers certain rights in respect of fixations of performances on phonograms. If Members have already met this obligation at the date of acceding to TRIPS, then performers will be right holders in phonograms and entitled to the benefits, if any, of Article 14(4). A second interpretation applies to the circumstances of a state that, as of the date of becoming a Member, has not provided for performers' rights in phonograms: performers are therefore not right holders and paragraph (4) does not apply. The International Bureau of WIPO has suggested a third interpretation:

> As regards other possible right holders in phonograms—such as performers whose performances, and authors the performances of whose works are fixed in phonograms—the expression 'any other right holders in phonograms as determined in a Member's law' indicates that Members are free to extend or not to extend that right to those right holders.[13]

On this third interpretation, Members can determine for themselves whether to provide performers with an exclusive right of rental. Presumably Members will choose the interpretation that best fits their national circumstances.

The second point to be determined is whether the limitation in Article 11 so restricts the application of the rental right to performers that it is worthless. Article 11 provides that, in respect of computer programs, the obligation to provide a right of rental does not apply when the computer program is not the essential object of the rental transaction. If this limitation is applied *mutatis mutandis* to phonograms, it would mean that if a rental transaction took place and the goods rented included a phonogram containing a performance, but the phonogram was only incidental to the transaction, Article 14(4) would not apply. It is hard to think of examples—perhaps the lease of a car that included a cassette or a CD providing instruction on the running of the car would qualify.

The final point to consider is that the possibility of Article 14(4) applying to performers is reduced because the second sentence of that provision allows Members to take advantage of an existing situation. The second sentence of Article 14(4) provides:

> If on 15 April, 1994 [the date of the signing of the TRIPS Agreement] a Member has in force a system of equitable remuneration of right holders in respect of the rental of phonograms, it may maintain such system provided that the commercial rental of phonograms is not giving rise to the material impairment of the exclusive rights of reproduction of right holders.

[13] World Intellectual Property Organisation, *Implications of the TRIPS Agreement on Treaties Administered by WIPO* (World Intellectual Property Organisation, Geneva, 1997) [70]. See also A Kérever, 'The New WIPO Treaties: the WIPO Copyright Treaty and the WIPO Performances and Phonograms Treaty' (1998) 32 *Copyright Bulletin* 3, 11.

The effect of this provision is that Members who, at the operative date, had granted a remuneration right to right holders in phonograms are permitted to maintain that system rather than to afford right holders an exclusive right of rental. That concession is subject to a material impairment test: namely, that widespread copying of phonograms is not going on to the detriment of the ability of right holders to control the exploitation of their phonograms. The provision is more obviously directed at the protection of producers of phonograms, who are the named beneficiaries under Article 14(4), than to performers or other right holders.

The unsatisfactory end result of the way in which Article 14(4) is drafted is that it is unclear whether Members are obliged to provide performers with a rental right. The scope of such a right, if obligatory, is also unclear. The provision is so hedged with uncertainty that failure to provide a rental right is unlikely to be regarded as a breach of a Member's obligations under TRIPS.

C WPPT

The essential elements of rental were noted above as being a transfer of possession for a limited period of time for commercial purposes. These elements were confirmed in the definition of 'rental of a phonogram' that was part of the Basic Proposal but which was not included in the final form of the WPPT. That definition stated that: '"rental of a phonogram" means any transfer of the possession of a copy of a phonogram for consideration for a limited period of time.'[14]

The Basic Proposal notes that the right of rental can be considered to be part of a general right of distribution but 'for practical reasons' it was dealt with in that document, and subsequently in the WPPT, as a separate issue.[15] Article 9 of the WPPT is divided into two paragraphs. The first paragraph sets out the scope of the right of rental and relates back to Article 8 and the right of distribution. Article 9(1) provides:

> Performers shall enjoy the exclusive right of authorizing the commercial rental to the public of the original and copies of their performances fixed in phonograms as determined in the national law of Contracting Parties, even after the distribution of them by, or pursuant to, authorization by the performer.

The rental right granted to performers under the WPPT is an exclusive right. Although the definition of rental in the Basic Proposal was not carried forward into the Treaty, Article 9(1) concerns a commercial transaction, thereby excluding the public lending right. It also makes it clear that the rental right survives after the distribution of the phonograms in which performances are fixed. Article 9 is therefore an exception to the exhaustion principle.

[14] Art 2(f) of the draft Treaty: Basic Proposal, above n 10.
[15] *Ibid* [9.03].

There are two main limitations on the scope of the right of rental. The first is that the exclusive right is limited to 'the original and copies of performances' fixed in phonograms.[16] This restriction to phonograms should be of concern to performers, but it is at least consistent with the other articles in the WPPT dealing with fixations of performances and there is nothing exceptional in that. Performers should be more concerned with the second limitation. The protected performances are qualified by the words: 'as determined in the national law of Contracting Parties'. (This qualification is not included in Article 13 of the WPPT, which provides for a right of rental for producers of phonograms.) It has been suggested by Cresswell that the effect of this qualifying phrase is to render the obligation to grant a rental right to performers 'less than absolute.'[17] He bases his suggestion on matters raised in the debate over the place of the rental right in the WCT. If he is correct, it is another example of the WCT influencing the interpretation of the WPPT. The debate resulted in the adoption of an Agreed Statement that applies to Article 7 of the WCT, which provides for a rental right for authors. The Agreed Statement states:

> It is understood that the obligation under Article 7(1) does not require a Contracting Party to provide an exclusive right of commercial rental to authors who, under that Contracting Party's law, are not granted rights in respect of phonograms. It is understood that this obligation is consistent with Article 14(1) of the TRIPS Agreement.

Cresswell's argument depends on three steps: (i) The words in question, 'as determined in the national law of Contracting Parties', also appear in Article 7 of the WCT. (ii) The Agreed Statement is intended as an aid in interpreting that Article and appears to read down its application. (iii) Cresswell's final step is:

> Given the understanding with regard to the interpretation of [Article 7(1) of the WCT], and that those words were included in art.9 [of the WPPT] at the insistence of countries who were concerned that performers should not have a greater right than authors, the obligation imposed by art.9 must be less than absolute in regard to countries that do not give a rental right to performers in respect of their sound recordings.[18]

It is a difficult argument to follow, especially since there is no connection between the Treaties—that is, a state is free to accede to one Treaty and not to the other.[19] While it is not suggested that it is an incorrect interpretation of the negotiations, it should be noted that it is still only an opinion as to the

[16] The Agreed Statement, that copies means tangible copies, discussed in respect of the right of distribution in Art 8 of the WPPT also applies to Art 9 and reinforces this limitation.

[17] Cresswell, above n 11, 13. Cresswell was the leader of the Australian delegation to the Geneva Diplomatic Conference.

[18] *Ibid.*

[19] Art 1(3) of the WPPT and Art 1(1) of the WCT.

interpretation of the provision.[20] Ultimately, recourse must be had to Articles 31 and 32 of the Vienna Convention on the Law of Treaties, which provide, respectively, for the general rule of interpretation of treaties and for supplementary means of interpretation.

Leaving Cresswell's suggestion aside, it is possible to interpret those qualifying words as meaning that Contracting States are free in their national legislation to determine which types of performances, if any, the right of rental will apply to. There is support for this interpretation from the suggestion that the Agreed Statement should not be considered as an integral part of the WCT and, on this basis, Contracting Parties are not obliged to provide authors with a right of rental.[21] If this interpretation is correct, then it is a major limitation, as it could conceivably mean that a state would not apply the right of rental at all. It is an interpretation that does not sit well with the aim set out in the Preamble of the WPPT: 'to develop and maintain the protection of the rights of performers.'

The second major limitation on the rental right is provided in Article 9(2), which is similar to the second sentence of Article 14(4) of TRIPS (quoted above). Article 9(2) provides:

> Notwithstanding the provisions of paragraph (1), a Contracting Party that, on April 15, 1994, had and continues to have in force a system of equitable remuneration of performers for the rental of copies of their performances fixed in phonograms, may maintain that system provided that the commercial rental of phonograms is not giving rise to the material impairment of the exclusive right of reproduction of performers.

It would seem, therefore, that if a country falls into the category set out in paragraph (2) it need not have regard to paragraph (1), provided of course, that it can satisfy the same material impairment test in Article 14(4) of TRIPS. The end result is that the apparently exclusive right of rental can be watered down to a right of remuneration. However, if a country chooses to provide a right of rental after acceding to the WPPT, it must provide an exclusive right.

IV RIGHT OF MAKING AVAILABLE

The right of making available has its origin in the development of digital technology. It is unique in terms of performers' rights to the WPPT, although there

[20] It is the interpretation put on the provision in an Australian Government discussion paper: see Attorney-General's Department and the Department of Communication and the Arts, *Performers' Intellectual Property Rights Scope of extended rights for performers under the Copyright Act 1968* (Attorney-General's Department and the Department of Communication and the Arts, Canberra, 1997) [3.28].

[21] Kéréver suggests that the Agreed Statement does not meet the conditions to be recognised as an integral part of the WCT that are set out in Art 31 of the Vienna Convention on the Law of Treaties: Kéréver, above n 13, 12.

is a corresponding provision in Article 8 of the WCT that is called 'the right of communication to the public'. More than any other provision in the WPPT, the right of making available is designed to meet the challenge of introducing new rules on an international basis to provide performers and producers of phonograms with effective and uniform protection. The first two paragraphs of the Preamble to the WPPT state:

> Desiring to develop and maintain the protection of the rights of performers and producers of phonograms in a manner as effective and uniform as possible.
>
> Recognising the need to introduce new international rules in order to provide adequate solutions to the questions raised by economic, social, cultural and technological developments.

The right of making available takes the protection of performers much further than they could have envisaged when they first began to agitate for protection against the unauthorised use of their performances. The making available right protects performers against the unauthorised exploitation of their performances in an interactive digital environment. It is apparently only a matter of time before technology and commerce will enable a consumer to order a copy of a fixed performance and have it delivered to the computer or other receiving device of his or her choice at the time and place of his or her choice.

> The electronic or digital 'record shop' can be compared to a record manufacturing plant or a CD factory. The functions of the manufacturing and distribution portions of the music industry and retail record shops may be replaced by a database open to the public for the direct delivery of music productions via communications networks to home computers.[22]

The situation envisaged in this quotation from the Basic Proposal in 1996 has already moved much closer to reality in respect of musical works.[23] However, the technical problem of bandwidth and the likelihood of increased piracy will probably delay the introduction of services providing access to audiovisual works.

There is an enormous social and technological gap between (i) the situation in which a performance is presented without the assistance of technology to an audience that is present in the flesh, and (ii) the presentation of a performance

[22] Basic Proposal, above n 10, [11.05].

[23] On 5 October 2001, the Recording Industry Association of America, Inc, the National Music Publishers' Association, Inc and the Harry Fox Agency, Inc reached an agreement concerning the licensing of digital music services including 'on-demand streams' and 'limited downloads'. An on-demand stream is defined in para 1 of the agreement as 'an on-demand, real-time digital transmission of a sound recording of a single musical work to allow a user to listen to a particular sound recording chosen by the user at a time chosen by the user, using streaming technology'. Limited download is defined as 'a digital transmission of a time-limited or other use-limited download of a sound recording of a single musical work to a local storage device (eg the hard drive of the user's computer or portable device)'. The agreement is available on the Recording Industry Association of America, Inc. ('RIAA') website: <http://www.riaa.com/Music-Intro.cfm>.

to an audience whose members can individually determine, by means of digital technology, the time and place at which a performance will be accessed so that it can be viewed or heard immediately or at a later time. The right of making available addresses some of the legal issues associated with that gap.

A Rome Convention

There is no right of making available in the Rome Convention.

B TRIPS

There is no right of making available in TRIPS.

C WPPT

The delegates to the Geneva Diplomatic Conference recognised the difficulties of fitting issues associated with the on-demand delivery of electronic copies into the coverage of the traditional rights.[24] The problem of devising a right acceptable to the international community led to a compromise solution dubbed the 'umbrella solution.'[25] In brief, an umbrella provision is one that leaves to national law the decision as to the legal qualification or the characterisation of the rights covered in the provision:

> Mr Kushan (United States of America) expressed support for Article 10 of the Draft Treaty No. 1 and Articles 11 and 18 of Draft Treaty No. 2, concerning the rights of communication to the public and making available to the public, which were key to the ability of owners of rights to protect themselves in the digital environment. He stressed the understanding—which had never been questioned during the preparatory work and would certainly not be questioned by any Delegation participating in the Diplomatic Conference—that those rights might be implemented in national legislation through application of any particular exclusive right, also other than the right of communication to the public or the right of making available to the public, or combination of exclusive rights, as long as the acts described in those Articles were covered by such rights.[26]

[24] See the statement of the United States delegate referring to particular problems, Summary Minutes, above n 12, [302].

[25] M Ficsor, 'The Spring 1997 Horace S. Manges Lecture—Copyright for the Digital Era: The WIPO "Internet" Treaties' (1997) 21 *Columbia-VLA Journal of Law and the Arts* 197, 210–211.

[26] Summary Minutes, above n 12, [301].

Article 10 of the WPPT provides:

> Performers shall enjoy the exclusive right of authorizing the making available to the public of their performances fixed in phonograms, by wire or wireless means, in such a way that members of the public may access them from a place and at a time individually chosen by them.

There are a number of important points to be made about Article 10:

(i) Article 10 provides performers with an exclusive right. However, Contracting Parties are free to determine the legal characterisation of the right and to implement the obligation in the legal terminology that they choose.[27]

(ii) Although Article 10 responds to the latest technology, it is consistent with the remainder of the Treaty in that it restricts protection to performances fixed in phonograms.

(iii) The term 'making available' is not defined, but the right covers the grant of access to performances that, at the point at which they are accessed, are not embodied in a tangible article. It is to be distinguished from Article 8, the right of distribution, that relates to performances fixed in a tangible form.[28]

(iv) The provision is described in terms that are technology neutral as opposed to being technology specific. The characteristics of digital technology are not explicitly referred to, although the means used to make the performance available must encompass interactive capability. The reference in the new right to 'making available . . . by wire or wireless means' is capable of being interpreted broadly enough to cover new developments that may supplant present technology. The problems of comparing new technology with old technology have therefore been avoided.

(v) The key to the provision lies in the last clause of Article 10. The relevant act—that is the one that is to be reserved to performers in national legislation—is to authorise the making available of the performance to the public in an on-demand interactive system. While there may appear to be an issue as to who constitutes the public, the commercial environment that the right was intended to meet (namely the digital record shop available to shoppers anywhere in the world and at any time) should dictate that the constitution of the public is unlikely to be a real issue.[29] The relevant act occurs when, without a performer's consent, a performance

[27] Basic Proposal, above n 10, [11.09] and [11.11].

[28] *Ibid* [11.02]. Note the discussion of this provision at the Geneva Diplomatic Conference: Summary Minutes, above n 12, [299]. Cresswell paraphrases the right as one 'to authorise or prohibit the introduction of . . . sound recordings into on-line networks': Cresswell, above n 11, 8.

[29] There was agreement at the Geneva Diplomatic Conference that 'public' should be widely interpreted: see Summary Minutes, above n 12, [321].

> performed by that performer is made available to members of the public in the circumstances described in Article 10. The actual number of people who may access that performance and the circumstances from which they access the performance is irrelevant. This interpretation stems from the phrase 'from a place and at a time individually chosen by them'. Once a copy of the performance has been made available, it does not matter that the copy of the performance is not accessed: it is sufficient if there is a possibility of it being accessed.

Although liability of individuals is not a matter for international treaties, it is worth noting the Agreed Statement that was adopted in respect of the parallel provision in Article 8 of the WCT.[30] The text of that Statement reads:

> It is understood that the mere provision of physical facilities for enabling or making a communication does not in itself amount to communication within the meaning of this Treaty or the Berne Convention. It is further understood that nothing in Article 8 precludes a Contracting Party from applying Article 11*bis*(2).

There was concern expressed at the Diplomatic Conference that Article 8 of the WCT and Articles 10 and 14 of the WPPT imposed liability on intermediaries, such as Internet Service Providers, in circumstances in which they could not be expected to monitor the material that was made available.[31] (Article 14 of the WPPT provides phonogram producers with a right of making available.) The Agreed Statement was intended to provide some comfort for these bodies. Although the Statement was not adopted in respect of Articles 10 and 14 of the WPPT, it can be taken as confirmation that the focus of Article 10 is on the act of first offering the transmission of the performance to the public and not on providing server space, communication connections or facilities for carrying and routing signals.

[30] Art 8 of the WCT provides that authors 'shall enjoy the exclusive right of authorising any communication to the public of their works, by wire or wireless means, including the making available to the public of their works in such a way that members of the public may access these works from a place and at a time individually chosen by them'.

[31] Other organisations that may be at risk include 'most organisations involved with networked information including ISPs, bulletin board operators, anyone with a web-site or intranet, subscription television, interactive television, libraries and educational bodies': J Wodetski, 'What About the Copyright User? Implications of the New WIPO Treaties' in D Saunders and B Sherman (eds), *From Berne to Geneva: Recent Developments in International Copyright and Neighbouring Rights* (1997) 108. The liability of ISPs is the subject of major provisions in recent United States and Australian copyright legislation: Title II of the Digital Millenium Copyright Act 1998 (US) and ss 26, 39, 42, 87 and 95 of the Copyright Amendment (Digital Agenda) Act 2000 (Cth). The liability of ISPs has also recently been considered in the context of defamation. The defendants in *Godfrey v Demon Internet Ltd* [2001] QB 201 carried on business as an Internet Service Provider. They failed to remove an article, defamatory of the plaintiff, which was received and stored by them on their news server. Once the defendants became aware of the defamatory content of the posting they could not avail themselves of the defence of innocent dissemination.

V MORAL RIGHTS

The comment was made in an earlier chapter that moral rights, which are an established feature of copyright, translate easily into the context of performers' rights because they cover areas where industry practice has traditionally applied.[32] This is true, but it is important to remember that there are other factors to consider, only some of which apply also to authors, and therefore moral rights may not fit so easily into performers' rights. A performance is inherently derivative: it is the interpretation of another work (not necessarily a work of copyright) and it often takes a form that is dictated by another (a producer or director). A performance also takes place not at the behest of the performer but because the producer has made the arrangements (even if performer and producer are the same person).

A Rome Convention

There are no moral rights in the Rome Convention. There was a body of support for the inclusion of a moral right in the Hague Draft, but it would have been unacceptable to a number of delegates. Those in support therefore agreed to drop their demand for a moral right. There was no provision for moral rights in the Hague Draft and no provision for them in the Convention.[33]

While there is no specific obligation to provide a moral right, Article 11 of the Rome Convention provides for a restricted right to be identified. It specifies how the requirements as to formalities for the protection of phonograms are to be complied with. If the principal performers are not identified on the copies of the phonograms or on their containers, then the name of the person who owns the performers' rights in the country of fixation must be included in the formalities notice.[34]

[32] Ch 4, n 53 and accompanying text.

[33] Report of Mr W Wallace, Rapporteur General, 'Comité d'experts sur la protection des artistes interprètes ou exécutants, des producteurs de phonogrammes et des organismes de radiodiffusion' (Réunion de la Haye, 9–20 mai, 1960) (1960) *Le Droit D'Auteur* 167 [40].

[34] The minimum obligations in respect of the notice are that: it should be applied to the copies of phonograms or their containers; it should consist of the symbol Ⓟ and the year of first publication; it should identify the producer or the owner of the producer's rights; and it should identify the principal performers or the owner of the rights of those performers.

B TRIPS

There is no provision for moral rights in TRIPS. The United States opposed the inclusion of moral rights and Article 9(1) reflects the United States position.[35] Article 9(1) provides:

> Members shall comply with Articles 1 through 21 of the Berne Convention (1971) and the Appendix thereto. However, Members shall not have rights or obligations under this Agreement in respect of the rights conferred under Article 6*bis* of that Convention or of the rights derived therefrom.

Members are obliged to comply with the economic rights under the Berne Convention but rights or obligations under or derived from Article 6*bis* of that Convention are excluded. (The rights conferred under Article 6*bis* are the right of attribution and the right of integrity.) TRIPS does not specify what the rights are that are derived from Article 6*bis*. It has been suggested that Article 10(3) and Article 11*bis*(2) of the Berne Convention fall into this category.[36] Both provisions involve the application of moral rights. Article 10(3) restates the right of attribution; it obliges people who quote or otherwise use works in accordance with the other provisions of Article 10 of the Berne Convention to acknowledge their sources.[37] Article 11*bis*(2) permits contracting states to provide for a system of compulsory licences in place of an author's exclusive right of broadcasting. Such a system is subject to a number of restrictions, including the requirement that it should not be prejudicial to the moral rights of the author. It would seem that Members are not obliged, under TRIPS, to comply with the requirement under Article 10(3) to mention an author's name; and the restriction that a system of compulsory licensing of broadcasts under Article 11*bis*(2) should not prejudice an author's moral rights does not apply.

C WPPT

The impetus for moral rights being included in the WPPT was the development of digital technology that makes it possible to transmit, receive and manipulate performances with an ease that would have been unthinkable a few years ago.[38]

35 JC Ross, 'Trade-Related Aspects of Intellectual Property Rights' in TP Stewart (ed), *The GATT Uruguay Round: a Negotiating History (1986–1992) Vol II* (Kluwer Law and Taxation Publishers, Deventer, Boston, 1993) 2288–2289.

36 WIPO, *Implications of the TRIPS Agreement on Treaties Administered by WIPO*, above n 13, [21].

37 Masouye, above n 1, [10.11].

38 This was acknowledged in a document presented to the first meeting of the Committee of Experts that met to consider the need for a new performers' treaty. It was not challenged after that point: Memorandum Prepared by the International Bureau of WIPO 'Questions Concerning a Possible Instrument for the Protection of the Rights of Performers and Producers of Phonograms' INR/CE/I/2 (Committee of Experts on the Possible Protection of the Rights of Performers and Producers of Phonograms, First Session, Geneva, 28 June to 2 July 1993) [29].

In the meetings of the Committees of Experts held before the Geneva Diplomatic Conference, three factors were identified as important to the drafting of the moral rights provisions: (i) Those provisions should be as broad as possible to enable each state to implement moral rights having regard to its own legal traditions and culture. (ii) In respect of performers and performances, it is more difficult to identify circumstances that constitute a modification or other derogatory action prejudicial to honour or reputation than it is to identify those circumstances in respect of authors and works. (iii) It was noted that parody is more usually expressed in performances than it is in works. It was concluded that, in the case of performers, moral rights should be expressed in a way that takes account of only the most serious cases.[39]

In fact, Article 5(1) of the WPPT closely resembles Article 6*bis*(1) of the Berne Convention. It provides:

> Independently of a performer's economic rights, and even after the transfer of those rights, the performer shall, as regards his live aural performances or performances fixed in phonograms, have the right to be identified as the performer of his performances, except where the omission is dictated by the manner of the use of the performance, and to object to any distortion, mutilation or other modification of his performances that would be prejudicial to his reputation.

Article 5(1) provides for the right of attribution and the right of integrity. The opening words of this provision acknowledge that a performer's moral rights are quite separate from his or her economic rights. This separation is consistent with the theory that the moral rights are based on the importance of protecting the performer's personality, and that while the moral rights may protect a performer's economic interests, they are independent of them. It is not clear whether the following words, 'and even after the transfer of those rights', mean that the rights are inalienable. This has been the subject of conjecture in respect of Article 6*bis* of the Berne Convention and it can be assumed that there will be the same uncertainty in respect of Article 5(1).[40] There is no help to be found in the Basic Proposal: that document merely records that there is nothing concerning inalienability or inter vivos transfer in the provision.[41]

The application of the moral rights to 'live aural performances' is a curious provision. In itself, a live aural performance is an intriguing concept. The difficulties associated with the concept of a 'live performance' have already been canvassed.[42] There are two possible interpretations in the present context. One

[39] Memorandum Prepared by the International Bureau of WIPO 'Questions Concerning a Possible Instrument for the Protection of the Rights of Performers and Producers of Phonograms' INR/CE/III/2 (Committee of Experts on the Possible Protection of the Rights of Performers and Producers of Phonograms, Third Session, Geneva, 12 to 16 December 1994) [33].

[40] Masouye, above n 1, [6*bis*.6]; S Ricketson, *The Berne Convention for the Protection of Literary and Artistic Works: 1886–1986* (Centre for Commercial Law Studies, Kluwer, London, 1987) [8.104].

[41] Basic Proposal, above n 10, [5.07].

[42] Ch 4, n 58, and accompanying discussion.

is that a live aural performance is an unfixed performance presented by a person who is present in the same area as the audience but who is not visible, perhaps off-stage. The other is that a live aural performance is an unfixed performance that is broadcast or communicated to the public by purely audio media so that there is no visual component. In any event, the situations in which performers are likely to exercise their moral rights in respect of unfixed performances are limited. An example of the exercise of the right to object to any distortion would be to ensure that equipment being used to broadcast an unfixed performance or to communicate it to the public was in good order, thereby ensuring the quality of the performance.[43] Such matters are better dealt with in the contractual arrangements between the performer and producer and between the producer and the owners of the venue and the equipment. Performers will also be more concerned to ensure that fixations of their performances are not mistreated, as they are longer lasting than their unfixed performances. Article 5(1) also has the unfortunate result that performers of unfixed performances that are not aural, such as performances by mimes or performances using sign language, need not be protected in national legislation. But otherwise performers of all qualifying performances will be protected in their unfixed form.

Article 5(1) does not specify how the right of attribution is to be exercised but the way it is drafted does provide an opportunity to limit the scope of the provision, in that there is no obligation to identify a performer where that omission is dictated by the manner of the use of the performance. This is clearly a practical solution for performances such as those broadcast on the radio: it can be assumed that the listening public does not want to be told the names of the performers in an advertisement or the names of all the members of a symphony orchestra. If they want to know, there are ways of finding out. The Basic Proposal does not address the matter. However, in an earlier WIPO document, the International Bureau of WIPO made suggestions that are intended to provide guidance. They suggested that solo performers, artistic leaders of performers (such as conductors) and principal performers should be named. In respect of performances by several performers, the name jointly used, such as the name of an orchestra, should be used.[44] While it is up to national legislation to decide the final form of the right to be identified, the words of Article 5 are wide enough to include those suggestions.

The right of integrity in the WPPT is narrower than the Berne Convention provision on which it is based. Article 5(1) of the WPPT contains the phrase 'distortion, mutilation or other modification', but not the phrase 'or other derogatory action'. Also, the reference to 'prejudicial to his reputation' is narrower than the corresponding provision in the Berne Convention, which speaks

[43] Another example might be a concern to ensure that a broadcast of an unfixed performance is not distorted by the inclusion of advertisements or other material at a crucial point.

[44] Memorandum Prepared by the International Bureau of WIPO, INR/CE/III/2, above n 39, [31].

of an author's 'honour or reputation'. The latter phrase extended the ambit of the right in the Berne Convention to include an author's reputation as an individual as well as his or her reputation as an author.[45] It is arguable, therefore, that the narrower right granted to performers is restricted to protecting performers solely in their capacity as performers.

In practice, these factors should not lead to legislation by Contracting Parties that is more restrictive than that accorded to authors. In any event, the major issue with the right of integrity of a performance arises not at the level of the drafting of the WPPT or the drafting of national legislation. It arises when a performer decides that a performance has been dealt with in a way that is prejudicial to his or her reputation. Not all modifications will be prejudicial to a performer's reputation. In any event, even outside of express contractual agreements, there must be leeway for the producer to modify the constituent elements of a production to meet overall artistic or financial objectives. The WPPT gives no assistance in determining where the line lies between permissible and impermissible modifications. Even with guidance from national legislation, the courts will have to decide whether the impugned use by a producer merely constitutes reproduction to which the performer has consented, or whether it has gone further and amounts to a use that is prejudicial to the performer's reputation.[46] If, however, a performer agrees to a fixation of a performance in the full knowledge that it may be dealt with in various ways, such as being used in trailers advertising a cinematographic film, then the performer should not be able to object to such treatment if it does occur. In the case of distortion, mutilation or modification by a third party, the right of reproduction will normally be applicable and it is open to question whether the right of integrity is the better means of controlling acts of this kind.

VI CONCLUSIONS

There are three economic rights that, together with the moral rights, constitute the extended performers' rights. The purpose of this chapter was to complete the exercise of determining the scope of protection under the international

[45] Ricketson, above n 40, [8.110].

[46] The moral rights of the well-known performer, George Michael, were considered in *Morrison Leahy Music Ltd v Lightbond Ltd* [1993] EMLR 144. In that case the defendant had produced a phonogram containing a medley of words and music from five compositions. The second plaintiff was the author and the first plaintiff was the copyright owner. The phonogram started with five seconds of fill-in music, then ten seconds from one of the five compositions, thirty two seconds from another, and so on. Morrit J held, at 150–151, that it was arguable whether this constituted 'modification' or whether it constituted 'distortion or mutilation'. However, on the basis that damages would be an inadequate remedy, he granted an interlocutory injunction.

instruments by the analysis of those rights. While that analysis concentrated on the relevant provisions of the WPPT, there were clear indications that, apart from the issue of the transmission of on-demand customised fixations of performances, the remainder of the issues covered in that Treaty had been considered before.

For convenience sake, the extended rights have been analysed as a separate group. In a discussion of the system of performers' rights established by the three international instruments, they must be considered in conjunction with the primary economic rights. In assessing the scope of protection provided by the primary economic rights, the question was asked whether those rights provided performers with the means to control the use of their performances. That question needs to be asked again: given the foreseeable future state of technology and the existence of the primary economic rights, do performers have the means to control the exploitation of their performances?

In answering that question, the first step is to determine whether the extended rights plug the gaps that were identified by the analysis of the primary economic rights in the previous chapter. The answer is both 'yes' and 'no':

(i) States that sign the WPPT are obliged to implement moral rights for performers, although there are issues concerning the application of those rights.
(ii) Apart from the broadcasting right, which is a right of remuneration, the WPPT has confirmed that performers should be granted exclusive rights, and has put performers on an equal footing with producers of phonograms in this regard.
(iii) The pragmatic approach to the audiovisual issue has been continued and the lack of control over audiovisual performances remains a serious gap in the protection afforded to performers.
(iv) The need to harmonise protection has, at least, been recognised.

The second step is to assess the rights that are available to performers under the three international instruments. There is no doubt that the bundle of performers' rights now parallels authors' rights in many ways; this is a dramatic change from the handful of rights granted under the Rome Convention, which were pitched at a level lower than authors' rights. The rights of performers in that Convention were also pitched at a level lower than the rights granted to phonogram producers and broadcasters. Performers and producers of phonograms are treated equally in the WPPT. The need to update performers' rights at the same time as moves were taken to update copyright has also been recognised by the international community. This recognition is most obvious in the grant of the right of making available.

The analysis of the scope of performers' rights has shown, however, that there are still gaps to be filled:

(i) Other forms of protection, particularly contract, are available to supplement the extended rights, but as was noted in respect of the primary economic rights, this supplemental protection is only a stop-gap.
(ii) The protection of performances that are embodied in audiovisual media is set at a very low level compared to performances embodied in audio media.
(iii) The protection available to performers is uneven. Although the WPPT provides performers with a large bundle of rights, it has not come into force and those rights are not fully applied in the developed world, let alone in the developing world.[47]

Apart from the uneven application of the rights provided in the international instruments, another factor contributes to the unevenness of the international protection of performers: the instruments themselves allow contracting states to make limitations and exceptions and reservations to the protection that they provide. Those provisions in the Rome Convention, TRIPS and the WPPT are analysed in the next chapter.

[47] The United Kingdom has introduced a performers' right of rental, s 182C of the Copyright, Designs and Patents Act 1988 (UK). This provision was not implemented in compliance with the WPPT, but rather in compliance with obligations under the EC Directive on rental and lending rights and on piracy: Council Directive 92/100/EC of 19 November 1992 on rental right and lending right and certain rights related to copyright in the field of intellectual property. There has been more progress in implementing the provisions of the WCT—notably, the Digital Millenium Copyright Act 1998 (US) and the Copyright Amendment (Digital Agenda) Act 2000 (Cth).

11

Limitations and Exceptions and Reservations to the Guaranteed Rights

I INTRODUCTION

IT IS CLEAR from the discussion in the previous two chapters that the performers' rights provided for under the international instruments are now extensive. For the various reasons discussed below, it has been thought desirable to permit contracting states to modify the application of performers' rights in national legislation by limitations and exceptions and by reservations which reduce the level of protection that is available to performers. Those provisions, which are an integral part of the application of performers' rights, are analysed in this chapter.

The first section of this chapter consists of a short discussion of limitations and exceptions and reservations in the context of performers' rights. Particular reference is made to the important 'three-step test'. This discussion is followed by an analysis of the relevant provisions in the three international instruments.

II THE USE OF LIMITATIONS AND EXCEPTIONS AND RESERVATIONS IN INTERNATIONAL INSTRUMENTS

A Limitations and Exceptions

Intellectual property rights are granted on the basis that the benefit provided to individuals, such as performers, exceeds the costs to other individuals and to the state itself. It is important, therefore, to ensure that those rights do not extend beyond the purposes of protection. The grant of performers' rights involves balancing the interests of interested parties—notably, performers, producers, authors and the general public. It is a balance that may have to be reviewed from time to time to ensure that it remains up to date with developments in technology and in the use of performances. The international instruments permit limitations and exceptions to the protection that they provide performers, and those limitations and exceptions have a significant role to play within that balancing exercise, something Hugenholtz has called 'fine-tuning.'[1] The boundaries of the rights granted under the international instruments are set by those limitations and exceptions, by specifying that certain uses are outside the control of the performer.

As with other areas of performers' rights, the way in which the issue of limitations and exceptions is treated in the literature of copyright has lessons for performers' rights. Ricketson has suggested that, as well as compulsory licences, there are two main ways of limiting the protection of copyright, and those two ways are also applicable to performers' rights.[2] They are:

(i) The exclusion of protection for particular categories of performances on the basis that there are clear public policy grounds that they should not be protected. An example would be to exclude performances from protection on the basis of content, such as performances that incite racial hatred or that are obscene or blasphemous.
(ii) Allowing certain uses so that performers' rights do not unreasonably restrict the legitimate interests of the public in the free dissemination of those performances. An example would be to broadcast a part of a performance for the purpose of news or criticism.

There is also a pragmatic side to the practice of allowing exceptions in international conventions and treaties. They may be included to take account of the particular circumstances important to individual states or they may be a response where states acknowledge that the right holder cannot control the use, such as the private copying of performances. (Private copying is becoming an increasingly problematic exception as technology facilitates high-quality home copying from broadcasts and from the Internet. Private copying may be the main means of exploitation in the future.) The seemingly inevitable consequence of permitting exceptions and reservations is a lack of harmony and uniformity in the approach adopted by contracting states. This consequence comes on top of variations made by those states in the interpretation of the provisions in the instruments, including those dealing with limitations and exceptions.

The rights that are set out in the international instruments are the conventional minima and, as such, they are mandatory. There is no obligation to make them subject to exceptions in national legislation. If exceptions are implemented, then they must not be broader than the relevant instrument permits. Exceptions can be formulated in two ways; both of these ways are found in the international instruments that provide for performers' rights and both owe their inclusion in those instruments to the example of the Berne Convention.

[1] PB Hugenholtz, 'Fierce Creatures, Copyright Exemptions: Towards Extinction?' (Paper presented at: Rights, Limitations and Exceptions: Striking a Proper Balance, IFLA/IMPRIMATUR Conference, Amsterdam, 30–31 October 1997) 4.

[2] S Ricketson, *The Berne Convention for the Protection of Literary and Artistic Works: 1886–1986* (Centre for Commercial Law Studies, Kluwer, London, 1987) [9.1].

The first approach involves an attempt to list all, or all the important, exceptions that the resulting legislation should cover. The usual exceptions include private use, the use of short excerpts for news or reporting, and use for scientific, judicial or educational purposes. The obvious complaints that may result from an enumerative approach are that a particular list is too narrow (possibly because, as is often the case, it was a compromise occasioned by the difficulty of obtaining agreement to an enumeration of exceptions), or that it is so extensive as to be cumbersome.

The other approach is to draft a general provision that covers all the permitted instances in a generic fashion, leaving contracting states to provide for exceptions in national legislation. It can be said that this approach suffers from the need to interpret the provision and the uncertainty that this interpretation engenders.

1 *The Three-Step Test*

The most important general provision in the field of copyright and neighbouring rights is Article 9(2) of the Berne Convention. It provides:

> It shall be a matter for legislation in the countries of the Union to permit the reproduction of such works in certain special cases, provided that such reproduction does not conflict with a normal exploitation of the work and does not unreasonably prejudice the legitimate interests of the author.

This provision limits the scope of exceptions that contracting states may implement in national legislation. If an exception for a particular use is to be included in national legislation it must meet the so-called 'three-step test': (i) The limitation or exception must be confined to certain special cases. (ii) It should not conflict with the normal exploitation of the work. (iii) It should not unreasonably prejudice the legitimate interests of the author. 'These conditions are cumulative, and each raises problems of interpretation.'[3] To pick up on just one of these problems in the context of performers and performances: what are the legitimate interests of a performer in a performance that has been arranged and financed by somebody else (the producer), scripted by somebody else (the author), created and artistically arranged by somebody else (the director) and ultimately paid for by the consumer? The answer to the question will depend on whether the person answering is a performer or one of the other people mentioned. It will be a matter of time before a conclusion can be reached as to whether the benefits of the three-step test outweigh the problem of the differences of opinion as to its scope.

The three-step test in Article 9(2) permits members of the Berne Union to limit copyright's exclusive right of reproduction. Its importance for performers'

[3] *Ibid* [9.6].

rights lies in the fact that it has been incorporated in both TRIPS and the WPPT as a provision of horizontal application to all performers' rights and not just to the right of reproduction. It has also had an indirect effect on the exceptions permitted by the Rome Convention. There are several ways of looking at a provision like Article 9(2): those who support a narrow range of exceptions may regard it as uncertain and therefore capable of loose interpretation; those who support a wide range of exceptions may see it as unduly restrictive. Whichever view is preferred, the result will be that someone, be it an academic or a legislator or a judge, will have to work out whether specific instances fall within the scope of the general provision, thereby effectively enumerating the permitted exceptions.

Presumably, the reason Article 9(2) has become so influential in the field of performers' rights is that it was believed that a test formulated to deal with issues concerning the use of works was equally applicable to the use of performances.[4] Of course, performances are not works and it must be asked whether the introduction of this test into the performers' rights instruments will really assist contracting states to adopt a principled approach to permitted exceptions.

B Reservations

The decision to declare a reservation is optional. A reservation enables a state that wishes to become a party to a treaty to declare that it will exclude or modify the operation of certain provisions of the treaty and declare the extent to which they will exclude or modify those provisions. If a state does not make a reservation in respect of a provision, then it must implement that provision in full. 'Reservation' is defined in the Vienna Convention on the Law of Treaties. Article 2(1)(d) states:

> 'reservation' means a unilateral statement, however phrased or named, made by a State, when signing, ratifying, accepting, approving or acceding to a treaty, whereby it purports to exclude or to modify the legal effect of certain provisions of the treaty in their application to the State.

Why allow reservations? The answer is severely pragmatic. When a treaty is being concluded there may be states that are so opposed to a provision that they are not prepared to sign the agreement, and also states that are determined

[4] The Basic Proposal notes that the interpretation of the three-step test as it appears in Art 16(2) of the WPPT 'may follow the established interpretation of Art 9(2)': Chairman of the Committees of Experts on a Possible Protocol to the Berne Convention and on a Possible Instrument for the Protection of the Rights of Performers and Producers of Phonograms, 'Basic Proposal for the Substantive Provisions of the Treaty for the Protection of Performers and Producers of Phonograms to be Considered by the Diplomatic Conference' CRNR/DC/5 ('Basic Proposal') (Diplomatic Conference on Certain Copyright and Neighbouring Rights Questions, Geneva, 2 to 20 December 1996) [13.04].

that the provision will remain in the agreement. In the face of such an impasse, a reservation may be included in the agreement to ensure that the greatest possible number of states will accede to the instrument.[5]

III ROME CONVENTION

The conventional minima in Article 7 of the Rome Convention are subject to quite extensive provisions permitting Contracting States to provide for exceptions. Article 15 includes both specific exceptions and a general exception provision. Exceptions in respect of a number of uses had been agreed upon in the Hague Draft and they are included in Article 15(1), which provides:

> Any Contracting State may, in its domestic laws and regulations, provide for exceptions to the protection guaranteed by this Convention as regards:
>
> (a) private use;
>
> (b) use of short excerpts in connection with the reporting of current events;
>
> (c) ephemeral fixation by a broadcasting organisation by means of its own facilities and for its own broadcasts;
>
> (d) use solely for the purposes of teaching or scientific research.

The exceptions in this provision draw on the Berne Convention for inspiration, although they are unqualified: that is, they are not required to take into account the effect of the respective uses of the performances on the interests of performers, which is something that is required in the Berne three-step test:

(i) Private use is use other than public use or use for profit. This exception recognises the difficulty of policing private reproductions.[6] (Private use of copyright works is generally regarded as falling within the scope of Article 9(2) of the Berne Convention and would therefore be subject to the three-step test.[7])

[5] Prior to the Diplomatic Conference that concluded the WPPT, Argentina proposed that reservations should be allowed in the new treaty because it was concerned that consensus might not be achieved regarding the level of protection to be granted: Document Prepared by the International Bureau of WIPO, 'Comparative Table of Proposals and Comments Received by the International Bureau' INR/CE/V/11 (Committee of Experts on the Possible Protection of the Rights of Performers and Producers of Phonograms, Fifth Session, Geneva, 1 to 9 February 1996) [XIV].

[6] A point that was made at the Rome Diplomatic Conference: 'Summary Records of the Proceedings', *Records of the Diplomatic Conference on the International Protection of Performers, Producers of Phonograms and Broadcasting Organisations* (ILO, UNESCO and BIRPI, Geneva, 1968) [1531].

[7] Ricketson above n 2, [9.11]; C Masouye (W Wallace trans), *Guide to the Berne Convention for the Protection of Literary and Artistic Works (Paris Act, 1971)* (World Intellectual Property Organisation, Geneva, 1978) [9.10].

(ii) The exception for use in connection with reporting current events is modelled on Article 10*bis*(2) of the Berne Convention.[8] The wording of the exception in Article 15(1) of the Rome Convention suggests that such use should be carefully monitored to ensure that it is short and that its use can be justified for news purposes.
(iii) The exception for ephemeral fixations by broadcasters is modelled on Article 11*bis*(3) of the Berne Convention. It covers copies made for purely technical reasons by the broadcaster itself and made solely for its own use.[9]
(iv) The exception for the use of performances for teaching or scientific research looks to Article 10(2) of the Berne Convention, but is wider than that provision.[10]

Because clauses (a) to (d) deal with exceptions to the norm that states may wish to implement to suit their individual circumstances, the wording of each clause is open to interpretation.

The advantage of the enumerative approach is that it provides a degree of certainty and clarity. If a particular use is listed, then some thought will have been given to its scope and its potential effect. Enumerating a list also has a role in providing for exceptions that particular states wish to implement for particular uses. This was the situation with the exception covering scientific research in Article 15(1)(d), which was included at the instigation of the Indian delegation. Its inclusion is an example of a developing state obtaining a concession peculiar to its circumstances.[11] However, the difficulty in settling on a comprehensive list of exceptions led to agreement at the Rome Diplomatic Conference that the enumeration of specific exceptions would be supplemented by a general provision referring to the exceptions permitted in a state's copyright legislation. The general provision is contained in Article 15(2), which provides:

> Irrespective of paragraph (1) of this Article, any Contracting State may, in its domestic laws and regulations, provide for the same kinds of limitations with regard to the protection of performers, producers of phonograms and broadcasting organisations, as it provides for, in its domestic laws and regulations, in connection with the protection of copyright in literary and artistic works. However, compulsory licences may be provided for only to the extent to which they are compatible with this Convention.

The circumstances that prevailed at the Rome Diplomatic Conference provide a useful background to the interpretation of Article 15(2). Authors and their sup-

[8] C Masouye (W Wallace trans), *Guide to the Rome Convention and to the Phonograms Convention* (World Intellectual Property Organisation, Geneva, 1981) [15.3].
[9] *Ibid* [15.4].
[10] *Ibid* [15.5].
[11] In this case as urged by India: 'Summary Records of the Proceedings', above n 6, [1548], [1550] and [1552].

porters were determined that the beneficiaries of the Rome Convention would not be treated better than authors. As well as providing a general formula, therefore, Article 15(2) had another aim: 'But the paragraph was intended to act as a hint to the member States that they should in principle consider treating copyright and neighbouring rights equally in this respect.'[12] If performers are considered as merely vessels for disseminating works it is logical that performers' rights should be subject to the same exceptions that apply to the authors of the works.

As noted, the specific exceptions owe much to the Berne Convention; however, by linking any further exceptions to copyright in literary and artistic works, Article 15(2) had yet another effect. For Contracting States that are also members of the Berne Union, the inclusion of that paragraph ensures that the three-step test in Article 9(2) of the Berne Convention has at least an influential effect on the exceptions that they include in their performers' rights legislation. Unlike TRIPS or the WPPT, the wording of Article 15 of the Rome Convention does not include the three-step test, nor does it refer to the test itself. However, if states have acceded to the Berne Convention then the exceptions and limitations in their copyright legislation relating to the right of reproduction are required to comply with that test. If that is the case, then, according to Article 15(2) of the Rome Convention, the inclusion of those exceptions in performers' rights legislation by those states should proceed only if that same test is applied to the legitimate interests of performers.

Finally, Article 15(2) is subject to a specific limitation as to the provision of compulsory licences. Even if a state has provided for the compulsory licensing of copyright works, it may not provide for a similar system in respect of performances unless it is compatible with the provisions of the Rome Convention. It was settled in the discussions of Working Party II of the Rome Diplomatic Conference that the requirement of consent in Article 7(1) meant that a compulsory licence system was incompatible with that Article as the consent of the performer would not be required under the compulsory licence system, thereby effectively overriding the performer's possibility of authorising the use.[13] Masouye suggests, however, that compulsory licence systems may be possible, provided a similar limitation on the rights of authors is in place in respect of the acts covered in Article 7(2), because that provision regulates situations after a performer's consent has been obtained.[14] It is open to Contracting States to adopt this interpretation.

[12] Masouye, above n 8, [15.9].

[13] 'Report of the Rapporteur-General', *Records of the Diplomatic Conference on the International Protection of Performers, Producers of Phonograms and Broadcasting Organisations* (ILO, UNESCO and BIRPI, Geneva, 1968) 43; 'Summary Records of the Proceedings', above n 6, [1100].

[14] Masouye, above n 8, 15.11.

Turning to reservations, the only reservations that may be made to the provisions in the Rome Convention are those permitted by the Convention. This is explicitly provided for in Article 31:

> Without prejudice to the provisions of paragraph 3 of Article 5, paragraph 2 of Article 6, paragraph 1 of Article 16 and Article 17, no reservation may be made to this Convention.[15]

Although reservations do not play a large part in the Rome Convention, the significance of a reservation under Article 16(1)(a) to the right of remuneration has been discussed above.[16]

IV TRIPS

There are two provisions in TRIPS that deal with exceptions. There is a specific provision in Article 14(6). It provides:

> Any Member may, in relation to the rights conferred under paragraphs 1, 2 and 3, provide for conditions, limitations, exceptions and reservations to the extent permitted by the Rome Convention.

It is clear, therefore, that the exceptions and reservations permitted by Articles 15 and 16 of the Rome Convention have been incorporated into TRIPS in relation to the rights in TRIPS that parallel the rights granted by the Rome Convention. It would also seem that the limitation on compulsory licensing of the rights granted in Article 7(1) of the Convention carries over to the rights granted in Article 14(1) of TRIPS. Nothing more needs to be added to the above discussion of those exceptions and reservations other than to note that the reservations permitted by Article 16(1)(a) of the Rome Convention are not relevant in a discussion of TRIPS because they relate to equitable remuneration for secondary uses, which is not included under TRIPS.

There is also a provision of general application in TRIPS which is derived from Article 9(2) of the Berne Convention. Article 13 of TRIPS provides:

> Members shall confine limitations or exceptions to exclusive rights to certain special cases which do not conflict with a normal exploitation of the work and do not unreasonably prejudice the legitimate interests of the right holder.

Although the three-step test in TRIPS extends horizontally to 'exclusive rights' without exception, the effect of this provision on performers' rights will be

[15] Arts 5 and 17 refer to the points of attachment for phonogram producers and Art 6 to the points of attachment for broadcasting organisations.

[16] See the discussion in ch 9, n 59, and accompanying discussion.

limited.[17] The rights granted to performers in Article 14(1) are not exclusive rights and, in any event, they are subject to the specific application of Article 14(6). It would make for unwieldy drafting to suggest that the effect of Article 13 is to require that exceptions that are permitted under Article 14(6) should also be measured against the three-step test. Of the rights granted to performers by TRIPS, only the rental right is an exclusive right (if one accepts the argument discussed in the previous chapter that performers are entitled to a rental right by Article 11 of TRIPS). As the rental right is not included in the Rome Convention, any exceptions that a Member makes to a right of rental for performers must meet the requirements of the three-step test.

Article 14(6) applies to reservations permitted by the Rome Convention. The general provision as to reservations to rights other than those governed by the Rome Convention is Article 72 of TRIPS. It prohibits a Member from entering a reservation in respect of any provision of TRIPS without the consent of other Members. Its only application to performers' rights is, like Article 13, in respect of a right of rental.

V WPPT

In the WPPT, the practice of enumerating unqualified exceptions was abandoned. The Treaty includes two general provisions as to exceptions and limitations, taking one from the Rome Convention and the other from the Berne Convention. Article 16(1) provides:

> Contracting Parties may, in their national legislation, provide for the same kinds of limitations or exceptions with regard to the protection of performers and producers of phonograms as they provide for, in their national legislation, in connection with the protection of copyright in literary and artistic works.

This provision replicates the first sentence of Article 15(2) of the Rome Convention and the comments previously made in respect of Article 15(2) are therefore applicable here. Article 16(1) of the WPPT does vary from the Rome Convention model in one respect: the restriction on compulsory licensing in Article 15(2) of the Convention is not included in the WPPT. However, any compulsory licensing scheme that affected the rights granted in the WPPT would

[17] How much further Art 13 of TRIPS extended the three-step test was apparently debated at some length at the Geneva Diplomatic Conference: C Cresswell, 'Copyright Protection Enters the Digital Age: The New WIPO Treaties' (1997) 15 *Copyright Reporter* 4, 16. A recent United States Department of Commerce publication described the effect of Art 13 as 'narrowly circumscribing the limitations and exceptions that WTO member countries may impose': The Report of the Working Group on Intellectual Property Rights, *Intellectual Property and the National Information Infrastructure* (Department of Commerce, Patent and Trade Mark Office, Washington, 1995) 134, n 437 and accompanying text.

either have to be provided for in respect of the corresponding right in copyright, or it would have to meet the three-step test in paragraph (2) of Article 16.

In the second general provision, the WPPT adopted the three-step test from the Berne Convention. Article 16(2) provides:

> Contracting Parties shall confine any limitations of or exceptions to rights provided for in this Treaty to certain special cases which do not conflict with a normal exploitation of the performance or phonogram and do not unreasonably prejudice the legitimate interests of the performer or of the producer of the phonogram.

A strict interpretation of Article 16 is that the two paragraphs are cumulative, which effectively makes Article 16(1) redundant: that is, any exceptions made to the rights granted under the Treaty, whether they parallel exceptions to the protection of literary or artistic works or not, must meet the three-step test. This is certainly the view taken by the International Bureau of WIPO.[18] Whether the states that accede to the WPPT accept this interpretation is, of course, another matter. An equally valid interpretation is that paragraphs (1) and (2) of Article 16 are quite distinct and therefore paragraph (2) does not govern paragraph (1), even though paragraph (2) functions as a general limit on the exceptions that may be made to the rights granted by the WPPT.

Article 16(2) is another example of the way in which the negotiations over the WCT influenced the form of the WPPT. Considerable concern was expressed at the Geneva Diplomatic Conference that the three-step test, if incorporated into the WCT, would restrict the application of established exceptions to rights in copyright, and this apprehension spilled over into the discussions of the WPPT.[19] 'The main concern of critical delegations was that it would introduce inconsistency between exceptions and limitations under the CT [*sic*] those allowed under Berne, which the CT complements.'[20] These concerns were allayed by the inclusion of an Agreed Statement which applies, *mutatis mutandis*, to Article 16 of the WPPT. The text of the Agreed Statement states:

> It is understood that the provisions of Article 10 [Article 16 of the WPPT] permit Contracting Parties to carry forward and appropriately extend into the digital environment limitations and exceptions in their national laws which have been considered acceptable under the Berne Convention. Similarly, these provisions should be understood to permit Contracting Parties to devise new exceptions and limitations that are appropriate in the digital network environment.

[18] 'It is obvious that any limitations and exceptions—existing or new—in the digital environment are only applicable if they are acceptable under the "three-step test" indicated in Art 16(2) of the Treaty.' See International Bureau of WIPO, 'New Trends in the Protection of Copyright and Neighbouring Rights: The WIPO Performances and Phonograms Treaty (1996)' WIPO/CR/GE/97/4b (Introductory Seminar on Copyright and Neighbouring Rights, Geneva, 8 to 10 October 1997) 7.

[19] Summary Minutes, Main Committee I of the Diplomatic Conference on Certain Copyright and Neighboring Rights Questions CRNR/DC/102 ('Summary Minutes') (Diplomatic Conference on Certain Copyright and Neighboring Rights Questions, Geneva, 2 to 20 December 1996) [489–494].

[20] Cresswell, above n 17, 15.

> It is also understood that Article 10(2) [Article 16(2) of the WPPT] neither reduces nor extends the scope of applicability of the limitations and exceptions permitted by the Berne Convention.

At the core of the Statement is the concession that Contracting Parties may 'carry forward and appropriately extend into the digital environment limitations and exceptions in their national laws which have been considered acceptable under the Berne Convention.' It is also important that the Statement noted that the development of new exceptions and limitations appropriate to the digital environment is not ruled out. The final sentence of the Agreed Statement can be interpreted as supporting the stand-alone status of Article 16(1).

The effect of this Agreed Statement is hard to gauge.[21] The view taken by a senior official of WIPO is that Article 16(2), read together with the Agreed Statement, means that the extension of exceptions and limitations acceptable under the Berne Convention 'should not be considered an automatic and mechanical exercise; it is all subject to the application of the three-step test.'[22] The position taken here by Ficsor is that, because the exploitation of performances in the digital environment is different from exploitation in the traditional, analog environment, the nature of the unreasonable prejudice that may be caused to performers, which is the key element of the three-step test, may also be different. Therefore, the existing exceptions and limitations should be subjected to the three-step test before they are carried forward to the digital environment. Ficsor's view needs to be treated with care. It is surely dangerous to make sweeping statements about the application of the Berne three-step test to performers' rights for a number of reasons: (i) The test has traditionally been applied to rights established under the copyright regime and, even there, its application is controversial. (ii) The application of the test to performers' rights in TRIPS is not settled. (iii) There is no agreed interpretation of the Agreed Statement. (iv) The application of rights, and exceptions to those rights, in the environment of digital technology is very new; there is therefore no history of how the test has been interpreted in national legislation. One thing is clear, no matter how the three-step test is finally applied to performers' rights, the debate on its application in the context of performers' rights has hardly begun.

The inclusion of the three-step test in Article 16, whether directly in paragraph (2) or indirectly through the application of copyright exceptions by virtue of paragraph (1), has ensured that the rights granted in the WPPT are not subject to unrestricted limitation. One obvious example is that any exception for private use, a matter of some concern at the Geneva Diplomatic Conference, is

[21] Note that Kéréver is particularly critical of the Statement. He suggests that either it exceeds the limits set out in Art 31 of the Vienna Convention on the Law of Treaties or it is superfluous. A Kéréver, 'The New WIPO Treaties: the WIPO Copyright Treaty and the WIPO Performances and Phonograms Treaty' (1998) 32 *Copyright Bulletin* 3, 9–10.

[22] M Ficsor, 'The Spring 1997 Horace S. Manges Lecture—Copyright for the Digital Era: The WIPO "Internet" Treaties' (1997) 21 *Columbia-VLA Journal of Law & the Arts* 197, 215.

now subject to the three-step test. This will be seen to benefit performers and, perhaps, the people responsible for exploiting their performances.

So far as reservations are concerned, Article 21 of the WPPT follows the example of the Rome Convention by providing that the only reservations permitted are those to the right of remuneration. It provides:

> Subject to the provisions of Article 15(3), no reservations to this Treaty shall be permitted.

This provision has provoked a quizzical comment that is equally applicable to the Rome Convention.

> One wonders how effective a performances and phonograms treaty is if a country does not have to grant performance rights to performers and can still be a party to it.[23]

VI CONCLUSIONS

The purpose of this chapter was to analyse the articles in the Rome Convention, TRIPS and the WPPT that provide for limitations and exceptions and reservations. It is clear from the analysis of these provisions that while a state may recognise that performers need to be able to control the uses that are made of their performances, performers have to yield a measure of control in certain circumstances. The analysis undertaken in this chapter also disclosed that the need to balance competing interests within the different cultural and legal structures of contracting states means that the provisions relating to limitations and exceptions are extensive in their effect. They are so extensive, in fact, that the three-step test places a limitation on limitations and exceptions. By contrast, the reservations provisions are restricted in their effect: reservations are not generally permitted in the instruments.

Apart from those general points, three important features of the provisions permitting limitations and exceptions are worthy of specific comment:

(i) The influence of the copyright treaties, specifically the Berne Convention and the WCT, on the form of limitations and exceptions in the instruments concerned with performers' rights is very strong. It was shown above that both the Rome Convention and TRIPS (the latter through the incorporation of provisions of the Rome Convention) look to the Berne Convention for inspiration. Article 16(1) of the WPPT looks to the Rome Convention, which in turn, looks to the Berne Convention. The WCT was clearly influential on the drafting of Article 16(2) of the WPPT.

[23] RF Martin, 'The WIPO Performances and Phonograms Treaty: Will the US Whistle a New Tune?' (1997) *Journal of the Copyright Society of the USA* 157, 181.

(ii) There are two ways of approaching the provision of limitations and exceptions: there is an enumerative approach and a general approach. In the WPPT, the general approach in the form of the three-step test has been preferred. This preference at international level does not, however, prevent a contracting state from adopting an enumerative approach in national legislation.

(iii) There is an understandable desire on the part of states that support the international system of performers' rights to make the coverage of the international instruments as wide as possible. This conflicts with the pragmatic need to allow limitations and exceptions to the rights granted, with the consequence that those rights are unevenly applied.

In respect of reservations, similar comments can be made about the need to balance the concerns of contracting states against the level of protection that is afforded to performers. Performers' rights should not exceed the required level of protection. If, however, contracting states are able to reduce the level of that protection by the employment of limitations and exceptions and reservations, perhaps the mandatory conventional minima need to be set at a lower level or the duration of the rights should be reconsidered.

12

Duration of the Rights

I INTRODUCTION

THERE ARE TWO aspects to the duration of intellectual property rights. The first and most important is the term of the right, that is, how long does it last? The second aspect of duration is the application in time of the right; in other words, from what point in time does the right take effect? Associated with the latter question is the issue of retroactivity; is the subject matter protected in relation to activities that took place before the right was established in law?

This chapter analyses the provisions in the international instruments that provide for the duration of performers' rights. Because these provisions place a time limit on the exercise of the rights that are granted to performers, they act as limitations on the exercise of those rights and are part of the balance between right holders and users of performances. The present analysis therefore conveniently follows the discussion of limitations and exceptions and reservations in the previous chapter. By comparison with other issues in performers' rights, the duration of performers' rights is a matter that has provoked little argument, as recent treaty negotiations have shown.[1]

II TERM OF PROTECTION AND APPLICATION IN TIME

A Term of Protection

The transitory nature of a performance means that duration is an issue only for fixed performances.[2] A right in respect of an unfixed performance, such as the

[1] There is only a short record of the discussion of the term of protection at the Geneva Diplomatic Conference. All the recorded speakers were in favour of a 50 year term except the delegate of Peru who favoured a 70 year term: Summary Minutes, Main Committee I of the Diplomatic Conference on Certain Copyright and Neighboring Rights Questions, CRNR/DC/102 ('Summary Minutes') (Diplomatic Conference on Certain Copyright and Neighboring Rights Questions, Geneva, 2 to 20 December 1996) [336]–[357].

[2] This point was noted by delegates to the Rome Diplomatic Conference: 'Summary Records of the Proceedings', *Records of the Diplomatic Conference on the International Protection of Performers, Producers of Phonograms and Broadcasting Organisations* (ILO, UNESCO and BIRPI, Geneva, 1968) [567.1] and [568].

right to authorise or to prohibit the first fixation, must be exercised before the performance is made; as soon as the relevant exploitation of an unfixed performance has occurred, the duration of those rights is irrelevant. It is the duration of the rights in respect of fixations that is crucial to the right holder.

The current trend to extend the term of performers' rights is probably linked to the pressure to extend the term of copyright. If this is the case, there is a danger that extensions will be made to the term of performers' rights, both in international instruments and in national legislation, merely because performers' rights are seen as neighbouring rights and therefore as being linked to copyright. The United States Congress has recognised three main reasons for extending the copyright term of protection.[3] They include the reasons that are most commonly raised in support of extending the term of performers' rights and are therefore a valuable reference point.[4]

(a) The first reason is uniformity of world standards. On the surface this seems an attractive argument, but it owes little to principle and more to agreements among powerful states over trade concerns. It can lead to the longest term becoming the norm and to a continuing upward harmonisation of the term of performers' rights. This, it is suggested, would place an undesirable restriction on the use of performances.

(b) The second reason is that protection should be sufficient to provide creators with a fair return for themselves and their dependants. The rights of an author's heirs to share in the income generated by a work is a significant argument raised in terms of the duration of the copyright term *post mortem auctoris*. The same argument can be raised in respect of performers' rights, that they are rights in the nature of property rights and it should be possible to transfer them to a performer's heirs to provide a source of income. Of course, this argument ignores the fact that an author and, in some jurisdictions, a performer can easily assign those rights before his or her death.[5] It also ignores the argument that intellectual property rights that are based on the personality of the creator should protect the creator, not the creator's assignees or heirs.

[3] OG Hatch, 'Toward a Principled Approach to Copyright Legislation at the Turn of the Millenium' (1998) 59 *University of Pittsburgh Law Review* 719, 728–739. Senator Orrin G Hatch was, at the time of writing the article, Chairman of the Senate Committee on the Judiciary in the United States Senate.

[4] See also B Sherman and L Bently, *Performers' Rights: Options for Reform* (Department of Communications, Information Technology and the Arts, Canberra, 1995) [12.6]; Australian Copyright Council, *Performers' Copyright* (Australian Copyright Council, Redfern, Sydney, 1996) [5.9].

[5] In the United Kingdom, performers' property rights are transmissible by assignment, by testamentary disposition or by operation of law, s 191B of the Copyright, Designs and Patents Act 1988 (UK). In certain other jurisdictions they are not assignable: eg Australia, by virtue of s 248N of the Copyright Act 1968 (Cth).

(c) The third reason is that technology has resulted in a longer life for fixations of performances. An answer to this argument is that technology has merely increased the technical life of a fixed performance. It has not guaranteed that there will be any continuing interest in or popularity of a particular performance. Technical developments have also resulted in more frequent instances of fixations of performances being altered in a number of ways—for example, by sampling. However, the development of technology should not be a reason for extending the term of protection beyond the economic life of the performance. The fact that technology has improved merely places a heavier burden on a performer, if he or she is the right holder, to be more vigilant in policing the use of a performance during his or her lifetime.

While there are advantages in looking to the example of copyright, the last word on linking performers' rights to the term of protection granted to works of copyright is simple: performances are not works.

B APPLICATION IN TIME

The second aspect of the duration of performers' rights—the application of the rights in time—requires a definite date from which intellectual property rights take effect, for the sake of clarity and certainty. It is also important to be clear as to the application of those rights backwards in time. A problem with the enactment of any new performers' rights, especially those that apply retroactively, is that existing arrangements or agreements that are based on the law before that enactment took place may have to be renegotiated.

There are three main options as to the retroactive application of performers' rights:

(i) It is possible to provide that the rights will apply retroactively without limitation.
(ii) The other absolute approach is that the rights will not apply retroactively.
(iii) The third option is more usual: it is that the provision of the rights will apply to performances made before the rights were enacted, but only in respect of actions that occur after the rights were enacted.

III ROME CONVENTION

The Report of the Rapporteur-General records that various proposals were put to the Rome Diplomatic Conference as to how long the term of protection should be for performers. These ranged from a low of 10 years to a high of

30 years. Another suggestion was a term of 25 years with a possible renewal for a further 25 years.[6] The term chosen was between the extremes. Article 14 provides:

> The term of protection to be granted under this Convention shall last at least until the end of a period of twenty years computed from the end of the year in which:
>
> (a) the fixation was made—for phonograms and for performances incorporated therein;
> (b) the performance took place—for performances not incorporated in phonograms;
> (c) the broadcast took place—for broadcasts.

The term of protection, 'at least twenty years', is considerably shorter than that available to authors under the Berne Convention at the same time.[7] The relatively short term can probably be attributed to a concern on the part of the delegates to the Rome Diplomatic Conference to ensure the pre-eminence of authors and copyright over the right holders in neighbouring rights.[8] Like the other provisions in the Rome Convention, the term of protection is set at the minimum. It is open to Contracting States to extend this period.

For performers, Article 14 provides two answers to the question of when the term of protection starts: (a) For phonograms and for the performances incorporated in them, the starting point is the end of the year in which the fixation was made. (b) For performances not incorporated in phonograms, the starting point is the end of the year in which the performance was made. For all practical purposes, this provision should be read as meaning the end of the year in which the performance was fixed; the wording of this provision is wide enough to cover unfixed performances, but it has already been noted that it is not necessary to stipulate a term of protection for an unfixed performance. The wording also covers performances fixed in audiovisual media; it was explained during the debate over this provision that 'sub-paragraph (b) concerned audio-visual fixations—which were not necessarily motion pictures—made without the consent of the performer.'[9] The reason that it applies only to performances fixed without consent in audiovisual media is simple: in respect of performances fixed in audiovisual media with the consent of the performer, Article 19 applies and

[6] 'Report of the Rapporteur-General', *Records of the Diplomatic Conference on the International Protection of Performers, Producers of Phonograms and Broadcasting Organisations* (ILO, UNESCO and BIRPI, Geneva, 1968) 51.

[7] In 1961, the term of protection under Art 7(1) of the Berne Convention (Brussels Act, 1948) was 50 years *post mortem auctoris*.

[8] Art 1 of the Rome Convention safeguards copyright. It provides: 'Protection granted under this Convention shall leave intact and shall in no way affect the protection of copyright in literary and artistic works. Consequently, no provision of this Convention may be interpreted as prejudicing such protection.'

[9] 'Summary Records of the Proceedings' above n 2, [568].

Article 7, which grants the rights that performers enjoy under the Convention, has no further application.[10]

Another issue of duration that was addressed at the Rome Diplomatic Conference was the problem to be faced when states implemented conflicting terms of protection. An answer to this problem is the rule of comparison of terms, and this rule had been included in the Hague Draft.[11] Under such a rule, the state in which protection is sought is not obliged to grant protection for a longer period than the period fixed by the state of origin. Thus, if State A protects its nationals for a period of 70 years and State B protects its nationals for a period of 50 years, a national of State B enjoys protection for a term of 50 years in State A. (It is always open to State A to protect nationals of other states for as long as it protects its own nationals.)

It was decided at the Diplomatic Conference, however, that comparison of terms was of real importance only in respect of the secondary uses of phonograms and the obligation to pay equitable remuneration under Article 12. It was decided that this situation was adequately covered by the provision as to material reciprocity of duration in Article 16(1)(a)(iv).[12] Although, the problem of conflicting terms also arose in respect of a limited number of situations relating to the reproduction of a fixation, it was decided that those situations did not constitute sufficient grounds for providing for a comparison of terms. The rule in the Hague Draft was therefore not included in the Convention.[13]

As to retroactive application, the Rome Convention is simple and direct. Article 20(2) follows the second option canvassed above. It provides:

> No Contracting State shall be bound to apply the provisions of this Convention to performances or broadcasts which took place, or to phonograms which were fixed, before the date of coming into force of this Convention for that State.

A Contracting State is not obliged to apply the provisions of the Convention to performances that took place before the state acceded to the Convention. It is therefore an option, not an obligation, to provide retroactive protection in national legislation.

[10] See the discussion of Art 19 in ch 9, n 34, and accompanying text.

[11] Art 13(1) of the Hague Draft proposed that: 'The period of the protection granted, under the terms of this Convention, to performers, makers of phonograms and broadcasters, shall be determined by the law of the country where the protection is claimed. However, no Contracting State shall be obliged to grant protection for a longer period than that fixed by the law of the country of origin.'

[12] 'Report of the Rapporteur-General', above n 6, 50. Art 16(1)(a)(iv) is discussed in ch 9, n 65 and accompanying text.

[13] E Ulmer, 'The Rome Convention on Neighboring Rights. Part III' (1963) *10 Bulletin. Copyright Society of the U.S.A.* 219, 238–9.

IV TRIPS

The term of protection provided to performers in TRIPS is more generous than the term provided in the Rome Convention. Article 14(5) provides:

> The term of protection available under this Agreement to performers and producers of phonograms shall last at least until the end of a period of 50 years computed from the end of the calendar year in which the fixation was made or the performance took place.

The starting point for the computation of the term of protection—'the end of the calendar year in which the fixation was made or the performance took place'—is stated more precisely in this provision than it is in the Rome Convention.

TRIPS is also more generous to performers because it provides for the retroactive application of its provisions. Article 14(6) applies the provisions of Article 18 of the Berne Convention, *mutatis mutandis*, to the rights of performers and producers of phonograms. Article 18(1) of the Berne Convention sets out the general principle of retroactivity; it provides protection for works that existed at the time the Convention came into force and in respect of which the term of protection had not expired. Applying that principle to TRIPS, performers have rights in their performances embodied in phonograms that existed when TRIPS became applicable and in respect of which the 50 years term of protection had not expired.[14] The conditions referred to in paragraphs (2), (3) and (4) of Article 18 of the Berne Convention will also apply, *mutatis mutandis*.[15] TRIPS does not, however, give rise to obligations in respect of acts that occurred before the TRIPS Agreement became applicable; that is explicit in Article 70(1).[16]

V WPPT

The WPPT provides that performers shall enjoy economic rights and moral rights, and the duration of those rights is dealt with in separate provisions. The duration of performers' economic rights is dealt with in Article 17(1) and in Article 22. Article 17(1) provides:

[14] This provision is reinforced by Art 70(2) of TRIPS, which provides, in part, that: 'In respect of this paragraph and paragraphs 3 and 4 . . . obligations with respect to the rights of producers of phonograms and performers in existing phonograms shall be determined solely under Art 18 of the Berne Convention (1971) as made applicable under paragraph 6 of Art 14 of this Agreement.'

[15] Art 18(2) bars protection being granted anew if protection has lapsed in the country in which it was originally protected. Art 18(3) provides that contracting states may implement transitional measures to safeguard acquired rights. Art 18(4) provides for new accessions and other events that are likely to bring this Article into operation.

[16] Art 70(1) of TRIPS provides: 'This Agreement does not give rise to obligations in respect of acts which occurred before the date of application of this Agreement for the Member in question.'

> The term of protection to be granted to performers under this Treaty shall last, at least, until the end of a period of 50 years computed from the end of the year in which the performance was fixed in a phonogram.

The WPPT follows TRIPS in providing that the duration of the economic rights is 50 years. In stipulating the point from which the term of protection is calculated, the WPPT reverts to the looser wording of the Rome Convention and specifies that the term is calculated from the end of the year in which the performance is fixed in a phonogram.

In a memorandum prepared for a Committee of Experts that met before the Geneva Diplomatic Conference, the International Bureau of WIPO suggested that there were two reasons for extending the term of protection from the 20 years provided in the Rome Convention to 50 years. The first was the effect of technology and the other was the example of TRIPS in providing for a 50-year term.[17] (Both reasons were criticised in an earlier section of this chapter.) According to the Basic Proposal,

> The reasons for setting the term of protection at this proposed level are obvious. There is a clear trend towards a fifty-year term of protection for performers and producers of phonograms.[18]

It is not clear, however, whether the reasons are so obvious that they do not need to be stated or whether there is in fact only one reason, namely, the need to harmonise protection in line with the trend to 50 years. On either interpretation, the approach lacks a principled basis. It has been suggested above that international harmony of legislation is not really a good enough reason, on its own, to extend the term of protection. If there are other obvious reasons, they should not have been left unstated.

Article 22(1) provides for the retroactive protection of performers in respect of both economic and moral rights. It provides:

> Contracting Parties shall apply the provisions of Article 18 of the Berne Convention, *mutatis mutandis*, to the rights of performers and producers of phonograms provided for in this Treaty.

The discussion of Article 18 in respect of the retroactive application of performers' rights under TRIPS is relevant here and does not need to be repeated. The difference between the provisions in the WPPT and TRIPS is that the

[17] Memorandum Prepared by the International Bureau of WIPO, 'Questions Concerning a Possible Instrument for the Protection of the Rights of Performers and Producers of Phonograms' INR/CE/III/2 (Committee of Experts on the Possible Protection of the Rights of Performers and Producers of Phonograms, Third Session, Geneva, 12 to 16 December 1994) [77].

[18] Chairman of the Committees of Experts on a Possible Protocol to the Berne Convention and on a Possible Instrument for the Protection of the Rights of Performers and Producers of Phonograms, 'Basic Proposal for the Substantive Provisions of the Treaty for the Protection of Performers and Producers of Phonograms to be Considered by the Diplomatic Conference' CRNR/DC/5 ('Basic Proposal') (Diplomatic Conference on Certain Copyright and Neighbouring Rights Questions, Geneva, 2 to 20 December 1996) [21.06].

WPPT does not include an express provision of non-retroactivity that parallels Article 70(1) of TRIPS. Nonetheless, it is unlikely that the rights provided under the WPPT would be seen as applying to acts that took place before a state acceded to the Treaty.[19]

Article 5(2) of the WPPT, which is the provision providing for the duration of performers' moral rights, is modelled on Article 6*bis*(2) of the Berne Convention. It provides:

> The rights granted to a performer in accordance with paragraph (1) shall, after his death, be maintained, at least until the expiry of the economic rights, and shall be exercisable by the persons or institutions authorised by the legislation of the Contracting Party where protection is claimed. However, those Contracting Parties whose legislation, at the moment of their ratification of or accession to this Treaty, does not provide for protection after the death of the performer of all rights set out in the preceding paragraph may provide that some of these rights will, after his death, cease to be maintained.

The basic term of protection for moral rights, including the time of application, is therefore the same as for economic rights, although there is an indication in the words 'at least until the expiry of the economic rights' that the term of moral rights could well be extended in national legislation beyond that granted to economic rights. There is also an internal exception in Article 5(2) that parallels Article 6*bis*(2) of the Berne Convention: Contracting Parties whose laws do not provide for the protection after the performer's death of the moral rights set out in Article 5(1) may restrict their protection after the death of the performer to 'some' of those rights. As only two moral rights are made obligatory in Article 5(1), this provision must mean that the duration of either the right of attribution or the right of integrity may be limited to the life of the performer. The limitation maintains the harmony of this provision with the copyright provision.[20]

The retroactive application of moral rights is dealt with further in Article 22(2), which may be implemented notwithstanding the operation of Article 22(1). Article 22(2) provides:

> Notwithstanding paragraph (1), a Contracting Party may limit the application of Article 5 of this Treaty to performances which occurred after the entry into force of this Treaty for that Party.

By virtue of that provision, Contracting Parties are permitted to limit the application of the moral rights provisions to performances that took place after the WPPT entered into force for each individual state. The inclusion of moral rights

[19] International Bureau of WIPO, *Implications of the TRIPS Agreement on Treaties Administered by WIPO* (WIPO, Geneva, 1997) [231].

[20] There was agreement early on in the preparatory meetings that preceded the Geneva Diplomatic Conference that the duration of performers' moral rights should be the same as that accorded to authors: Memorandum Prepared by the International Bureau of WIPO, above n 17, [34].

in the WPPT was not unconditionally welcomed at the Geneva Diplomatic Conference.[21] The restriction of the application of the moral rights provisions may have been a gesture of conciliation to those delegations that opposed moral rights.

VI CONCLUSIONS

In this chapter, the provisions in the three international instruments relating to the duration of performers' rights were considered. The answer to the question of the term of protection has tended to favour the interests of right holders over the interests of users of performances. In respect of the term in years of those rights, the provisions are quite specific: the term of protection under the Rome Convention is 20 years and under TRIPS and the WPPT it is 50 years. The provisions are less specific as to the retroactive application of the rights.

The most important issue concerning the duration of performers' rights is the extension of the term of those rights. The increasing sophistication of the technology of exploitation is a factor that has been raised in justification of an extended term of protection for performers. In other words, so the argument goes, because technology can extend the commercial life of a fixed performance, performers need protection for the term of that extended life.[22] However, the flaw in this argument is that it pre-supposes that performers will retain their rights in a performance for the commercial life of that performance, something that seems quite unlikely.

The other argument cited in favour of extending the term of protection is the need for international harmonisation.[23] If this argument is accepted, it will mean that the term of performers' rights will gradually increase without any evidence that the increased term will benefit performers, producers or the public. It seems that the most likely impact of an increased term of protection is to further limit the public's access to performances protected under the regime of rights. It is suggested that there is a real need to debate the merits of extending the term of protection beyond 20 years.

[21] See the comments of the delegates from the United States, the United Kingdom and Australia: 'Summary Minutes', above n 1, [408], [409] and [434].
[22] Memorandum Prepared by the International Bureau of WIPO, above n 17, [77].
[23] Basic Proposal, above n 18, [21.06].

13

An Audiovisual Performances Treaty?

I INTRODUCTION

THE MODE OF exploitation of a performance, whether by means of audio or audiovisual media, should not affect the protection available for that performance. However, the analysis of the provisions of the three international instruments in the preceding chapters has shown that the level of protection afforded to performances in audiovisual media has been established at a significantly lower level than the protection afforded to performances in audio media.

The focal point of consideration in this chapter is the proposed audiovisual instrument that was the subject of discussion and negotiation at the Diplomatic Conference on the Protection of Audiovisual Performances in Geneva from 7 to 20 December 2000. The next section of this chapter describes the background to the proposed audiovisual instrument in the same manner used in the historical interlude to describe the background to the Rome Convention and the other instruments. The main difference between the proposed audiovisual instrument and the WPPT was that the former made express provision for the transfer of the rights granted under the Treaty. The other substantive provisions were in the same language. The remainder of the chapter is, therefore, largely concerned with an analysis of those important transfer provisions.

II BACKGROUND

The deadlock over audiovisual performances that threatened the Geneva Diplomatic Conference was overcome by excluding those performances from the extended protection of the WPPT. This was a practical response and it enabled the WPPT to be concluded even if it denied protection to a considerable number of performers. However, the need for international protection for audiovisual performances was also recognised. A resolution adopted at the conclusion of the Diplomatic Conference stressed that there was an 'urgent need to agree on new norms for the adequate legal international protection of audiovisual performances.'[1] The next step in the international protection of performers' rights was therefore to prepare an instrument that would fill the gap in protection, either as a protocol to the WPPT or as a separate treaty. A series of meetings were convened in Geneva, beginning in September 1997 and culminating in April 2000, and regional consultations were held in the regions or in Geneva. Finally, an Extraordinary Session of the WIPO General Assembly approved the convening of a Diplomatic Conference on the Protection of Audiovisual Performances in Geneva from 7 to 20 December 2000.

The provisions of the proposed new instrument were set out in the Basic Proposal for the Substantive Provisions of an Instrument on the Protection of Audiovisual Performances to be considered by the Diplomatic Conference ('audiovisual basic proposal').[2] The delegations attending the Conference were able to reach 'provisional agreement' on 19 out of the 20 articles in the audiovisual basic proposal. However, the fundamental issue of the transfer of rights proved to be too great a stumbling block, and the Diplomatic Conference closed without adopting the new audiovisual instrument.

The Diplomatic Conference did note that 'provisional agreement has been reached on 19 Articles', and recommended to the Assemblies of the Member States of WIPO that they should reconvene the Diplomatic Conference for the purpose of reaching agreement on outstanding issues.[3] The WIPO General Assembly, meeting in Geneva, 24 September to 3 October 2001, was therefore invited to discuss the recommendation and to decide whether the Conference should be reconvened. Neither the European Community nor the United States, the two main protagonists at the Conference, spoke in favour of reconvening the Conference. The consensus of the meeting was that efforts to overcome differences should be progressed by informal meetings. The General Assembly decided that the issue should remain on the agenda of the General Assembly in 2002.[4] The future of the audiovisual instrument is therefore uncertain.

Another problem awaits delegates if the Diplomatic Conference is reconvened sometime in the future, for the effect of reaching 'provisional agreement' is not clear. Provisional agreement is not final agreement and while it can be

[1] 'Resolution Concerning Audiovisual Performances Adopted by the Diplomatic Conference on December 20, 1996' CRNR/DC/99 (Diplomatic Conference on Certain Copyright and Neighboring Rights Questions, Geneva, 2 to 20 December 1996).

[2] Chairman of the Standing Committee on Copyright and Related Rights, 'Basic Proposal for the Substantive Provisions of an Instrument on the Protection of Audiovisual Performances to be Considered by the Diplomatic Conference' IAVP/DC/3 ('Audiovisual Basic Proposal') (Diplomatic Conference on the Protection of Audiovisual Performances, Geneva, 7 to 20 December 2000).

[3] Memorandum of the Director General, 'Diplomatic Conference on the Protection of Audiovisual Performances' A/36/9 (Assemblies of the Member States of WIPO, Thirty-Sixth Series of Meetings, Geneva, 24 September to 3 October 2001).

[4] 'General Report Adopted by the Assemblies' A/36/15 (Assemblies of the Member States of WIPO, Thirty-Sixth Series of Meetings, Geneva, 24 September to 3 October 2001) [170]–[185].

presumed that there will be no desire to re-open negotiations on the articles on which such agreement was reached, that option is still a possibility.

III THE AUDIOVISUAL BASIC PROPOSAL

The preamble to the audiovisual basic proposal set out the objective of the new instrument as being: 'to develop and maintain the protection of the rights of performers in their audiovisual performances'. It then went on to recognise the need for 'new international rules' particularly in view of 'the development and convergence of information and communication technologies on the production and use of audiovisual performances.'[5]

The audiovisual basic proposal was unique for three reasons: it represented the first time an attempt had been made to solve the problems of audiovisual performers; it was the first time that a transfer provision had formed part of an international instrument concerned with performers' rights; and, it was also the first time that performers' rights, on their own, had been the subject matter of a proposed international instrument.[6]

A General Features of the Audiovisual Basic Proposal

The audiovisual basic proposal followed the model of the basic proposal that had formed the basis of the WPPT. It was drafted in the form of administrative and final provisions and included 'alternative solutions' in a number of places. The provisions of the audiovisual basic proposal largely repeated, *mutatis mutandis*, the provisions of the WPPT. This is understandable, given that the objective of extending protection to audiovisual performances stemmed from and responded to essentially the same technological developments that led to the WPPT. (The definitions were naturally different.[7]) The rights to be accorded to audiovisual performers therefore included the same rights that had been accorded to performers in their audio performances. Those rights, which have been discussed in the preceding chapters were moral rights; economic rights of performers in their unfixed performances; right of reproduction; right of distribution; right of rental; right of making available of fixed performances; right of

[5] Audiovisual Basic Proposal, above, n 2.

[6] Apart from performers, both the Rome Convention and TRIPS are concerned with the protection of broadcasters and phonogram producers; the WPPT is concerned with the protection of performers and phonogram producers.

[7] For example, 'fixation' in Art 2(c) of the WPPT is restricted to 'the embodiment of sounds'; the equivalent definition agreed by the Diplomatic Conference referred to 'audiovisual fixation' as meaning 'the embodiment of moving images, whether or not accompanied by sounds'. See Art 2(b) of the Draft WIPO Audiovisual Performances Treaty presented to the Assemblies of the Member States, Memorandum of the Director General, above n 3.

broadcasting and communication to the public. Other substantive provisions, including the duration of the rights and the limitations, exceptions and reservations to those rights reflected the provisions of the WPPT. If an international instrument had been agreed at the Diplomatic Conference in 2000, it would therefore have brought audiovisual performers, at the international level, up to the same level of protection accorded to audio performers.[8]

Although there were several areas on which agreement could not be guaranteed, including national treatment and the right of broadcasting and communication to the public, the most contentious issue at the Conference was always going to be the transfer of the economic rights.[9] The official position of the two most important delegations, the European Community and the United States, was that they supported the negotiation of a new international instrument. However, they were far apart in respect of the management of the economic rights that would be granted under the instrument, specifically in respect of the transfer of those rights.

The position adopted by the European Community and its Member States has been consistently based on principle: the international protection of performers' rights should cover both audio and audiovisual performances; and the content and scope of the rights in audiovisual performances should be similar to those granted under the WPPT to performers in their audio performances.[10] This position was reaffirmed in the Introductory Speech made by the delegate for the European Community at the Diplomatic Conference in 2000:

> The European Community and its Member States wish to reaffirm the utmost relevance of the protection of audiovisual performances, particularly in the digital environment. We reiterate our attachment to solutions that should provide for an updated and high level of protection and allow the necessary flexibility to be acceptable to all

[8] In at least one aspect, protection would actually have been greater. Under Art 15(1) of the WPPT, performers are provided with a right of equitable remuneration in respect of the direct or indirect use of phonograms for broadcasting or communication to the public. The equivalent provision agreed upon by the Diplomatic Conference in 2000 would have provided performers with an exclusive right to authorise the broadcasting or communication to the public of their performances fixed in audiovisual fixations, although Contracting Parties could notify WIPO that they would instead establish a right to equitable remuneration. See Arts 11(1) and 11(2) of the Draft WIPO Audiovisual Performances Treaty presented to the Assemblies of the Member States, Memorandum of the Director General, above n 3.

[9] The provision relating to national treatment that was agreed upon by the Diplomatic Conference included a provision that permitted the application of material reciprocity in respect of the exclusive right of broadcasting and communication to the public or the right of equitable remuneration. There is no equivalent provision in the WPPT. See Arts 4(2), 11(1) and 11(2) of the Draft WIPO Audiovisual Performances Treaty which was presented to the Assemblies of the Member States as part of the Memorandum of the Director General, above n 3.

[10] For example, see the statement made to the Diplomatic Conference in 1996, Summary Minutes, Main Committee I of the Diplomatic Conference on Certain Copyright and Neighboring Rights Questions CRNR/DC/102 ('Summary Minutes') (Diplomatic Conference on Certain Copyright and Neighboring Rights Questions, Geneva, 2 to 20 December 1996) [469]: '[Mr Reinbothe] said that his Delegation believed that no distinction and no discrimination should be made between performers' rights with respect to sound performances and audiovisual performances.'

> countries, and, at the same time, avoid any unjustified differentiation on the basis of the nature of the performance.[11]

The position taken by the United States has also been consistent—it has emphasised the need to provide certainty for audiovisual producers and the need to determine when and how exclusive rights are to be transferred from the performer to the producer. The issues raised by audiovisual productions were summed up in a submission by the United States to the WIPO Standing Committee on Copyright and Related Rights on the subject of the transfer of performers' rights.

> Unlike literary or musical works, audiovisual works involve contributions of many different individuals who may be of different nationalities. In addition, audiovisual works are increasingly produced and financed across national borders which makes consistency and certainty of transfer and rights ownership rules extremely important.[12]

Since the discussions at the Diplomatic Conference in 1996 that resulted in the WPPT, the United States has sponsored the proposition that extended protection should be accorded to performers of audiovisual performances only if such protection was subject to a presumption of the transfer of the economic rights by a performer to the producer of an audiovisual fixation.[13]

As it turned out, provisional agreement was reached on all the provisions, bar the transfer provision, in a form that reflected the WPPT. The following discussion is therefore restricted to the alternative solutions relating to the transfer of the economic rights.

B The Transfer Provision

The importance of balancing the overarching objective of improving the international rules and norms governing the protection of audiovisual performers against the producers' need for legal certainty in the production and distribution of audiovisual works was addressed in Article 12 of the audiovisual basic proposal. This was drafted in the form of Alternatives E to H.[14] The solutions varied from one extreme of a rebuttable presumption of transfer of the performers' economic rights to the producers of the audiovisual works to the other extreme of having no transfer provision in the instrument at all.

[11] Introductory Speech of the European Community to the Diplomatic Conference: <http://europa.eu.int/comm/internal_market/en/intprop/intprop/news/diplomat.htm>.

[12] 'Submission of the United States of America on Transfer', Submitted by the United States of America, SCCR/4/4 (Standing Committee on Copyright and Related Rights, Fourth Session, Geneva, 11 12 and 14 April 2000) [2].

[13] Summary Minutes, above n 10 [465] and [466].

[14] Alternatives A and B were alternative solutions to 'Art 1: Relation to Other Conventions and Treaties'; Alternatives C and D were alternative solutions to 'Art 4: National Treatment'.

—Alternative E: **Transfer**

> Once a performer has consented to the incorporation of his performance in an audiovisual fixation, he shall be deemed to have transferred all exclusive rights of authorization provided for in this Treaty with respect to that particular fixation to its producer, subject to written contractual clauses to the contrary.

Alternative E was the option that the United States backed and it reflected that country's emphasis on the need for certainty for producers within its cinematographic film industry. Performers in American films are usually employed on a 'work made for hire' basis under which the producer, as the employer, is considered to be the author of any work and therefore owns all of the rights comprised in the copyright.[15] The 'work made for hire' doctrine reflects arguments raised by the cinematographic film industry that: (i) It is impossible to identify all the people who make creative contributions to a film. (ii) The producer is the one who makes the financial investment and carries the corresponding risks. The application of the doctrine to performers' rights would serve to ensure that all the intellectual property rights would be assembled in the hands of the producer.

Under Alternative E, a performer who has consented to the incorporation of a performance in an audiovisual fixation is deemed to have transferred his or her exclusive rights with relation to that particular fixation to its producer. The concept of a rebuttable presumption of transfer has been criticised by performers' organisations as being unfair to performers and as forcing some states to reduce the level of protection of audiovisual performers.[16] However, an analysis of the provision demonstrates that it does have limitations. (i) The transfer of rights is only triggered by the performer when he or she consents to the incorporation of a performance in an audiovisual fixation. (ii) The presumption of transfer is restricted to the exclusive rights of authorisation in the audiovisual basic proposal; it does not extend to a right of remuneration or to moral rights. (iii) The

[15] §201(b) of the Copyright Act 1976 (US). The alleged consequence of including performers whose performances are exploited in audiovisual media as right holders in the WPPT has been described in a leading American copyright text in the following words: 'That inclusion could have wrought havoc to the Hollywood studio community, given that performers in American movies typically function on a work for hire basis by which all copyright interest inures to the benefit of the pertinent studio.' D Nimmer, 'A Tale of Two Treaties Dateline: Geneva—December 1996' in M Nimmer and D Nimmer, *Nimmer on Copyright: A Treatise on the Law of Literary, Musical and Artistic Property and the Protection of Ideas* (Mathew Bender, New York, 1978–Release 42–6/97) 24. The footnotes to this quotation have been omitted.

[16] See the comments of Mr Hoberg-Petersen, the representative of FIA, Summary Minutes, (Main Committee I), IAVP/DC/37 ('Audiovisual Summary Minutes') (Diplomatic Conference on the Protection of Audiovisual Performances, Geneva, 7 to 20 December 2000) [262]. However, prior to the Diplomatic Conference, the United States claimed that its proposal enjoyed 'the wide support of performers, producers and distributors in the U.S.'. See the statement on the transfer of rights in: Agenda Item 4: Protection of Audiovisual Performances, 'Submission of the United States', SCCR/3/7 (Standing Committee on Copyright and Related Rights, Third Session, Geneva, 16 to 20 November 1999).

presumption of transfer is rebuttable; it is subject to a written agreement to the contrary. (iv) The performer's rights in respect of the exploitation of a live performance are unaffected.

The most telling criticism of the rebuttable presumption of transfer can be stated simply: it would change the effect of the economic rights provisions from the protection of performers to the protection of producers. (The EC has stated on a number of occasions that the purpose in negotiating an instrument protecting audiovisual performances was to protect performers and not to provide protection for producers.[17]) A further criticism of this provision was that, in many countries, it would require a change to domestic law. On another level, a presumption of transfer can be also criticised for placing the onus on performers to be aware of the law and aware of their ability to contract out of the provision. It therefore forces the performer to be the one that raises the issue in any contractual negotiations. This would place extra pressure on performers who are already in a weak bargaining position.

—Alternative F: **Entitlement to Exercise Rights**

> In the absence of written contractual clauses to the contrary, once the performer has consented to the audiovisual fixation of his performance, the producer shall be deemed to be entitled to exercise the exclusive rights of authorization provided for in this Treaty with respect to that particular fixation.

Alternative F was based on Article 14*bis*(2) of the Berne Convention which provides for a rule, known as 'the presumption of legitimation', covering the interpretation of contracts relating to cinematographic works and the exploitation of those works.[18] Alternative F goes further than Article 14*bis*(2), for it provides for a 'presumption of entitlement'—namely, that the producer is entitled to exercise the rights accorded to the performer. The performer, however, retains ownership of the rights. Other features of this alternative are: (i) The presumption is subject to the provisions of an applicable contract in writing. (ii) It takes effect when the performer consents to the audiovisual fixation of a particular performance. (iii) The presumption only applies to the exclusive rights of authorisation in the audiovisual basic proposal; it does not extend to a right of

[17] See the statement on the transfer of rights in: Agenda Item 4: Protection of Audiovisual Performances, 'Further Submission by the European Community and its Member States on a Protocol Concerning Audiovisual Performances', SCCR/2/3 (Standing Committee on Copyright and Related Rights, Second Session, Geneva, 4 to 11 May 1999) [2]; 'Submission on behalf of the European Community and its Member States on the Protection of Performers' Rights in Their Audiovisual Performances', SCCR/4/2 (Standing Committee on Copyright and Related Rights, Fourth Session, Geneva, 11 12 and 14 April 2000) [5]. In the Introductory Speech to the Diplomatic Conference, above n 11, the European Community labelled the mandatory transfer of performers' rights at international level as being 'unacceptable'.

[18] Alternative F did not include a similar provision to Art 14*bis*(3) which severely limits the application of the presumption of legitimation.

remuneration or to moral rights. (iv) It does not affect the performer's rights in respect of the exploitation of a live performance.

There are similarities between Alternative F and Alternative E and performers have levelled similar criticisms at this option.

> Alternative F carries with it all the injustice and adverse effects . . . regarding Alternative E. It will equally weaken the bargaining position of audiovisual performers and it will disrupt established contract patterns and force some States to lower existing levels of protection the same way as a presumption of transfer of rights.[19]

One way to read Alternative F is that it provides the producer with a degree of certainty without actually depriving the performer of the right to exercise the exclusive rights against other parties. The provision does not interfere with the freedom of the performer and producer to enter into a contract that transfers the exclusive rights, however it is friendlier to performers than Alternative E in that it shifts the burden onto the producer to initiate negotiations should the producer wish to have the certainty of acquiring those rights. Because the provision functions as a presumption, it is still incumbent on the performer to be aware of the applicable legal position.

—Alternative G: **Law Applicable to Transfers**

> (1) In the absence of contractual clauses to the contrary, a transfer to the producer of an audiovisual fixation of a performance, by agreement or operation of law, of any of the exclusive rights of authorization granted under this Treaty, shall be governed by the law of the country most closely connected with the particular audiovisual fixation.[20]

Alternative G represented an attempt to formulate a compromise that would allow the greatest number of states to sign the instrument, including the states that are the most important sources of audiovisual works.[21] The provision recognised that performers' economic rights in their audiovisual performances may be transferred and that such transfer may be provided for in domestic legislation. Nevertheless, it did not oblige contracting states to include transfer provisions in their legal systems. It is arguable that a contracting state may provide in its domestic legislation that performers' rights shall not be transferred or waived and still comply with a provision of this nature.

[19] International Federation of Actors 'Comments on the WIPO Basic Proposal prepared for the Diplomatic Conference, December 2000': <http://www.fia-actors.com/new/wipo_2000_comments_eng.htm>.

[20] The 'law of the country most closely connected to the audiovisual fixation' is determined by three points of attachment set out in para (2) of Alternative G: the contracting state in which the producer has its headquarters or habitual residence; the contracting state of which the majority of the performers are nationals; the principal contracting state in which the photography takes place.

[21] Alternative G was the option favoured by certain performers and broadcasters. This is clear from the statements of the representatives of FIA and the Association of Commercial Television in Europe ('ACT'), Audiovisual Summary Minutes, above n 16, [262] and [276].

In contrast to Alternatives E and F, Alternative G did not require contracting states to amend their domestic laws. Other salient features of this alternative include: (i) It is subject to a contractual arrangement to the contrary. (ii) The transfer of rights can be achieved by agreement (but not necessarily agreement in writing) or by operation of law (such as a statutory presumption of transfer). (iii) It is restricted to the exclusive rights granted under the instrument and therefore does not include any right of remuneration or moral rights. (iv) The transfer is governed by the law of the country most closely connected with the audiovisual fixation. (v) The proposed provision does not affect the performer's exploitation of a live performance.

The notes to Alternative G in the audiovisual basic proposal suggest that the provision is intended, in part, to provide business certainty.[22] In fact, the implementation in domestic law of Alternative G would be subject to the interpretation of the provision adopted by individual states. The rules relating to the country most closely related to the fixation could therefore lead to confusion and uncertainty for both performer and producer. For example, the headquarters or habitual residence of the producer is the principal point of attachment that determines the country most closely connected with the audiovisual fixation. As the term 'producer' is not defined, the drafting of this provision enables the producer to choose the country that the producer determines has the most appropriate legal system for his requirements.

—Alternative H: **No Such Provision**

> The alternative of having no provision concerning the transfer of rights is the approach taken in the WPPT and the other instruments that provide for performers' rights. In the absence of a transfer provision, a contracting state need not implement transfer provisions relating to performers' economic rights in domestic law but it would not be precluded from doing so.

This was the option favoured by the European Community.[23] It represented their stated position that the audiovisual instrument was intended to improve the protection of performers not the protection of producers and their aim that it should reflect, so far as practicable, the provisions of the WPPT. During the course of the Diplomatic Conference, the European Community backed down from its original position and proposed an amendment to Article 12 which recognised that contracting states could provide that exclusive rights of authorisation in respect of a specific audiovisual fixation could be transferred from the performer to the producer. The amendment also contained an agreed statement relating to Article 12, which drew on Alternative G, and which recognised

[22] Audiovisual Basic Proposal, above n 2, [12.13].
[23] Audiovisual Summary Minutes, above n 16, [346].

the right of contracting states to provide that performers' rights are inalienable and unwaivable.[24]

IV CONCLUSIONS

In essence, the arguments for and against the extended protection of audiovisual performances fall into two categories. (i) Optimists who advocate a principled approach that favours performers argue that a distinction in terms of protection cannot and should not be maintained between performances embodied in audiovisual fixations and performances embodied in audio fixations. The nature of an intellectual product, whether it is a performance or a work of authorship or an invention, should determine whether protection is available; that is, whether the performance or work or invention meets the qualifying factors for protection under the law. The means that are adopted to exploit the product should, in principle, be irrelevant. (ii) The arguments of pessimists against extending the rights of audiovisual performers to the level provided for audio performers are based on the need to ensure that producers of audiovisual fixations have legal certainty so that they can successfully exploit the performances embodied in those fixations. In the view of supporters of this argument, there are significant differences between the audio industry and the audiovisual industry, including different models of financing, production and exploitation that are said to justify different treatment.[25]

Although considerable progress towards a consensus had been made in the preparatory meetings, success at the Diplomatic Conference depended on a compromise being negotiated that would satisfy the European Community and the United States as the proponents of the two entrenched positions—the principled approach versus the demand for legal certainty—concerning the transfer of the economic rights. In the event, a successful compromise could not be achieved.

The failure to conclude a new instrument at the Diplomatic Conference devoted to the interests of performers was a disturbing outcome. Until then, the trend at an international level had been to provide performers with increased protection. For audiovisual performers, the failure of the Diplomatic Conference has established an unfortunate precedent of failure and their position has

[24] Proposal by the European Community and its Member States, 'Amendment to Art 12 of the Basic Proposal for the Substantive Provisions of an Instrument on the Protection of Audiovisual Performances to be Considered by the Diplomatic Conference', IAVP/DC/12 (Diplomatic Conference on the Protection of Audiovisual Performances, Geneva, 7 to 20 December 2000). The wording of Art 12 in the EC proposal was: 'Contracting Parties may provide that exclusive rights of authorization provided for in this Agreement are transferred, with respect to a particular audiovisual fixation, from the performer to the producer of that particular fixation.'

[25] The arguments for and against providing extended protection to audiovisual performances are discussed above, ch 4, n 63 and accompanying text.

been further weakened by the decision taken at the meeting of the WIPO General Assemblies, in effect, to put to one side the question of an audiovisual instrument.

Nevertheless, both performers and producers can take comfort from the achievements of the Diplomatic Conference. Agreement was reached that the scope of economic rights to be provided to audiovisual performers should reflect those in the WPPT; and it was agreed that audiovisual performers should be entitled to moral rights. Producers have gained international recognition of the importance of the transfer of those rights; it now remains for the international community to decide on an appropriate transfer system to be established on an international basis.

Unfortunately for those who support protection for audiovisual performers, other developments have undermined the need for another international instrument. The Screen Actors Guild and the American Federation of Television and Radio Artists, on the one hand, and the Alliance of Motion Picture and Television Producers, on the other hand, have recently negotiated a new motion picture and television production agreement.[26] The success of these negotiations demonstrated that if performers are properly organised they can achieve domestic protection under collective bargaining agreements on a level that equates to the protection provided for in the international instruments.

There are, however, major problems with depending on collective agreements to achieve protection: (i) Performers have to be sufficiently organised to be able to exercise sufficient bargaining power and even that is not a guarantee of success.[27] (ii) Even if performers are able to achieve their aims by way of negotiation with producers, the control of the exploitation of their performances that performers are able to achieve by this means will be limited to control over the activities of parties to any agreements. (iii) Unless foreign performers are members of unions or guilds in other countries, they will not enjoy the benefit of agreements made with producers in those countries.

Collective agreements provide protection that is narrowly based. The purpose of international instruments such as the Rome Convention, TRIPS and the WPPT is not to prescribe the protection that states should accord to their own citizens. The purpose of those instruments is to provide for the protection of performers in states in which they are not citizens by establishing minimum standards of protection that contracting states may apply to the protection of the citizens of other states. If it is accepted that audiovisual performances should be protected at a higher level, and recent statements by both the

[26] Highlights of the agreement include: significant increases in basic cable residuals and new provisions for the Internet. Details of the agreement are available at: <http://www.sag.com>; <http://www.aftra.org>; <http://www.amptp.org>.

[27] Negotiations over a new system of cinematographic film payments between the United Kingdom entertainers' trade union, Equity, and the Producers Alliance for Cinema and Television, ('PACT') began in July 2000. They were unresolved as of December 2001. See Equity 'Films Dispute Latest', <http://www.equity.org.uk/actors_strike/index.htm>.

European Community and the United States are in agreement on this point,[28] then an adequate level of protection for foreign performers can only be achieved by means of an international instrument that provides protection that is international in scope, that provides uniform protection for performers in both the audio and audiovisual industries and that is effective. Unfortunately, there is nothing to suggest that a new audiovisual instrument would be any more successful than the WPPT in attracting signatories—particularly if it does not have the wholehearted support of both the European Community and the United States.[29]

As with other intellectual property rights, a balance must be established and maintained between creators and users. In the present context, the balance that needs to be established is between the rights to be accorded to performers to protect their performances and the interests that users, especially producers, have in exploiting the performances. Performers in audiovisual media would argue that the balance has been tipped in favour of users for too long, that such rights that they have been given have not been sufficient to meet the challenges of technology; and that until there is protection for audiovisual performances, a balance does not, in fact, exist.

A solution to the impasse between the performer-friendly views represented by the European Community's position and the producer-friendly position of the United States needs to deliver consistency between the protection of audio and audiovisual performances as well as certainty to producers in respect of the exploitation of performances. However, the prospects for meaningful protection of audiovisual performances are not great. Until a new instrument is concluded, the gap in the international protection of performers will continue to exist. The highpoint of the protection of audiovisual performances is defined by the Rome Convention, an instrument that did not adequately take account of the technology of its time, let alone the technology of the twenty-first century.

[28] In its final statement to the Diplomatic Conference, the United States delegation stated that it 'would continue in its commitment as it had been at the Diplomatic Conference, in sincerity, good faith, with good will and no hidden agenda to participate in the process of providing better protection for audiovisual performances.' Summary Minutes, (Plenary), IAVP/DC/36 (Diplomatic Conference on the Protection of Audiovisual Performances, Geneva, 7 to 20 December 2000) [103]. In a statement issued by the European Commission immediately after the Diplomatic Conference concluded, dated 20 December 2000, it was stated that: 'The European Community and its Member States remain faithful to the Resolution adopted in 1996, calling for the WPPT . . . to be complemented by an international instrument on the protection of audiovisual performers.' European Commission 'Commission Regrets Conference on the Protection of Audiovisual Performance's Failure to Conclude Treaty' <http://europa.eu.int/comm/internal_market/en/intprop/intprop/news/geneva.htm.>

[29] The WPPT finally entered into force on May 20, 2002. The major contracting state is the United States: World Intellectual Property Office, 'Intellectual Property Treaties' <http://www.wipo.org/treaties/ip/wppt/index.html>

Part IV

Conclusions

14

Conclusions

I INTRODUCTION

IN THIS, THE final chapter, the conclusions that can be drawn from this study of performers' rights will be summarised, first, in respect of the chapters in Part II, and then in respect of the chapters in Part III. Next, three specific problems identified in the discussion will be examined. The final task is to answer the question of the appropriateness of the system of performers' rights.

II CONCLUSIONS FROM PART II

In Part II, the basis for a system of rights that protects performers in states other than their own state of origin was put to the test. This involved questioning the two fundamental propositions that provide the foundations for performers' rights: (i) that performers face a problem of a lack of control; and (ii) that the correct solution lies in providing them with a system of rights that has international effect.

The subject matter to which the rights of protection extend in a system of performers' rights is a key consideration. The first question to be answered required an analysis of the current definitions of 'performance'. Those definitions were found to be lacking as definitions to be included in an international system of performers' rights. In answering the next question, why should they be protected, performers were called upon to justify their entitlement to a specific regime of rights—particularly in light of other protection that is available to them. Then followed a series of questions from whom or what do performers need protection, how should they be protected, where should that protection be available and how long should it last? In answering those questions, the origins of performers' rights were placed in the context of the relationship between performances and technological development. The technology of exploitation has enabled an increasing number of people—producers, bootleggers, pirates and consumers—to use performances in ways that performers have found difficult to control. From there, another series of questions examined the availability of other protection, the nature of a performer and the ownership of performers' rights were given. The current definitions of 'performers' were analysed and they were found to be inadequate for the purposes of inclusion in an international system of performers' rights.

The discussion in Part II led, therefore, to a number of important conclusions:

(i) All performances that meet the criteria of a principled definition should be protected, irrespective of factors such as the quality or merits of the performance, the content or the nature of the material that is presented, or the status of the performer. An associated conclusion was that performers perform performances; they can be identified by their performances and they should be defined by reference to their performances.

(ii) The natural right theory provides the strongest argument in favour of a regime of protection for performers. The theory that performers' rights provide an economic incentive to the production of performances was found to be wanting.

(iii) The proposition that performers need protection was confirmed. It was clear that, with the development of the means of fixing performances and of broadcasting and communicating them to the public, performers had lost control of the uses that are made of their performances which, in a commercial sense, had become commodities. The technology of exploitation is such that performers must be protected on an international basis.

(iv) Even without the implementation of statutory performers' rights, performers are already protected in a number of ways. The main forms of protection overlap with one another and together provide significant levels of protection. The problems involved in qualifying for that protection mean, however, that most performers can legitimately claim that those other forms of protection do not provide them with complete protection.

(v) As a corollary to the conclusions summarised in paragraphs (ii) and (iv), performers' rights should be accepted as a species of intellectual property rights. Performances meet the essential requirements for protection under such rights, being original products of the intellectual efforts of their makers. However, while there is an expectation that performers' rights will be implemented as exclusive rights, this is not an obligation under the Rome Convention or TRIPS.

(vi) Although there are other claimants to first ownership of performers' rights, performers should be recognised as the first right holders. A preferred element of a system of performers' rights is that the economic rights should be freely transferable.

In short, it can be concluded that performers face a serious problem that transcends national boundaries; therefore, the solution must address the problem on an international scale. That solution is to provide performers with a system of intellectual property rights that will enable them to control the uses that are made of their performances in states in which they are foreigners. Having established the need for protection and having discussed the issues that arise when such protection is made available, the investigation shifted to the analysis of the international instruments.

III CONCLUSIONS FROM PART III

In Part III, a detailed analysis was made of the performers' rights provisions in the Rome Convention, TRIPS and the WPPT, to determine how well they dealt with the issues raised in Part II. (The failed attempt to provide protection for audiovisual performances was also considered.) The conclusions from the analysis in chapters 7 to 13 have been grouped together and discussed below under three inter-related headings: 'International Protection', 'Uniform Protection' and 'Effective Protection'. Apart from those general findings, three specific problem areas were revealed which relate to the effectiveness and the uniformity of the protection provided by the three international instruments. This section of the chapter concludes with a discussion of those problem areas: audiovisual performances; ownership; and performances.

A International Protection

The technology of exploitation is such that efforts to ensure the protection of performers must take into account the ease with which both fixed and unfixed performances can be exploited across the globe. Performers should therefore be protected in other states as well as in their state of origin. Protection on an international scale can only be achieved by agreements between states. The question is raised whether the existing protection of performers is truly international. Obviously, the obligations under an international instrument are binding only on those states that have become parties to that instrument. The first step, therefore, is to consider the status of the international instruments.

As of 15 October 2001, 68 states have become parties to the Rome Convention; as of 1 January 2002, there was 144 Members of the WTO; the WPPT entered into force on 20 May 2002, that is three months after the deposit by 30 states of their instruments of ratification or accession.[1] Using the number of states that have become parties to the instruments as a measure, TRIPS (as an Annex to the WTO Agreement) is by far the most successful. Even so, while one might say that TRIPS provides international coverage, it cannot be called global. Important states, including the Russian Federation, are not yet Members of the WTO. It is also useful to remember that apart from the duration of

[1] WIPO, 'Intellectual Property Treaties' <http://www.wipo.org/eng/main.htm>; World Trade Organisation, 'Trading into the Future: The Introduction to the WTO' <http://www.wto.org/english/thewto_e/whatis_e/tif_e/tif_e.htm>.

performers' rights, the obligations under TRIPS are set at the lowest level of the three instruments. As for the other two instruments, they have been less successful. Although they provide a higher level of protection, the number of states that have become parties to the Rome Convention has always been an issue of concern.[2]

There will probably always be a conflict between the objective of obtaining the agreement of as many states as possible to becoming parties to the international instruments and the objective that protection should be uniform and set at a particular level. The inability or the refusal of some states to meet the requirement to implement that level of protection can have one of two consequences: (i) principles prevail and the states that promote a standard of protection successfully insist that the standard is maintained with the consequence that the numbers of states that become parties to an instrument is reduced; or (ii) pragmatism prevails and, in the interests of encouraging the agreement of as many states as possible, principles are compromised by allowing the standard of protection to be reduced.

Another reason for the failure to gain wider international protection for performers is that the protection of performers is not an issue that has been eagerly taken up by many states. The importance of State A becoming a party to an instrument like the Rome Convention is that it requires other contracting states to protect performers who are nationals of State A. If, however, State A is not concerned to obtain protection for its performers either at home or abroad, then there is no incentive to become a party to the Rome Convention. Smaller states are usually net importers of performers and fixed performances. For those states, the benefits of the protection of its performers overseas and the obligations to protect the performers of other Members under Article 14 of TRIPS came with the other benefits that Membership of the WTO conferred.[3] After all, the TRIPS Agreement came into being within the framework of the GATT.

Although the above findings paint a gloomy picture of the international protection of performers, some comfort can be taken from the fact that it is something that tends to improve over time—that is, as time goes on, more states will

[2] The issues with ratification of the Rome Convention were raised in fora such as the Committees of Experts that met before the conclusion of the Satellites Convention: 'Report of the Second Committee of Governmental Experts on Problems in the Field of Performers, Producers of Phonograms and Broadcasting Organizations Raised by Transmission Via Space Satellite' (Paris, 9 to 17 May 1972) (1972) *Copyright* 142.

[3] As an example of a small, developed state, prior to meeting its obligations under TRIPS, there was no provision for performers' rights in New Zealand legislation. In a paper published in 1989, the Department of Justice, which administers the copyright legislation in New Zealand, concluded that no need for performers' rights legislation had been shown: Law Reform Division, Law Reform Division, New Zealand Department of Justice, *The Copyright Act 1962—Options for Reform* (Department of Justice, Wellington, 1989) [10.11]. The United Kingdom and Australia are parties to the Rome Convention and had provided for performers' rights before the adoption of the WTO Agreement.

become parties to the various instruments and performers will be protected in a greater number of states.

B Uniform Protection

The Preamble to the WPPT refers to the development and maintenance of the protection of the rights of performers 'in a manner as effective and uniform as possible'. The concepts of effective protection and uniform protection are borrowed from the Preamble to the Berne Convention.[4] Uniform protection for performers assumes that where international protection for performers is available, all the states that are parties to the relevant agreement will provide the same range of rights to the performers of other contracting states. For a number of reasons the ideal of uniform international protection has not been achieved for performers. Those reasons are as follows:

(i) The three international instruments all have Rome-style national treatment. Contracting states are obliged to provide the performers of other states with the same protection that they provide to their own performers, but this protection is subject to a number of limitations: (a) Performers must meet the requisite criteria of eligibility and the definition of 'performers' in those instruments. (b) The obligation is to provide only the protection that is specified in the respective instruments. (c) The protection provided by the Rome Convention and TRIPS is subject to any limitations, exceptions or reservations permitted in the instrument in question; the fact that the WPPT is different in this respect is another factor that may affect the uniformity of protection. The elements of Rome-style national treatment mean that the national law of contracting states will vary according to the use that is made of the permitted limitations and exceptions and of the reservations. The result is that the protection available to foreign performers is uneven. Another result is that a state does not necessarily protect foreign performers in the same way that it protects its own nationals: it may grant foreigners protection at a higher or lower level.

(ii) The likelihood of uniform protection is also reduced because interpretation of the provisions in the instruments has not been standardised. Indeed, the Rome Convention and TRIPS invite a variety of interpretations

[4] Chairman of the Committees of Experts on a Possible Protocol to the Berne Convention and on a Possible Instrument for the Protection of the Rights of Performers and Producers of Phonograms, 'Basic Proposal for the Substantive Provisions of the Treaty for the Protection of Performers and Producers of Phonograms to be Considered by the Diplomatic Conference' CRNR/DC/5 ('Basic Proposal') (Diplomatic Conference on Certain Copyright and Neighbouring Rights Questions, 2 to 20 December Geneva, 1996) [0.03].

of the obligation to protect performers. It was noted in the discussion of Article 7(1) of the Rome Convention that the phrase, the 'possibility of preventing', was adopted to enable the United Kingdom to accede to the Convention and to implement it by providing protection in the form of criminal sanctions. By way of comparison, Section 2 of the Model Law on performers' rights, which provides a framework for states that wish to implement the Rome Convention, provides for exclusive rights.[5] The Rome Convention also invites an interpretation that will result in implementation of its provisions that differs from state to state. Apart from the conventional minima, which are mandatory, there are provisions that are permissive. The most notable of the latter is Article 9, which permits states to extend protection to performers who do not perform literary or artistic works.[6]

(iii) Finally, uniformity of protection is an objective that is unlikely to be achieved because there are three instruments and the levels of protection will differ from state to state depending on whether or not a state is a party to a particular instrument. The potential unevenness of the protection available to foreign performers can be demonstrated simply by considering which states are parties to which instruments.

What is the consequence of Rome-style national treatment? The protection that is available for performers is uneven, but at least there is some protection. At various points in this thesis, a pragmatic approach to the level of protection available to performers has been advocated. Because national treatment is such a contentious issue, it is again suggested that performers should be happy with what they have got. Apart from improved protection for performances exploited in audiovisual media, it is unrealistic to expect any better.

C Effective Protection

As noted above, the Preamble to the WPPT also borrows the concept of effective protection from the Preamble to the Berne Convention. What does 'effective protection' mean?

5 The Intergovernmental Committee of the International Convention for the Protection of Performers, Producers of Phonograms and Broadcasting Organisations done at Rome in 1961, *Model Law Concerning the Protection of Performers, Producers of Phonograms and Broadcasting Organisations with a Commentary on it* (ILO, UNESCO, WIPO; Geneva and Paris, 1974).

6 This point was given a culinary flavour by Masouye: 'As well as the basic *table d'hôte* menu—the conventional minima—there exist *à la carte* provisions which allow each country a choice of the obligations which it must undertake.' C Masouye (W Wallace trans), *Guide to the Rome Convention and to the Phonograms Convention* (World Intellectual Property Organisation, Geneva, 1981) [XXI].

In his commentary on the Berne Convention, Masouye suggests that by including a reference to 'effective protection' the delegates who negotiated the Convention sought to provide 'a high level of protection.'[7] Elsewhere, the term 'more effective' has been construed to mean:

> that the norms (standards) of protection are raised, where necessary, to the required level and that the enforcement of the intellectual property rights will be easier and the sanctions for infringement stricter.[8]

It is submitted that the second construction given to 'effective' should be followed. The effectiveness of a treaty should not be measured by whether it provides a high level of protection: it may be that performers require only a low level of protection. It will always be difficult to determine whether the level of protection is set too high, whether it is too low or whether it correctly balances the interests of performers against those of consumers and other users of performances. Protection is more likely to be viewed as being out of balance, however, if it is set too high than if it is set at a low level. The conventional minima form a floor beneath which contracting states must not go, subject to the implementation of permitted limitations and exceptions and to the declaration of reservations where they are permitted. But if the minimum level is too high, there is the risk that the rights will be viewed as overly burdensome. If the minimum level is set too low, it is always open to a contracting state to provide a higher level of protection than is provided for in the instrument or instruments to which it is a party.

Bearing in mind the importance of finding the correct level of protection, two general comments can be made about protection under the international instruments:

(i) The right to authorise or to prohibit the use of a performance overlaps with other protection, such as contract or copyright, that is wider in some respects than the protection available under a performer's exclusive right. Does this matter? If performers can justify protection then the source of that protection does not matter. It only matters if performers' rights merely duplicate other forms of protection, for then they add another and unnecessary layer of rights that leads to compliance costs for users. Performers' rights should correct a problem that is not otherwise addressed. Another consideration is that rights that are specifically intended to correct a problem, such as the effect of technology, should be simple and be able to be easily applied.

[7] C Masouye (W Wallace trans,) *Guide to the Berne Convention for the Protection of Literary and Artistic Works (Paris Act, 1971)* (World Intellectual Property Organisation, Geneva, 1978) [0.2].

[8] International Bureau of WIPO, 'Note, Committee of Experts on Model Provisions for Legislation in the Field of Copyright, First Session' (Geneva, 20 February to 3 March 1989) (1989) *Copyright* 146, 147.

(ii) The WPPT sets new standards for the protection of foreign performers. Apart from the narrow protection for performances exploited in audiovisual media, it cannot be said that the level of protection for performers is set too low in the WPPT. The bundle of rights in that Treaty includes all the important rights that are provided in the WCT—for example, the right of rental, the right of distribution and the right of making available. Have performers been accorded rights at too high a level? If performers' economic rights are transferable, one answer is that the level at which those rights is set is not an issue, because the majority of performers will be under pressure to transfer those rights to the producer. Even where rights are inalienable, performers will be under pressure to enter into arrangements that fetter the exercise of those rights; in most circumstances, this will entail the consent to a use of a performance that would otherwise be unlawful. Another answer is that the greater the scope of the rights, the greater the concessions that performers will be able to extract from producers because of their increased bargaining power. On this basis, performers can rightly argue that rights have not been set at too high a level.

D Specific Problems

1 *Audiovisual Performances*

It was suggested in an earlier chapter that, in principle, there should be no distinction between the protection available to performances exploited in audiovisual media and performances exploited in audio media.[9] However, the analysis of the international instruments disclosed that none of the international instruments deals adequately with the question of the protection of performances exploited in audiovisual media.

In respect of unfixed performances, protection for audiovisual performances can be summarised as consisting of limited rights for performers to control the broadcasting and the communication to the public of their performances where the activity is done without their consent.[10] Under the Rome Convention alone, performers are also granted the possibility of preventing the first fixation of a performance in audio and audiovisual media.[11]

In respect of fixed performances, protection is even more restricted. It is found only in the Rome Convention, which provides protection against the reproduction and the broadcasting and communication to the public of

[9] See ch 4 and the discussion of 'Performances Exploited in Audiovisual Media'.
[10] Art 7(1)(a) of the Rome Convention; Art 14(1) of TRIPS; Art 6(i) of the WPPT.
[11] Art 7(1)(b) of the Rome Convention.

performances fixed in audiovisual media.[12] The effectiveness of that protection is reduced by limitations in other provisions of the Convention, including the exclusion of protection for performances exploited by the cinematographic film industry.[13] The fact that Article 7 of the Rome Convention, the first of the international instruments, grants primary rights to performers in respect of their performances fixed in audiovisual media makes it that much harder to justify the exclusion of those performances from protection under TRIPS and the WPPT. Yet in neither TRIPS nor the WPPT is there any form of protection for audiovisual fixations of performances.

In an era marked by the convergence of technology, failing to provide rights in performances fixed in audiovisual media is an increasingly difficult position for the law to take. There was an opportunity at the Geneva Diplomatic Conference to provide comprehensive protection for audiovisual performances; the opportunity was rejected and the WPPT provides protection only for performances fixed in phonograms, to the exclusion of audiovisual fixations. This result has rightly been described as 'an enormous defeat for the interests of performers.'[14] It is anomalous that an international instrument that was intended to bring protection of performers up to a level that took account of current technological developments should exclude performances exploited in audiovisual technology that has been in use for over a century.[15]

The shortcomings of the WPPT could have been resolved at the Diplomatic Conference on the Protection of Audiovisual Performances. However, the failure to conclude the proposed audiovisual instrument at that Conference left the international protection of audiovisual performances in a difficult situation, even though 'provisional agreement' was reached on nearly all of the provisions in the proposed instrument. The issue of transfer of ownership in the economic rights to be attached to those performances has, for the immediate future, stymied the likelihood of a higher level of international protection for audiovisual performances.

[12] Art 7(1)(c) of the Rome Convention.

[13] Art 19 of the Rome Convention.

[14] M Crosby, 'Performers and the WIPO Performances and Programs (sic) Treaty' in D Saunders and B Sherman (eds), *From Berne to Geneva—Recent Developments in International Copyright and Neighbouring Rights* (Australian Key Centre for Cultural and Media Policy, Nathan, Qld, 1997) 113. The scope of protection for performances under the WPPT is partly set by the definition of a phonogram in Art 2(b). It states: '"phonogram" means the fixation of the sounds of a performance or of other sounds, or of a representation of sounds, other than in the form of a fixation incorporated in a cinematographic or other audiovisual work'. The Agreed Statement in respect of Art 2(b) states: 'It is understood that the definition of phonogram provided in Art 2(b) does not suggest that rights in the phonogram are in any way affected through their incorporation into a cinematographic or other audiovisual work.'

[15] The Preamble to the WPPT refers to the need for new international rules to provide answers to 'the questions raised by economic, social, cultural and technological developments'. It goes on to refer to the impact of 'the development and convergence of information and communication technologies on the production and use of performances and phonograms'.

Moreover, it is to be regretted that the recognition of the need to protect audiovisual performances takes the form of developing yet another instrument that will form another layer of rights needing to be interpreted. While it has not yet been decided whether the new instrument, if it is concluded, will be a protocol to the WPPT or a stand-alone treaty, an audiovisual instrument will add to the problems of providing protection on an international scale, of uniform protection and of effective protection.

2 *Ownership*

Ownership of the economic rights and the transferability of those rights are not referred to in the international instruments, other than by way of a few oblique references. One can argue that performers are clearly the right holders and since the transfer of ownership of rights is not prohibited then it must be permitted. However, leaving the matter like this is unsatisfactory, because silence in a treaty does not promote uniform protection. In the absence of provisions as to the ownership of rights, it is always open to one state to make those rights transferable and for another to make them inalienable.

The fact that extensive rights go some way to redressing the imbalance of bargaining power between performers and producers is a good reason for their implementation. Performers' rights can form an important weapon for performers to exploit in their negotiations with producers and employers. The transfer of the rights to a producer leads to a benefit for performers by enabling them to negotiate higher levels of remuneration. If those rights are inalienable, however, they may constitute an obstacle to the exploitation of a performance, given that entrepreneurs may not wish to invest in a product they cannot control. An effective regime of rights must address these issues.

However, the impasse that developed over the transfer provisions in the proposed audiovisual instrument shows what a contentious issue the transfer of the economic rights can be. Clearly, silence on the issue of transfer is an option that is no longer acceptable to the United States, at least in respect of rights granted to performers in audiovisual media. The demand for certainty of ownership has already led to the failure of one diplomatic conference.

3 *Performances*

Although the definition of 'performers', and with it the subject matter of protection under the WPPT, has been extended to include performers who perform expressions of folklore, two important consequences flow from the provisions relating to 'performers' and 'performances' in the international instruments. The first is the obvious one: that is, only some performers and performances are protected. The importance of including all performances as the subject matter of protection has been referred to above. A person who is considered to be a performer in State A should be protected in State B if both states are parties to the same treaty. The second is that those provisions contribute to the unevenness of protection by acknowledging explicitly, in the case of the Rome Convention, and implicitly, in the case of TRIPS and the WPPT, that it is acceptable to extend the protection granted in national law to include any performer or performance.[16]

The extended definition of 'performers' in the WPPT does show that change is possible. The unhappy dependence on literary and artistic works as a criterion of performances has been abandoned. The time has come to acknowledge the reality of modern culture. Sports performances are specifically excluded from protection under the Australian legislation that has provided examples for discussion throughout this book.[17] Yet, as a category of performances that arguably do not derive from literary or artistic works, they are probably the most popular of all performances across the globe. Without the recognition that all performers and all performances deserve protection, the system of performers' rights does not provide complete coverage.

IV THE APPROPRIATENESS OF PERFORMERS' RIGHTS PROTECTION

Performances are a continuing form of human activity that are made in a wide range of circumstances, but primarily in education, entertainment and ritual. It is clear that performers need protection; although the real need for protection is to prevent the unauthorised first fixation of their performances. Bootlegging, and other unauthorised activities involving the use of an unfixed performance, are the activities that performers cannot easily prevent by other means of protection.

Do performers need other rights that provide more extensive protection? If the system of performers' rights finds its justification in the natural right theory, then moral rights form an integral element in that system. It has already been pointed out that the right of attribution is a statutory acknowledgement of practices that are standard in the entertainment industry. Besides a right of first fixation, other economic rights have their place. If ownership of economic rights enables performers, either individually or collectively, to negotiate remuneration and other benefits that they would not otherwise be able to extract from producers, then they fulfil an important purpose. A direct advantage is available to a performer who uses the rights to negotiate a higher level of benefits. Although he or she may be required to surrender his or her performers'

[16] Art 9 of the Rome Convention.

[17] S 248A(2) of the Copyright Act 1968 (Cth). Refer to the discussion in ch 2, n 10, and accompanying text. Sports performances are not specifically excluded from protection under the United Kingdom legislation, however, to be protected they would have to fit into one of the categories of 'performance' in s 180(2) of the Copyright, Designs and Patents Act 1988 (UK).

rights in return for those benefits, he or she will continue to have an indirect advantage because the producer will enforce those rights against bootleggers and pirates, both on the domestic scene and internationally; the producer will therefore be in a better position to guarantee a continued flow of remuneration to the performer.

It is easy to find fault with treaties such as the Rome Convention, TRIPS or the WPPT. Certainly, there are major flaws in the current system of protection represented by those instruments: it is not truly global in its application, its application is uneven, it does not provide complete coverage for all performers and its protection of performances exploited in audiovisual media is inadequate. However, appropriateness should not be equated with an ideal: a system of rights can be flawed yet still provide an appropriate level of protection. It can be concluded, therefore, that the current system of performers' rights is an appropriate system of protection for performers, subject to the proviso that the economic rights should be freely transferable.

Having reviewed the findings and come to the conclusion that the international system of performers' rights is appropriate, albeit flawed, there is one final question: where does that leave performers' rights? It is over 40 years since the conclusion of the Rome Convention and the conclusion of the WPPT has been followed by the failure to include audiovisual performances in the international regime of performers' rights. While it is too late to suggest, with any likelihood that the international community will listen, that performers' rights should be completely rethought, it is submitted that there is room for reform, or at least a tidy-up of the current system. This could be achieved within the boundaries of a review of TRIPS. The advantage of the WTO forum is, of course, that it would be incumbent on the Members of the WTO to implement the reforms.

Bibliography

This is a list of all the works cited in this book.

I REPORTS AND DOCUMENTS OF WIPO

A Records and Related Documents of the Diplomatic Conferences

Records of the Diplomatic Conference on the International Protection of Performers, Producers of Phonograms and Broadcasting Organisations (ILO, UNESCO and BIRPI, Geneva, 1968)

Summary Minutes, Main Committee I of the Diplomatic Conference on Certain Copyright and Neighboring Rights Questions CRNR/DC/102 (Diplomatic Conference on Certain Copyright and Neighboring Rights Questions, Geneva, 2 to 20 December 1996)

'Resolution Concerning Audiovisual Performances Adopted by the Diplomatic Conference on December 20, 1996' CRNR/DC/99 (Diplomatic Conference on Certain Copyright and Neighboring Rights Questions, Geneva, 2 to 20 December 1996).

Chairman of the Standing Committee on Copyright and Related Rights, 'Basic Proposal for the Substantive Provisions of an Instrument on the Protection of Audiovisual Performances to be Considered by the Diplomatic Conference' IAVP/DC/3 (Diplomatic Conference on the Protection of Audiovisual Performances, Geneva, 7 to 20 December 2000)

Proposal by the European Community and its Member States, 'Amendment to Article 12 of the Basic Proposal for the Substantive Provisions of an Instrument on the Protection of Audiovisual Performances to be Considered by the Diplomatic Conference', IAVP/DC/12 (Diplomatic Conference on the Protection of Audiovisual Performances, Geneva, 7 to 20 December 2000).

Summary Minutes, (Main Committee I), IAVP/DC/37 (Diplomatic Conference on the Protection of Audiovisual Performances, Geneva, 7 to 20 December 2000)

Summary Minutes, (Plenary), IAVP/DC/36 (Diplomatic Conference on the Protection of Audiovisual Performances, Geneva, 7 to 20 December 2000)

Memorandum of the Director General, 'Diplomatic Conference on the Protection of Audiovisual Performances' A/36/9 (Assemblies of the Member States of WIPO, Thirty-Sixth Series of Meetings, Geneva, 24 September to 3 October 2001).

'General Report Adopted by the Assemblies' A/36/15 (Assemblies of the Member States of WIPO, Thirty-Sixth Series of Meetings, Geneva, 24 September to 3 October 2001)

B Preparatory Documents for Conferences

Report of Mr Wallace, Rapporteur General, 'Comité d'experts sur la protection des artistes interpretes ou exécutants, des producteurs de phonogrammes et des organismes de radiodiffusion' (Réunion de la Haye, 9–20 mai 1960) (1960) *Le Droit D'Auteur* 167

'Report of the Second Committee of Governmental Experts on Problems in the Field of Performers, Producers of Phonograms and Broadcasting Organizations Raised by Transmission Via Space Satellite' (Paris, 9 to 17 May 1972) (1972) *Copyright* 142

'Report Adopted by the Assembly' International Union for the Protection of Literary and Artistic Works (Berne Union) B/A/XIII/2 (Assembly, Thirteenth Session (3rd Extraordinary), Geneva, 21 to 29 September 1992)

Memorandum Prepared by the International Bureau of WIPO, 'Questions Concerning a Possible Instrument for the Protection of the Rights of Performers and Producers of Phonograms' INR/CE/I/2 (Committee of Experts on the Possible Protection of the Rights of Performers and Producers of Phonograms, First Session, Geneva, 28 June to 2 July 1993)

Memorandum Prepared by the International Bureau of WIPO, 'Questions Concerning a Possible Instrument for the Protection of the Rights of Performers and Producers of Phonograms' INR/CE/III/2 (Committee of Experts on the Possible Protection of the Rights of Performers and Producers of Phonograms, Third Session, Geneva, 12 to 16 December 1994)

Discussion Paper prepared by the International Bureau of WIPO, 'Questions of the Rights of Performers in Audiovisual Fixations of their Performances', INR/CE/IV/3, (Committee of Experts on a Possible Instrument for the Protection of the Rights of Performers and Producers of Phonograms, Fourth Session, Geneva, 4 to 8 and 12 September 1995)

Document Prepared by the International Bureau of WIPO, 'Comparative Table of Proposals and Comments Received by the International Bureau' INR/CE/V/11 (Committee of Experts on the Possible Protection of the Rights of Performers and Producers of Phonograms, Fifth Session, Geneva, 1 to 9 February 1996)

Chairman of the Committees of Experts on a Possible Protocol to the Berne Convention and on a Possible Instrument for the Protection of the Rights of Performers and Producers of Phonograms, 'Basic Proposal for the Substantive Provisions of the Treaty for the Protection of Performers and Producers of Phonograms to be Considered by the Diplomatic Conference' CRNR/DC/5 (Diplomatic Conference on Certain Copyright and Neighbouring Rights Questions, Geneva, 2 to 20 December 1996)

'Draft Report' AP/CE/I/4 (Committee of Experts on a Protocol Concerning Audiovisual Performances, Geneva, 15, 16 and 19 September 1997)

'Draft Report' AP/CE/2/9 Prov, (Committee of Experts on a Protocol Concerning Audiovisual Performances, Geneva, 8 June to 12 June 1998)

Agenda Item 4: Protection of Audiovisual Performances, 'Further Submission by the European Community and its Member States on a Protocol Concerning Audiovisual Performances', SCCR/2/3 (Standing Committee on Copyright and Related Rights, Second Session, Geneva, 4 to 11 May 1999)

Agenda Item 4: Protection of Audiovisual Performances, 'Submission of the United States', SCCR/3/7 (Standing Committee on Copyright and Related Rights, Third Session, Geneva, 16 to 20 November 1999)

'Submission on behalf of the European Community and its Member States on the Protection of Performers' Rights in Their Audiovisual Performances', SCCR/4/2 (Standing Committee on Copyright and Related Rights, Fourth Session, Geneva, 11, 12 and 14 April 2000)

'Submission of the United States of America on Transfer', Submitted by the United States of America, SCCR/4/4 (Standing Committee on Copyright and Related Rights, Fourth Session, Geneva, 11, 12 and 14 April 2000)

Director General of WIPO, 'Agenda, Dates, Venue and Other Organisational Questions of the Diplomatic Conference IAVP/PM/5 (Preparatory Committee for the WIPO Diplomatic Conference on the Protection of Audiovisual Performances and Related Rights, Geneva, 12 and 14 April 2000)

C Reports and Documents

'Annotated Principles of Protection of Authors, Performers, Producers of Phonograms and Broadcasting Organisations in Connection with the Distribution of Programs by Cable' (1984), *Copyright* 131

The Intergovernmental Committee of the International Convention for the Protection of Performers, Producers of Phonograms and Broadcasting Organisations done at Rome in 1961, *Model Law Concerning the Protection of Performers, Producers of Phonograms and Broadcasting Organisations with a Commentary on it* (ILO, UNESCO, WIPO; Geneva and Paris, 1974)

International Bureau of WIPO, '1967, 1982, 1984: Attempts to Provide Intellectual Property Protection for Folklore by Intellectual Property Rights' UNESCO-WIPO/FOLK/PKT/97/19 (Paper presented at the UNESCO-WIPO World Forum on the Protection of Folklore in Phuket, Thailand, 8 to 10 April 1997)

International Bureau of WIPO, *Implications of the TRIPS Agreement on Treaties Administered by WIPO* (WIPO, Geneva, 1997)

International Bureau of WIPO, 'Note, Committee of Experts on Model Provisions for Legislation in the Field of Copyright, First Session' (Geneva, 20 February to 3 March 1989) (1989) *Copyright* 146

International Bureau of WIPO, 'New Trends in the Protection of Copyright and Neighbouring Rights: The WIPO Performances and Phonograms Treaty (1996)' WIPO/CR/GE/97/4b (Introductory Seminar on Copyright and Neighbouring Rights, Geneva, 8 to 10 October 1997)

'Notifications Concerning Treaties Administered by WIPO in the field of Copyright, Rome Convention, Accession, Australia' (1992) *Copyright* 301

'Report of the Committee of Governmental Experts on the Intellectual Property Aspects of the Protection of Expressions of Folklore' (1982) *Copyright* 278

'Report of the Committee of Governmental on Model Provisions for National Laws on Employed Authors (Geneva, 27 to 31 January 1986)' (1986) *Copyright* 72

'Report of the Group of Experts on the International Protection of Expressions of Folklore by Intellectual Property' (1985) *Copyright* 40

'Rome Convention for the International Protection of Performers, Producers of Phonograms and Broadcasting Organisations, Ratification by the United Kingdom of Great Britain and Northern Ireland (1963) *Copyright* 244

II OTHER REPORTS AND DOCUMENTS

Attorney-General's Department and the Department of Communication and the Arts, *Performers' Intellectual Property Rights Scope of extended rights for performers under the Copyright Act 1968* (Attorney-General's Department and the Department of Communication and the Arts, Canberra, 1997)

Paper prepared by the Bureau of Transport and Communications for the Department of Communications and the Arts, *Economic Effects of Extended Performers' Rights* (Department of Communications and the Arts, Canberra, 1996)

Copyright Law Review Committee, Commonwealth of Australia, *Report on Performers' Protection* (Australian Government Publishing Service, Canberra, May 1987)

S Globerman and MP Rothman, *An Economic Analysis of a Performers' Right* (Consumer and Corporate Affairs Canada, Ottawa, 1981)

Law Reform Division, New Zealand Department of Justice, *The Copyright Act 1962—Options for Reform* (Department of Justice, Wellington, 1989)

Music Industry Advisory Council, *Performers' Copyright* (MIAC Secretariat, Canberra, 1994)

The Report of the Working Group on Intellectual Property Rights, *Intellectual Property and the National Information Infrastructure* (Department of Commerce, Patent and Trade Mark Office, Washington, 1995)

B Sherman and L Bently, *Performers' Rights: Options for Reform* (Department of Communications, Information Technology and the Arts, Canberra, 1995)

Great Britain Department for Culture, Media and Sport, *Culture and Creativity: The Next Ten Years* (Department for Culture, Media and Sport, London, 2001)

III BOOKS (INCLUDING CHAPTERS IN BOOKS) AND MONOGRAPHS

A Abramson, 'The Invention of Television' in A Smith (ed) *Television An International History* (Oxford University Press, Oxford, 1995)

R Arnold, *Performers' Rights* 2nd edn (Sweet & Maxwell, London, 1997)

P Auslander, *Presence and Resistance—Postmodernism and Cultural Politics in Contemporary American Performance* (University of Michigan Press, Ann Arbor, 1994)

Australian Copyright Council, *Performers' Copyright* (Australian Copyright Council, Redfern, Sydney, 1996)

R Bagehot and N Kannar, *Music Business Agreements* 2nd edn (Sweet & Maxwell, London, 1998)

B Barber, 'Indexing: Conditionalism and its Heretical Equivalents' in AA Bronson and P Gale (eds), *Performance by Artists* (Art Metropole, Toronto, 1979)

W Baumol and WG Bowen, 'On the Rationale of Public Support' in R Towse (ed), *Baumol's Cost Disease The Arts and other Victims* (Edward Elgar, Cheltenham, UK, 1997)

W Benjamin (H Arendt ed, H Zohn trans), *Illuminations* (Fontana, London, 1973)

GHC Bodenhausen, *Guide to the Application of the Paris Convention for the Protection of Industrial Property As Revised at Stockholm in 1967* (United International Bureaux for the Protection of Intellectual Property, Geneva, 1968)

British Phonographic Industry Ltd and The Musicians' Union, *The BPI and the Musicians Union Agreement for the Engagement of Musicians* (August, 1996)

British Phonographic Industry Ltd, *BPI Statistical Handbook 2001* (BPI, London, 2001)

AW CAMPBELL, *Entertainment Law Cases and Materials* 4th edn (Austin and Winfield, San Francisco, 1997)

B CASEY, R DUNLOP and S SELWOOD, *Culture as Commodity—The Economics of the Arts and Built Heritage in the UK* (Policy Studies Institute, London, 1996)

M CHANAN, *Repeated Takes—A Short History of Recording and its Effects on Music* (Verson, London, 1995)

WR CORNISH, *Intellectual Property: Patents, Copyright, Trade Marks and Allied Rights* 4th edn (Sweet & Maxwell, London, 1999)

M CROSBY, 'Performers and the WIPO Performances and Programs (sic) Treaty' in D Saunders and B Sherman (eds), *From Berne to Geneva—Recent Developments in International Copyright and Neighbouring Rights* (Australian Key Centre for Cultural and Media Policy, Nathan, Qld, 1997)

G DAVIES, *Copyright and the Public Interest* (Wiley-VCH, Weinheim, 1994)

C FLESCH, 'The Orchestra Violinist' in G Seltzer (ed) *The Professional Symphony Orchestra in the United States* (Scarecrow Press, Meutchen, NJ, 1975)

S FOX, 'Learning to Live with 1s and 0s: Response to the New WIPO Treaties' in D Saunders and B Sherman (eds), *From Berne to Geneva: Recent Developments in International Copyright and Neighbouring Rights* (Australian Key Centre for Cultural and Media Policy, Nathan, Qld, 1997)

JM GAINES, *Contested Culture—The Image, the Voice and the Law* (University of North Carolina Press, Chapel Hill, 1991)

PE GELLER, 'Must Copyright be Forever Caught Between Marketplace and Authorship Norms' in B Sherman and A Strowel (eds) *Of Authors and Origins* (Clarendon Press, Oxford, 1994)

D GERVAIS, *The TRIPS Agreement: Drafting History and Analysis* (Sweet and Maxwell, London, 1998)

P GOLDSTEIN, *Copyright's Highway—The Law and Lore of Copyright from Gutenberg to the Celestial Jukebox* (Hill and Wang, New York, 1994)

LS GRAY and RL SEEBER, 'The Industry and the Unions: An Overview' in LS Gray and RL Seeber (eds), *Under the Stars Essays on Labor Relations in Arts and Entertainment* (ILR Press, Ithaca, 1996)

—— 'Looking Ahead' in LS Gray and RL Seeber (eds), *Under the Stars Essays on Labor Relations in Arts and Entertainment* (ILR Press, Ithaca, 1996)

S GREENFIELD and G OSBORN, *Contract and Control in the Entertainment Industry* (Ashgate, Aldershot, 1998)

D HARKER, *One for the Money: The Politics of Popular Song* (Hutchinson, London, 1980)

C HAWKINS, 'Overview of the New WIPO Standards' in D Saunders and B Sherman (eds), *From Berne to Geneva: Recent Developments in International Copyright and Neighbouring Rights* (Australian Key Centre for Cultural and Media Policy, Nathan, Qld, 1997)

C HEYLIN, *Bootleg—The Secret History of the Other Recording Industry* (St Martins Press, New York, 1994)

International Labour Organisation, 'Rights of Performers in Broadcasting, Television and the Mechanical Reproduction of Sound' in *Report III of the ILO Advisory Committee on Salaried Employees and Professional Workers Second Session* (International Labour Office, Geneva, 1951)

—— *Satellite and Cable Television—The Rights of Performers and Producers of Phonograms* (International Labour Office, Geneva, 1989)

—— *Conditions of Employment and Work of Performers* (International Labour Office, Geneva, 1992)

M Kirby, *A Formalist Theatre* (University of Pennsylvania Press, Philadelphia, 1987)

H Laddie, P Prescott, M Vitoria, A Speck and L Lane, *The Modern Law of Copyright* 3rd edn (Butterworths, London, 2000)

J Lahore, *Copyright and Designs* 3rd rev edn (Butterworths, Sydney, 1996)

J Lovering, 'The Global Music Industry Contradictions in the Commodification of the Sublime' in A Leyshon, D Matless and G Revill (eds), *The Place of Music* (Guildford Press, New York, 1998)

M McLean, *Maori Music* (Auckland University Press, Auckland, 1996)

C Masouye (W Wallace trans,) *Guide to the Berne Convention for the Protection of Literary and Artistic Works (Paris Act, 1971)* (World Intellectual Property Organisation, Geneva, 1978)

—— *Guide to the Rome Convention and to the Phonograms Convention* (World Intellectual Property Organisation, Geneva, 1981)

O Morgan, 'Performers' Rights' in B Brown et al, *Intellectual Property in New Zealand Copyright and Design* (Butterworths, Wellington, Issue No 3–March, 1997)

D Nimmer, 'A Tale of Two Treaties Dateline: Geneva—December 1996' in M Nimmer and D Nimmer, *Nimmer on Copyright: A Treatise on the Law of Literary, Musical and Artistic Property and the Protection of Ideas* (Mathew Bender, New York, 1978–Release 42–6/97)

W Nordemann, K Vinck, PW Hertin, (English version by G Meyer based on the translation by R Livingston), *International Copyright and Neighboring Rights Law: commentary with special emphasis on the European Community* (VCH Publishers, New York, 1990)

P Pavis (L Kruger trans), *Treatre at the Crossroads of Other Culture* (Routledge, London, New York, 1992) 67.

P Phelan, *Unmarked: The Politics of Performance* (Routledge, London, New York, 1993)

A Plant, 'The economic aspects of copyright in books' in A Plant, *Selected Economic Essays and Addresses* (Routledge Kegan Paul, London, Boston, 1974)

N Reber, *Film Copyright, Contracts and Profit Participation* (Weinheim, Wiley-VCH, 2000)

S Redhead, *Unpopular Cultures—The Birth of Law and Popular Culture* (Manchester University Press, Manchester, 1995)

S Ricketson, *The Berne Convention for the Protection of Literary and Artistic Works: 1886–1986* (Centre for Commercial Law Studies, Kluwer, London, 1987)

S Robinson, *The History of World Cinema* (Stein and Day, New York, 1981)

M Rose, 'The Author as Proprietor: Donaldson v Becket and the Genealogy of Modern Authorship' in B Sherman and A Strowel (eds), *Of Authors and Origins Essays on Copyright Law* (Clarendon Press, Oxford, 1994)

JC Ross, 'Trade-Related Aspects of Intellectual Property Rights' in TP Stewart (ed), *The GATT Uruguay Round: a Negotiating History (1986–1992) Vol II* (Kluwer Law and Taxation Publishers, Deventer, Boston, 1993)

R Schechner, *Performance Theory* (Routledge, New York, 1988)

T Schultheiss, 'Everything You Always Wanted to Know About Bootlegs, But Were Too Busy Collecting Them to Ask: A Treatise on the Wages of Sinning for Sound' in C Reinhart (ed), *You Can't Do That! : Beatles, Bootlegs and Novelty Records, 1963–80* (Pierian Press, Ann Arbor, 1981)

I Sinclair, *The Vienna Convention on the Law of Treaties* 2nd edn (Manchester University Press, Manchester, 1984)

SM Stewart, *International Copyright and Neighbouring Rights* 2nd edn (Butterworths, London, 1989)

D Throsby and B Thompson, *But What Do You Do for a Living? A New Economic Study of Australian Artists* (Australia Council, Strawberry Hill, NSW, 1994)

R Vasey, 'The World-Wide Spread of Cinema' in G Nowell-Smith (ed), *The Oxford History of World Cinema* (Oxford University Press, Oxford, 1996)

HL Vogel, *Entertainment Industry Economics: A Guide for Financial Analysis* 4th edn (Cambridge University Press, Cambridge, 1998)

C Wadlow, *The Law of Passing Off* 2nd edn (Sweet & Maxwell, London, 1995) and 1st Supplement (Sweet & Maxwell, London, 1997)

AL White, 'Introduction' in AL White (ed), *Lost in Music: Culture, Style and the Musical Event* (Routledge & Kegan Paul, London, 1987)

World Intellectual Property Organisation (ed), *Introduction to Intellectual Property Theory and Practice* (World Intellectual Property Organisation, London, Boston, 1997)

—— *Implications of the TRIPS Agreement on Treaties Administered by WIPO* (World Intellectual Property Organisation, Geneva, 1997)

J Wodetski, 'What About the Copyright User? Implications of the New WIPO Treaties' in D Saunders and B Sherman (eds), *From Berne to Geneva: Recent Developments in International Copyright and Neighbouring Rights* (Australian Key Centre for Cultural and Media Policy, Nathan, Qld, 1997)

IV JOURNAL ARTICLES AND CONFERENCE PAPERS

P Auslander, 'Legally Live Performance In/Of the Law' (1997) 41 (2) *TDR The Drama Review* 9

A Bertrand, 'The Moral Rights of Performers: French Law, International Law and Comparative Law' [1994] 4 *Entertainment Law Review* 114

LC Becker, 'Deserving to Own Intellectual Property' (1993) 68 *Chicago-Kent Law Review* 609

V Blanco Labra, 'The Three Subjects Protected by the Rome Convention' (1978) *Copyright* 25

GHC Bodenhausen, 'Protection of Neighbouring Rights' (1954) 19 *Law and Contemporary Problems* 156

J Boyle, 'The Search for an Author: Shakespeare and the Framers' (1988) *The American University Law Review* 625

S Breyer, 'The Uneasy Case for Copyright: A Study of Copyright in Books, Photocopies, and Computer Programs' (1970) 84 *Harvard Law Review* 281

Z Chafee, 'Reflections on the Law of Copyright: I' (1945) 45 *Columbia Law Review* 503

—— 'Reflections on the Law of Copyright: II' (1945) 45 *Columbia Law Review* 719

P Chesnais, 'The Rome Convention: Twenty-five Years Later' (1986) 20 (4) *Copyright Bulletin* 8

WR Cornish, 'The International Relations of Intellectual Property' (1993) *Cambridge Law Journal* 46

C Cresswell, 'Copyright Protection Enters the Digital Age: The New WIPO Treaties' (1997) 15 (1) *Copyright Reporter* 4

G Davies, 'The Rome Convention 1961—A Brief Summary of its Developments and Prospects' (1979) *European Intellectual Property Review* 154

J Dolan, J Roach, R Schechner, PB Zarilli and WB Worthen, 'Responses to WB Worthen's "Disciplines of the Text/Sites of Performance"' (1995) 39 (1) *TDR The Drama Review* 28.

JG Finell, 'How a Musicologist Views Digital Sampling' (1992) *New York Law Journal* 5

M Ficsor, 'The Spring 1997 Horace S. Manges Lecture—Copyright for the Digital Era: The WIPO "Internet' Treaties" (1997) 21 *Columbia-VLA Journal of Law and the Arts* 197

D Gaudel, 'The Eternally Excommunicated—The Situation of Performers in France' (1980) 103 *Revue Internationale du Droit D'Auteur* 92

D J Gervais, 'The Trips Agreement' [1999] *European Intellectual Property Review* 156

JC Ginsburg, 'Surveying the Borders of Copyright' (Paper presented at the *WIPO Worldwide Symposium on the Future of Copyright and Neighboring Rights*, Paris, 1 to 3 June 1994) 221

P Goldstein, 'Copyright and its Substitutes' (1997) *Wisconsin Law Review* 865

D Gruzauskas, 'Performers' Rights: The Right of Personality and the Possibility of a Proprietary Right' (1995) 6 *Australian Intellectual Property Journal* 92

O G Hatch, 'Toward a Principled Approach to Copyright Legislation at the Turn of the Millenium' (1998) 59 *University of Pittsburgh Law Review* 719

E C Hettinger, 'Justifying Intellectual Property' (1989) 18 *Philosophy and Public Affairs* 31

B Holland, 'Composers' Whys Affect the Whats' *New York Times* New York, United States of America, 11 August 1996, Section 2, 24

PB Hugenholtz, 'Fierce Creatures, Copyright Exemptions: Towards Extinction?' (Paper presented at: Rights, Limitations and Exceptions: Striking a Proper Balance, IFLA/IMPRIMATUR Conference, Amsterdam, 30–31 October 1997)

J Hughes 'The Philosophy of Intellectual Property' (1988) 77 *The Georgetown Law Journal* 287

HC Jehoram, 'The Relationship between Copyright and Neighbouring Rights' (1990) 144 *Revue Internationale du Droit d'Auteur* 81

—— 'Hybrids on the Borderline between Copyright and Industrial Property Law' (1992) 153 *Revue Internationale du Droit d'Auteur* 75

A Kéréver, 'The New WIPO Treaties: the WIPO Copyright Treaty and the WIPO Performances and Phonograms Treaty' (1998) 32 *Copyright Bulletin* 3

Mr JUSTICE LADDIE, 'Copyright: Over-strength, Over-regulated, Over-rated?' [1996] *European Intellectual Property Review* 253

S LEE, 'Jesus Draws' (10 August 1998) 162 *Forbes Magazine* 58.

A LUCAS, 'Summary of the Proceedings of the Symposium' (Paper presented at the WIPO Worldwide Symposium of the Future of Copyright and Neighbouring Rights Paris, France, 1–3 June 1994) 269

R F MARTIN, 'The WIPO Performances and Phonograms Treaty: Will the US Whistle a New Tune?' (1997) *Journal of the Copyright Society of the USA* 157

A MASON, 'Developments in the Law of Copyright and Public Access to Information' [1997] 11 *European Intellectual Property Review* 636

P MASOUYE, 'The Rome Convention: Realities and Prospects' (1985) *Copyright* 296

A MILLE (WIPO trans), 'Performers' Rights: A New Independent Institution of Intellectual Property Law' (1984) *Copyright* 289

DE PINOVER, 'The Rights of Authors, Artists, and Performers under Section 43(a) of the Lanham Act' (1993) 83 *Trade Mark Reporter* 38

J REINBOTHE, M MARTIN-PRAT and S VON LEWINSKI, 'The New WIPO Treaties: A First Resume' (1997) 4 *European Intellectual Property Review* 171

R REMBE, 'Authors and Performers: Equal Contribution: Equal Protection' (1986) 20(4) *Copyright Bulletin* 30

—— 'Time for A Performers' Convention' (1991) 25 (4) *Copyright Bulletin* 25

C RODRIGUES,, 'The Nature and Scope of Rules for Updating the Protection of Performers' Rights' (Paper presented at the International UNESCO Symposium on Copyright and Communication in the Information Society, Madrid, 11–14 March, 1996) 143

R SCHECHNER, 'A New Paradigm for Theatre in the Academy' (1992) 36 (4) *TDR The Drama Review* 7, 9

—— 'Comment' (1995) 39 (1) *TDR The Drama Review* 36

D SCHWARTZ, 'Strange Fixation: Bootleg Sound Recordings Enjoy the Benefits of Improving Technology' (1995) 47 *Federal Communications Law Journal* 611

N SERVENTY, 'The Protection of Performers' Rights in Australia' (1984) *University of New South Wales Law Journal Special Issue* 175

M SIMENSKY, 'Defining Entertainment Law' (1986) *The Entertainment and Sports Lawyer* 13, 13

N STEER, 'Moral Rights for Performers' (1994) 12 *Copyright Reporter* 19

SE STERK, 'Rhetoric and Reality in Copyright Law' (1996) 94 *Michigan Law Review* 1197

E THOMPSON, 'International Protection of Performers' Rights: Some Current Problems' (1973) 107 *International Labour Review* 303

—— 'Twenty Years of the Rome Convention' *Copyright* (1981) 270

—— 'Performers and technological change 25 years after the Rome Convention' (1986) 125 *International Labour Review* 575

E ULMER, 'The Rome Convention for the Protection of Performers, Producers of Phonograms and Broadcasting Organizations. Part I' (1963) 10 *Bulletin Copyright Society of the U.S.A.* 90

—— 'The Rome Convention on Neighboring Rights. Part II' (1963) *10 Bulletin Copyright Society of the U.S.A.* 165

—— 'The Rome Convention for the Protection of Performers, Producers of Phonograms and Broadcasting Organizations. Part III' (1963) 10 *Bulletin Copyright Society of the U.S.A.* 219

United States Department of Commerce, Patent and Trademark Office, 'Briefing on Request for Comments on the Chairman's Text of the Diplomatic Conference on Certain Copyright and Neighbouring Rights Questions, To be Held in Geneva from December 2 to 20, 1996', (Arlington, 12 November 1996)

M WALDORFF, 'Audiovisual Performers: Rights, Collective Bargaining and Multimedia Convergence' in ILO *Final Report Symposium on Multimedia Convergence Geneva, 27–29 January 1997* (1997) 124

J WALDRON, 'From Authors to Copiers: Individual Rights and Social Values in Intellectual Property' (1993) 68 *Chicago-Kent Law Review* 841

JS WOLSEY, 'Performers' Rights—The New Regime and Opportunities in Europe' (1994) 45 *Copyright World* 26

T ZELDIN, 'The Value of Creativity' (1997) *International Arts Manager* 21

V WORKS OF REFERENCE

WIPO Glossary of Terms of the Law of Copyright and Neigboring Rights (1980)

New Shorter Oxford Dictionary (1993)

VI ELECTRONIC SOURCES

'What is Aimster?' <http://www.aimster.com/whatis.phtml>

Free On-Line Dictionary of Computing <http://www.nightflight.com/foldoc/>

'Recording Industry World Sales 2000: CD albums up, overall unit sales down 1.2%' <http://www.ifpi.org/site-content/statistics/worldsales.html>

International Federation of Actors 'Comments on the WIPO Basic Proposal prepared for the Diplomatic Conference, December 2000': <http://www.fia-actors.com/new/wipo_2000_comments_eng.htm>.

Introductory Speech of the European Community to the Diplomatic Conference: <http://europa.eu.int/comm/internal_market/en/intprop/intprop/news/diplomat.htm>

C KOSELUK, 'Digital Acting' <http://www.sag.com/dgtlacting.html>

R LYMAN, 'Movie Stars Fear Inroads by Upstart Digital Actors' The New York Times (New York, United States of America), 7 July 2001, <http://www.nytimes.com/2001/07/08/technology/08FANT.html>

K ORSATTI, 'The Actor's Road to Empowerment' <http://www.sag.com/rdtoempwrmnt.html>

Webopaedia Online Dictionary and Search Engine <http://www.pcwebopaedia.com>

Agreement dated 5 October 2001, between the Recording Industry Association of America, Inc., the National Music Publishers' Association, Inc. and the Harry Fox Agency, Inc. <http://www.riaa.com/Music-Intro.cfm>.

Recording Industry Association of America, Inc., 'The Cost of a CD' <http://www.riaa.com/MD-US-7.ctm>

Screen Actors Guild, 'So You Wannabe an Actor?' <http://www.sag.com/wannabe.html>

Screen Actors Guild, '1998 Theatrical Motion Pictures and Television Contract Summary', <http://www.sag.org/theatrical-tv.html>

World Intellectual Property Office, 'Actions in Respect of Treaties Administered by WIPO not yet in Force' <http:// www.wipo.org/treaties/ip/index.html>
——, 'Intellectual Property Treaties' <http://www.wipo.org/treaties/ip/wppt/index.html>
Screen Actors Guild, <http://www.sag.com.>
American Federation of Television and Radio Artists <http://www.aftra.org>;
Alliance of Motion Picture and Television Producers <http://www.amptp.org>
Alliance of Canadian Cinema, Television and Radio Artists: <http://www.actra.ca>
World Trade Organisation, 'The Organisation: Members and Observers' http://www.wto.org/english/thewto_e/whatis_e/tif_e/org6_e.htm>
—— 'Trading into the Future: The Introduction to the WTO' <http://www.wto.org/english/thewto_e/whatis_e/tif_e/tif_e.htm>
Equity 'Films Dispute Latest', <http://www.equity.org.uk/actors_strike/index.htm>
European Commission 'Commission Regrets Conference on the Protection of Audiovisual Performance's Failure to Conclude Treaty' <http://europa.eu.int/comm/internal_market/en/intprop/intprop/news/geneva.htm>
International DanceSport Federation IDSF, 'IDSF and DanceSport now fully Recognised by IOC, <http://www.idsf.net/press97/idsfp172.htm>

Index

Agents:
  transfer of rights, 110
Agreement on Trade-Related Aspects of Intellectual Property Rights, *see* TRIPS Agreement
Aimster, 55
Arguments for performers' rights, 31–52
  Berne Union, 34
  bootlegging, 47–8
  copyright 35–48,
    see also Copyright
  Copyright Law Review Committee (CLRC), 32–3
  counter-arguments, 34
  economic incentive theory, *see* Economic incentive theory
  generally, 31–2
  intellectual property rights, 49
  International Labour Organisation, 33–4
  justification for system of protection, 49–51
  main arguments, 32–3
  natural rights theory, *see* Natural rights theory
  review, 48–52
  Screen Actors Guild, 34
  special, whether performers are, 51–2
  unemployment, 34
  UNESCO, 34
Assignment:
  economic rights, 114
Audiovisual Performances Treaty, 227–38
  assessment, 236–8
  background, 227–9
  basic proposals, 229–36
    features, 229–31
    generally, 229
    transfer provision, 231–6
  generally, 227
  transfer provision, 231–6
Auslander, P, 19
Australia:
  Copyright Law Review Committee (CLRC), 32–3, 35, 64
  protection of performers in, 64–6
  recording rights, 107, 108

Berne Convention:
  copyright, 83
  generally, 6
  national treatment, 85
  term of protection, 85
  see also Copyright
Berne Union:
  arguments for performers' rights, 34
Bootlegging:
  arguments against, 48
  arguments in favour of, 48
  copyright, 47–8
  definition, 47
  meaning, 47
  piracy distinguished, 62
  special case, whether, 47–8
  technology, 61–2
  value, 48
Broadcasting, 153–61
  definition, 56
  editing, 57
  fixed performances, 57
  manipulation, 57
  Rome Convention, 154–8
  technology, 56–7
  TRIPS Agreement, 158–9
  unfixed performances, 57
  WIPO Performances and Phonograms Treaty (WPPT), 159–61

Collecting societies:
  transfer of rights, 110
Commodities:
  performance as, 4
Communication to the public, right of, 153–61
  meaning, 56
  Rome Convention, 154–8
  technology, 56–7
  TRIPS Agreement, 158–9
  WIPO Performances and Phonograms Treaty (WPPT), 159–61
Consent:
  exploitation, to, 81–2
  use of performance, to, 115–16
Contract, 77–83
  consent to exploitation, nature, 81–2
  duration, 78
  first owner of rights, 77–8
  generally, 76
  inequality of bargaining power, 82–3
  meaning, 77
  nature of protection, 77–9
  negotiation, 83
  parties, 77

Contract,—*cont.*
  scope of protection, 78–9
  shortcomings of protection, 79–83
  technology and, 82
  terms, 78
    consent to exploitation, nature, 81–2
  third parties, 79–81
  worldwide protection, 78
Control of performance, 4
Copyright, 35–48, 83–7
  advantages of using, 83–4
  arguments for protection, 35–48
  basic rights, 85–6
  Berne Convention, 83, 85
  bootlegging, 47–8
  common law system, 36
  Copyright Law Review Committee (CLRC), 32–3, 35, 64
  economic incentive theory, 36–42
    basis, 36–7
    decision to invest in a performance, 37–8
    folklore, 40–2
    meaning, 36
    nature of decision to perform, 38–9
    special cultural significance, performance of, 40–2
  establishing ownership, 84–6
  first ownership, 83
  folklore, 40–2
  generally, 76
  justification for system, 35–6
  limitations and exceptions, 204
  minimum term of protection, 85
  moral rights, 86
  national treatment, 85
  natural right theory, 42–7
    advantages, 43
    economic interest, 44, 45–7
    meaning, 42–3
    originality, 44
    personality ratio, 43
    self-expression, 44, 45
  nature of protection, 84–6
  ownership of rights, 87
  performance, right of, 86
  rationale for protection, 35
  reproduction, right of, 85–6
  shortcomings of protection, 86–7
    ownership of rights, 87
    performances not directly protected, 86
Copyright Law Review Committee (CLRC), 32–3, 35, 64
Cornish, W R, 38
Course of trade, connection in, 88
  belittling performance, 88
  look-alikes, 89
  nature of protection, 89–92
  sound-alikes, 89
  well-known performances, 89
Culture:
  folklore, 40–2

Damage to reputation, *see* Unfair competition
Death of performer:
  transfer of rights, 115
Definition of performance, 13–29, 242
  approaches, 25–6
  assessment, 28–9
  common understanding of, 14–15
  communication, as form of, 28
  dictionary definition, 14
  entertainment, education, ritual, 28
  generally, 13
  hybrid approach, 14
  individual human activity, 27–8
  intended to influence, 28
  legal definition, 15–18
    international level, 15
    national level, 16–18
    Rome Convention, 15
    WIPO Performances and Phonograms Treaty (WPPT), 16
  national level, 16–18
  new, 26–9
  others, to, 28
  perceived without the aid of technology, 28
  performance theory, 18–25
    activity, 20
    audiences, 21–3
    characteristics of a performance, 24–5
    definition of performance in, 19–25
    done for another individual or group, 23–4
    done by individual or group, 20–1
    generally, 18–19
    in the presence of and for another individual or group, 21–3
  possible approaches, 25–6
  principled definition, 14–29
  Rome Convention, 15, 26
  Schechner, 20–5
  transitory nature, 27
  WIPO Performances and Phonograms Treaty (WPPT), 16, 26
Digital technology, use, 3
Distribution, right of, 181–5
  definition, 181
  exercise of right, 182
  exhaustion, 182
  generally, 181–2
  Rome Convention, 182
  TRIPS Agreement, 183

WIPO Performances and Phonograms Treaty (WPPT), 183–5
Duration of rights, 217–25
application in time, 219
assessment, 225
generally, 217
Rome Convention, 219–21
term of protection, 217–19
TRIPS Agreement, 222
WIPO Performances and Phonograms Treaty (WPPT), 222–5

Economic incentive theory, 36–42
basis, 36, 36–42
decision to invest in a performance, 36–7, 37–8, 40–2
folklore, 37–8
meaning, 36, 38–9, 40–2
nature of decision to perform, 36, 40–2
Economic rights, 153–80
assessment, 199–201
assignment, 114
broadcasting 153–61, *see also* Broadcasting
distribution 181–85, *see also* Distribution, right of
extended, 181–201
distribution 181–85, *see also* Distribution, right of
generally, 181
making available 190–94, *see also* Making available, right of
moral rights 195–9, *see also* Moral rights
rental 186–90, *see also* Rental, right of
first fixation 161–4, *see also* First fixation, right of
first ownership, 109
generally, 153
making available 190–4, *see also* Making available, right of
moral rights 195–9, *see also* Moral rights
primary, 153–80
assessment, 179–80
broadcasting 153–61, *see also* Broadcasting
communication to the public 153–61, *see also* Communication to the public, right of
first fixation 161–4, *see also* First fixation, right of
generally, 153
remuneration right 172–8, *see also* Remuneration right
reproduction, right of 164–71, *see also* Reproduction, right of
rental 186–90, *see also* Rental, right of
reproduction, right of 164–71, *see also* Reproduction, right of
technology and protection for performers, 69–70
transfer of ownership, 109
Effective protection, 246–8
Eligibility:
national treatment, 126–8
Encoding devices, 57
Exceptions, *see* Limitations and exceptions
Exploitation:
meaning, 3
technology, 3, 53, 241

First fixation, right of, 161–4
Rome Convention, 161–2
TRIPS Agreement, 162–3
WIPO Performances and Phonograms Treaty (WPPT), 163–4
First ownership of rights, 102–9, 242
approaches, 103
claimants, 104–8
common issues with transfer of ownership, 108–9
duration, 109
economic rights, 109
generally, 102–3
ideal system of rights, 103
joint ownership, 106–7
moral rights, 109
performers as, 104
producers, 104–6
recording rights, 107–8
significance, 102–3
Fixation:
consequences, 55–6
first, 55
first fixation 161–4, *see also* First fixation, right of
industry use, 56
Internet, 55
meaning, 54–5
morphing, 56
sampling, 56
technology, 54–6, 61
Folklore, 26
copyright, 40–2
culture, 40–2
definition, 40–1
expressions of, 40–1
Model Provisions for National Laws on the Protection of Expressions of Folklore against Illicit Exploitation and other Prejudicial Action, 41
use of term, 40–1

Foreign performers:
national treatment, *see* National treatment

Gaines, J M, 112–13
Goldstein, P, 14

Hettinger, E C, 42
Holder of rights:
performers 137–46, *see also* Performer
Hugenholtz, P M, 203–4

Improvisation, 84
Intellectual property rights, 242
arguments for performers' rights, 49
copyright, *see* Copyright
International Convention for the Protection of Performers, Producers of Phonograms and Broadcasting Organisations, *see* Rome Convention
International Federation of Actors (FIA), 4
International Labour Organisation:
arguments for performers' rights, 33–4
collectivist approach, 33
work protection approach, 33
International protection:
Agreement on Trade-Related Aspects of Intellectual Property Rights, *see* TRIPS Agreement
assessment, 243–5
connections between international instruments, 123–4
effective protection, 246–8
ensuring, 5–6
exceptions, *see* Limitations and exceptions
historical background, 119–24
International Convention for the Protection of Performers, Producers of Phonograms and Broadcasting Organisations, *see* Rome Convention
limitations and exceptions, *see* Limitations and exceptions
questions, formulating, 6–8
reservations, *see* Reservations
uniform protection, 245–6
WIPO Performances and Phonograms Treaty, *see* WIPO Performances and Phonograms Treaty (WPPT)
Internet, 5
fixation, 55
technology, 55

Joint ownership:
first ownership of rights, 106–7

Kirby, M, 19

Limitations and exceptions:
approaches, 204–5
assessment, 214–15
copyright, 204
Rome Convention, 207–9
three-step test, 205–6
TRIPS Agreement, 210–11
uses, 203–6
WIPO Performances and Phonograms Treaty (WPPT), 211–14
Live performances, 71–2
unfixed performance, as, 72

Making available, right of, 186–90
generally, 190–2
Rome Convention, 192
TRIPS Agreement, 192
WIPO Performances and Phonograms Treaty (WPPT), 192–4
Masouye, C, 209, 247
Moral rights, 195–9
copyright, 86
first ownership of rights, 109
generally, 195
Rome Convention, 195
technology and protection for performers, 69–70
transfer of ownership, 109
TRIPS Agreement, 196
WIPO Performances and Phonograms Treaty (WPPT), 196–9
Morphing, 56

Napster, 55
National treatment, 125–35, 241–3
copyright, 85
eligibility, 126–8
generally, 125
meaning, 101
Rome Convention, 128–30
TRIPS Agreement, 130–1
unfair competition, 91
WIPO Performances and Phonograms Treaty (WPPT), 131–4
Natural right theory, 42–7, 242
advantages, 44, 45–7
economic interest, 43
meaning, 43, 44
originality, 42–3
personality ratio, 44, 45
self-expression, 43
No play-no pay, 4

Originality, 44
Ownership, 250
first, *see* First ownership of rights
importance, 97

structure, 97–116
transfer of rights, *see* Transfer of rights

Paris Convention:
unfair competition, 89–92
Paris Union, 89
Passing off, 90–1
Pay-to-view television, 57
Performance, 149–51, 250–1
broadcasting, 3
communication, 3
definition, *see* Definition of performance
fixing, 3
generally, 149
limitations, 3
Rome Convention, 149–50
source, 5
time, existence in, 3
TRIPS Agreement, 150
WIPO Performances and Phonograms Treaty (WPPT), 151
Performer:
conduits for author's work, 102
death, 115
definition, 137–8, 151, 241–2
dictionary definition, 98
generally, 98
legal definition, 99
principled definition, 99–100
restriction of definition, 100–2
Rome Convention, 138–42
TRIPS Agreement, 143
WIPO Performances and Phonograms Treaty (WPPT), 143–6
first ownership, 104
holder of rights, 137–46
meaning, 98–102
national treatment, 101
nationality, 101
standards required by, 102
transfer of rights, 146–8
TRIPS Agreement, 143
Performers:
Rome Convention, 19
Performers' rights:
appropriateness of protection, 251–2
arguments for 31–52, *see also* Arguments for performers' rights
assessment, 93–5
categories of protection, 75–7
contract, *see* Contract
copyright, *see* Copyright
meaning, 5
technology and, *see* Technology
unfair competition, *see* Unfair competition
Piracy:
bootlegging distinguished, 62
meaning, 62
technology, 62
Producers:
first ownership of rights, 104–6
transfer of rights to, 110, 112–13
Production of performance:
meaning, 3–4

Recording rights:
Australia, 107, 108
definition of recording, 107–8
first ownership of rights, 107–8
New Zealand, 108
person having, 107
Remuneration right, 172–8
Rome Convention, 172–5
TRIPS Agreement, 176
WIPO Performances and Phonograms Treaty (WPPT), 176–8
Rental, right of, 186–90
generally, 186
Rome Convention, 186
TRIPS Agreement, 186–8
WIPO Performances and Phonograms Treaty (WPPT), 188–90
Reproduction, right of, 164–71
copyright, 85–6
right of, 85–6
Rome Convention, 164–7
technology, 54–6
TRIPS Agreement, 167
WIPO Performances and Phonograms Treaty (WPPT), 168–71
modification right, 171
temporary copies, 169–71
Reputation, damage to, *see* Unfair competition
Reservations:
assessment, 215
decision to take, 206
definition, 206
reasons for allowing, 206–7
Rome Convention, 210
TRIPS Agreement, 211
use, 206–7
WIPO Performances and Phonograms Treaty (WPPT), 214
Ricketson, S, 204
Rome Convention:
broadcasting, 154–8
communication to the public, right of, 154–8
definition of performance, 15, 26
definition of performer, 138–42
distribution, right of, 182
duration of rights, 219–21
first fixation, right of, 161–2

Rome Convention:—*cont.*
  generally, 6
  historical background, 119–21
  limitations and exceptions, 207–9
  making available, right of, 192
  moral rights, 195
  national treatment, 128–30
  performance, 149–50
  performers, 19
    definition, 138–42
  remuneration right, 172–5
  rental, right of, 186
  reproduction, right of, 164–7
  reservations, 210
  transfer of rights, 147

Sampling, 56
Schechner, R, 19, 20–5
Screen Actors Guild:
  arguments for performers' rights, 34
Secondary uses, 5
Star contracts:
  transfer of rights, 112–13

Technology, 53–73
  advances, 4
  Aimster, 55
  bootleggers, 61–2
  broadcasting, 56–7
  categories, 54–9
    broadcasting, 56–7
    communication to the public, 56–7
    current situation, 57–9
    fixation, 54–6
    generally, 54
    reproduction, 54–6
  communication to the public, 56–7
  consequences for performers, 62–4
  contract and, 82
  current situation, 57–9
  development, 57–9
  encoding devices, 57
  exploitation, 3, 53
  fixation, 54–6, 61
  generally, 53
  Internet, 55
  morphing, 56
  Napster, 55
  pay-to-view television, 57
  performances and, 53–64
  performer, producer relationship, 60–1
  piracy, 62
  protection of performers, 64–73
    audiovisual media, exploitation in, 72–3
    CLRC, 64–5
    duration, 70–1
    economic rights, 67–9
    international system, 65
    live performances, 71–2
    method, problem of, 66–7
    moral rights, 69–70
    scope, 66–70
  reproduction, 54–6
  sampling, 56
  scope of protection for performers, 66–70
  secondary uses, 61
  use, 4–5
  users, 59–62
    bootleggers, 61–2
    generally, 59–60
    performer, producer relationship, 60–1
    piracy, 62
    secondary uses, 61
Third parties:
  contract, 79–81
Transfer of rights, 110–16, 151–2
  agents, 110
  arguments against, 112
  assignment of economic rights, 114
  collecting societies, 110
  common issues with first ownership, 109–10
  compromise, 112
  consent to use of performance, 115–16
  death of performer, 115
  duration, 109
  economic rights, 109
  generally, 110
  interests of performer, actors acting in, 111–12, 113–14
  methods, 114–15
    assignment of economic rights, 114
    death of performer, 115
    rebuttable presumption of transfer, 114–15
  moral rights, 109
  performer, 146–8
  producers, to, 110, 112–13
  reasons for allowing, 111–12
  rebuttable presumption of transfer, 114–15
  Rome Convention, 147
  star contracts, 112–13
  transferee, 110–11
    categories, 110–11
    interests of performer, actors acting in, 110–12
  producers, 110
  TRIPS Agreement, 147
  unions, 110
  whether rights should be transferable, 111–15
  WIPO Performances and Phonograms Treaty (WPPT), 148

TRIPS Agreement:
  broadcasting, 158–9
  communication to the public, right of, 158–9
  definition of performer, 143
  distribution, right of, 183
  duration of rights, 222
  first fixation, right of, 162–3
  generally, 6
  historical background, 121
  limitations and exceptions, 210–11
  making available, right of, 192
  moral rights, 196
  national treatment, 130–1
  performance, 150
  remuneration right, 176
  rental, right of, 186–8
  reproduction, right of, 167
  reservations, 211
  transfer of rights, 147

Unemployment:
  arguments for performers' rights, 34
UNESCO:
  arguments for performers' rights, 34
Unfair competition, 87–93
  competition, 90
  definition, 89–90
  entitlement to protection, 90
  generally, 76
  national treatment, 91
  need for reputation, 92–3
  Paris Convention, 89–92
  passing off, 90–1
  performances not directly protected, 92
  reputation:
    meaning, 87–8
    need for, 92–3
  shortcomings of protection, 92–3
  term of protection, 90–1
Unions:
  transfer of rights, 110

Vogel, H L, 82–3

WIPO Performances and Phonograms Treaty (WPPT):
  broadcasting, 159–61
  communication to the public, right of, 159–61
  definitions:
    performance, 16, 26
    performer, 143–6
  distribution, right of, 183–5
  first fixation, right of, 163–4
  generally, 6
  historical background, 121–2
  independence, 123
  limitations and exceptions, 211–14
  making available, right of, 192–4
  moral rights, 196–9
  performance, 151
  performer, definition of, 143–6
  remuneration right, 176–8
  rental, right of, 188–90
  reproduction, right of, 168–71
    modification right, 171
    temporary copies, 169–71
  reservations, 214
  transfer of rights, 148
WPPT, *see* WIPO Performances and Phonograms Treaty (WPPT)